COMMITTEES OF INQUIRY

Committees of Inquiry

BY

GERALD RHODES

for the

ROYAL INSTITUTE OF PUBLIC ADMINISTRATION
LONDON · GEORGE ALLEN & UNWIN LTD
RUSKIN HOUSE   MUSEUM STREET

First published in 1975

© George Allen & Unwin Ltd, 1975

ISBN 0 04 351051 5

Printed in Great Britain
in 10 point Plantin type
by The Aldine Press, Letchworth, Herts

PREFACE

Committees of inquiry are a familiar and conspicuous feature of British government, and over many years they have played a prominent role in the policy-making process. Little work has been done, however, to try to establish just how important they are. This neglect becomes understandable only when account is taken of the difficulties involved.

These difficulties spring essentially from the fact that with the great extension of government activity during this century the range and variety of situations in which government actively seeks the help and advice of outsiders have also grown enormously. Large numbers of committees are appointed, ranging from the traditional royal commission concerned with important issues of policy to working-parties examining mainly technical questions. Many of these committees carry out inquiries and take evidence from interested parties and individuals, and their findings have a bearing on the resolution of policy questions. There is thus a two-fold problem of finding an acceptable definition of committees of inquiry, and of securing and effectively analysing information about a large number of committees concerned with a disparate range of questions.

The Institute, conscious of the importance of the subject, decided that it would be valuable to carry out research into it. At the same time, in view of the known difficulties, it was decided to depart from the usual practice of initiating a full-scale research project. Instead, it seemed worthwhile to explore systematically, and in some detail, the main problems encountered to try to establish, first, how far generalisation about committees of inquiry was feasible, and, second, the directions in which further research was possible or desirable.

The present study attempts to answer these questions on the basis of an examination of committees of inquiry appointed during the ten-year period 1959–68. It deals with the circumstances in which committees are used, their distinctive characteristics, and the consequences of committee reports, always bearing in mind that committees of inquiry are only one means by which government may seek help in resolving problems.

The research and writing of the present volume were undertaken by Gerald Rhodes. In view of the fact that this was not a full-scale project the Institute decided not to appoint the usual study group to advise him. Instead, a number of people with long experience and knowledge of the subject were invited to read and comment on the draft typescript. The following kindly agreed to this request:

Sir Charles Cunningham, formerly Permanent Under-Secretary of State, Home Office

T. D. Kingdom, formerly Controller, Government Social Survey Department

Sir Thomas Padmore, formerly Permanent Secretary, Ministry of Transport

Professor W. A. Robson, Professor Emeritus of Public Administration, University of London

Lady Sharp, formerly Permanent Secretary, Ministry of Housing and Local Government

The Institute is extremely grateful to them for undertaking this time-consuming task, and for the valuable comments which they made.

The Institute would also like to express its sincere thanks to the many senior officials and others who supplied information and offered comments on the work of particular committees.

The assistance received from these various sources undoubtedly helped to improve the accuracy of the work, but responsibility rests with the author for any errors which remain and for the views expressed.

The research was made possible by a grant from the Social Science Research Council. The Institute very much appreciates the support which the Council has given.

Finally, the Institute wishes to thank Gerald Rhodes, the Research Officer for the project, who met the challenge of this particularly difficult assignment with his customary skill and determination.

CONTENTS

CHAPTER 1

THE IMPORTANCE OF COMMITTEES OF INQUIRY

GENERAL VIEWS OF COMMITTEES OF INQUIRY

'The present policy on smallholdings was laid down 16 years ago under Part IV of the Agriculture Act, 1947. It is time that an independent body should take a look at the working of this policy, and I have therefore decided to set up a Committee of Inquiry to review the working of existing legislation. . . .' [1]

The words are those of Mr Christopher Soames, then Minister of Agriculture, Fisheries and Food, announcing the appointment of a Committee of Inquiry into Statutory Smallholdings in 1963, but they have a familiar ring and with only minor changes could serve to introduce many other committees of inquiry. It is indeed one of the familiar facts of political life that we have come to expect these ministerial announcements at intervals, sometimes suggesting reasons why a committee is desirable or necessary, but more often simply indicating the bare decision to appoint a committee, leaving those who are interested to draw their own inferences about the need for it.

Familiarity, if it does not always breed contempt, tends in this case to provoke scepticism. The most frequently heard comment on the appointment of a committee is that it is an excuse for the Government to put off a decision on an awkward problem. Certainly, one effect of setting up a committee of inquiry is that a government is unlikely to take any significant action in relation to the problem which it has entrusted to it until its report is received perhaps two or more years later. Even then action or reaction is not necessarily immediate. The Government may well say that it needs time to study the report thoroughly, and to consult with the interests concerned before deciding whether to accept its recommendations. Months or even years may pass with little or no action seeming to result from the committee's labours.

There is no lack of voices to draw attention to this supposed use (or

---

[1] H. C. Deb. 678, 29 May 1963, WA 128–9.

abuse) of committees of inquiry. Harold Laski's often quoted view, 'on the average, in our system, it takes nineteen years for the recommendations of a unanimous report of a Royal Commission to assume statutory form; and if the Commission is divided in its opinion, it takes, again on the average, about thirty years for some of its recommendations to becomes statutes', [1] finds its echo in Harold Wilson's more succinct and recent statement that a royal commission 'will take minutes and waste years'.[2]

Neither of these statements is to be taken as representing a considered expression of view on royal commissions, still less on committees of inquiry in general.[3] Nevertheless, the fact that such views are commonly expressed suggests a number of important questions for examination. In the first place, how true is it that royal commissions are a delaying and time-wasting device; and if it is true of all or most royal commissions, is it also true of other committees of inquiry; or if it is not generally true whether of royal commissions or other committees or both, what explanation can be given for the fact that the view is commonly expressed?

These questions have added point if we consider other views which have been put forward. Some, particularly American, scholars have taken a much more enthusiastic and optimistic view, at least of royal commissions, seeing them as a valuable instrument of rational decision-making in a democratic society.[4] Again, the question is how justified this optimism is and whether perhaps it is possible to take an optimistic view of the device in general, although at the same time acknowledging that sometimes it is wrongly used? To answer this requires detailed knowledge of the circumstances in which committees of inquiry are used and the purposes which they serve. Those for example who criticise the use of individual committees on the grounds that they have merely served to delay the introduction of necessary changes may do so because they know, or believe they know, what action should be taken to deal with a particular problem. They may or may not be right in the case of a particular committee; but even if they are it does not follow

[1] H. J. Laski, *Parliamentary Government in England* (Allen & Unwin, 1938), p. 117.

[2] At the Trade Union Congress 1964 (quoted in Richard A. Chapman (ed.), *The Role of Commissions in Policy-Making* (Allen & Unwin, 1973), p. 44).

[3] Laski was discussing the role of the House of Lords and arguing that nobody could accuse British governments of introducing important legislative changes 'with reckless haste'. For the context of Mr Wilson's statement, see previous reference.

[4] Cf. Charles J. Hanser, *Guide to Decision : The Royal Commission* (Bedminster Press, 1965).

that this is always or even generally the situation. 'Anything but Action?' [1] may be the rule or the exception. Or it may be the rule in the case of a certain class of problems, but not of others, and if so this may have given rise to the general view.

Given that committees of inquiry are so frequently used and that, particularly in the form of royal commissions, they have a long history, one might expect questions of this kind to have been resolved by research and analysis. The precise role of committees might be thought to be of interest not only for a greater theoretical understanding of the processes of government but for its bearing on practical questions such as whether committees are used as effectively as they might be. To take simply one example, that of cost. When a committee, though admittedly a particularly lengthy and complex one, can in the early 1970s cost directly nearly half a million pounds,[2] it may well provoke questions on whether the money was well spent, and whether appointing committees is necessarily the best way of resolving problems – if, indeed, the resolution of problems is the main aim in mind.

Until recently, however, little attention has been paid to the contemporary use of committees of inquiry in general, although certain aspects have attracted comment, especially their membership and methods of operation. This comparative neglect becomes more intelligible once one examines the difficulties involved. There are basically two closely-related difficulties. There is first the difficulty of finding a coherent, practical definition of what constitutes a committee of inquiry; secondly there is the difficulty of getting adequate and relevant information about individual committees.

More will be said about both these difficulties. Meanwhile, the consequences are somewhat paradoxical. There would be general agreement that committees of inquiry have some importance both in a narrow political sense and probably in some wider sense too. Attempts to specify the degree of importance and its nature tend, however, to be limited to a few detailed case-studies of particular committees or to examination of a particular class of committees, especially royal commissions. The assumption in both cases is that what is true of these committees is true of committees of inquiry in general. The assumption may be correct, but certainly has not been shown to be so. Unless and until it is, there must be considerable doubt about the validity of any conclusions drawn from

[1] See A. P. Herbert, 'Anything but Action?' in Ralph Harris (ed.), *Radical Reaction* (Hutchinson, 1961).

[2] The reference is to the Royal Commission on the Constitution, 1969–73 (Cmnd 5460); many indirect costs (e.g. the cost to those submitting memoranda to the Commission) are not included in the calculation.

these studies. What seems to be needed in fact is a systematic examination in detail of the whole range of committees of inquiry if valid and worthwhile generalisations are to be made.

The present study has the basic aim of considering whether such an examination is feasible, particularly in the light of the two major difficulties which have been referred to; and if it is not feasible, whether there are alternative ways of trying to answer the questions raised about committees of inquiry. Thus the study will be much concerned with the theoretical and practical problems of an analysis of committees of inquiry. At the same time those problems will be illuminated by the use of a good deal of information which has been collected about individual committees and which itself helps to indicate the scope and limits of a general discussion. The study will therefore suggest both what kinds of generalisation are possible and also the directions in which further work could profitably be undertaken. The remainder of this chapter elaborates on the scope of the study.

COMMITTEES AND POLICY-MAKING

If asked to suggest the salient characteristics of committees of inquiry most people would probably think of three in particular. Committees are appointed by governments to examine a particular problem; they are expected to gather information and views as widely and comprehensively as possible, but more especially by inviting written submissions from anyone interested in providing them; and they are expected to produce a report, which is then published, setting out their view of the problem and what, if anything, they think should be done about it.

These are not intended as an exhaustive list, still less as a definition of committees of inquiry. But they do suggest two important ideas associated with such committees. There is first the idea of government seeking advice or assistance with the underlying expectation that appointment of a committee will in some way enable it to deal with a problem better than it otherwise could. There is secondly the idea that the focus is on problems which involve or may involve government in taking action. It follows that any study of committees of inquiry is bound to be concerned with the ways in which they contribute to the development of public policy. Moreover, since they clearly are not the only influence on policy, investigation must also be concerned with any special or distinctive contribution which they may make in contrast with these other influences.

This immediately raises difficult problems over what is meant by the elusive word 'policy'. The difficulties arise mainly because policy is not simply a matter of determining aims and objectives but must inevitably be concerned also with ways and means of achieving those objectives.[1] Governments may need at different times, or at the same time, to have policies for dealing with unemployment or Commonwealth immigration or inadequate housing or road accidents. In some cases (e.g. Commonwealth immigration) much discussion and debate will turn on what the aims of government policy should be, and there may well be disagreement between the political parties on these lines; in other cases (e.g. inadequate housing) there will hardly be any dispute about what should be the overriding aim, but there may well be much controversy about the use and effectiveness of different means for achieving it. However, in every case policy will consist of both a statement of aims and a statement of the means to achieve it. A government which commits itself to a policy of control of immigration will also be judged by the kind of controls it proposes and the way it proposes to administer them, and these form part of its policy in just the same way as legislative and administrative proposals may embody a government's policy for dealing with road accidents.

It is of practical importance for the present study to have some means of distinguishing questions which are matters of policy from those which are not, the aim being to exclude from consideration any committees which may be appointed to look into the latter kind of question. For although it may be important to examine the relationship between committees examining different types of question, the main interest is in committees and their possible influence on policy.

However, from what has been said above, the conclusion must be that there is no firm criterion for distinguishing committees in this way. Most committees consider questions which have or could have a bearing on policy. They differ, certainly in the degree to which they bear on policy, but it is for this reason a matter for judgement how far a particular committee is to be regarded as being concerned with policy questions. Sometimes, there is little room for doubt. A committee like the Robbins Committee on Higher Education [2] is clearly concerned with issues of policy. Equally a committee concerned with the equipment and training of the ambulance service [3] has relatively so little concern with policy issues that it can be ignored for the present purpose.

Many committees are not so easily disposed of. When, for example,

[1] Cf. Nevil Johnson, 'Who Are the Policy-Makers?', *Public Administration* (Autumn 1965), p. 282.
[2] Cmnd 2154, 1963.
[3] Reports by the Working-Party on Ambulance Training and Equipment (HMSO, 1966 and 1967).

the Government appointed a committee of inquiry in 1968 into the causes of delays in commissioning electricity power stations,[1] the problem seemed superficially to be of a technical or administrative character rather than one of policy. Policy questions it might be thought centred on such things as how far energy needs should be met by electricity, and the type, number and location of power stations required for that purpose. Yet the importance of the subject, and especially the political importance of criticisms of the Central Electricity Generating Board and the Government for delays, had a direct bearing on important policy issues such as the organisation and structure of the electricity supply industry.

As will be seen later in this study, this brief discussion of policy is characteristic of much analysis applicable to committees of inquiry in that although the core of the discussion is reasonably clear and well defined, there is a considerable area of doubt, which can only be resolved by examining the circumstances, and especially the political circumstances, in which individual committees were appointed.

What we have in fact is a broad area of investigation in which committees are appointed to examine and analyse problems and to make proposals for dealing with them; and these problems concern in varying degrees and varying ways the aims of government and the various means, whether legislative or otherwise, which may be thought to contribute to those aims. Greater precision is hardly possible without a much more elaborate theoretical analysis than would be appropriate here. It is sufficient to make clear that at this stage the approach is deliberately broad rather than narrowly confined to major policy issues, however these may be defined. The reasons for this broad approach, and the problems of classification will, it is hoped, be made evident in later chapters.

A rather different question, much debated, is 'who makes policy?' and, in particular, whether ministers or officials or both determine policy. Again, so far as committees of inquiry are concerned, detailed analysis of individual committees, and in particular of the way in which committee reports are handled at the departmental and the political level, could help to illuminate this question. It should be stressed, however, that this is not a primary aim of the present study. Certainly, in looking at the complex process of policy-making in relation to specific issues, the need for this kind of information – and the difficulties of obtaining it – will be discussed. In any event, in the absence of access to official records, much of the relationship between official or depart-

[1] Cmnd 3960, 1969.

mental views and ministerial views must be founded on speculation or inference. The frequent references in this study to 'government' appointment of committees or 'government' reaction to their reports do not imply any specific theory about that relationship. Rather the aim has been more broadly to relate the influence of committees of inquiry to that of other external sources of information and advice.

WHAT COMMITTEES OF INQUIRY ARE

Given then that the aim is to examine in broad terms the contribution of committees of inquiry to policy-making, a first essential is to establish how frequently committees occur and what their range of subjects is. The way in which committees of inquiry are defined will have a bearing on these questions. It is clear, for example, from what has been said earlier, that royal commissions are often singled out for special comment. Royal commissions are, however, now rare particularly in comparison with the latter part of the nineteenth century. Excluding such semi-permanent bodies as the Royal Commission on Environmental Pollution, seven royal commissions were appointed by the Labour Government of 1964–70, and only one by the Conservative Government in its first three years of office (1970–3). Four of the Labour royal commissions were appointed in 1966 (tribunals of inquiry, local government in England and Scotland, assizes and quarter sessions), but apart from this exceptional year one has to go back to 1935 to find a year in which as many as four commissions were appointed; and right back to 1906 for the vintage year of this century when twelve were appointed.[1] This compares with seventy-four appointed in the ten years 1851–60 and an annual average of four in the period 1881–1900.[2]

Clearly there are advantages in confining discussion to royal commissions. They are simply defined by their nomenclature, and there are not too many of them to make analysis impossible. On the other hand, as has been suggested, to look only at royal commissions begs the question of whether they can be regarded as representative of committees of inquiry as a whole in such matters as their membership and methods of operation and the nature of the questions remitted to them, quite apart from their influence on policy-making.

But if the restriction of analysis to royal commissions represents an artificial limitation of the subject, the alternative seems to be to adopt a basically functional approach, that is, to stress inquiry as the primary

[1] See Hanser, op. cit., pp. 242–7.
[2] H. D. Clokie and J. W. Robinson, *Royal Commissions of Inquiry* (California, Stanford University Press, 1937), p. 79.

element in definition. That this is not such a simple and straightforward matter as it may at first sight appear will become evident from the discussion in the next chapter. The important point to note at this stage is that it broadens the field of investigation in such a way that it raises acutely some of the main theoretical and practical problems of this study.

By way of illustration, one may consider how far an intelligent, well-informed member of the public could be expected to be aware of some recent committees of inquiry. He could be expected, for example, to know that there had been inquiries in recent years into local government in England and in Scotland, both by royal commissions, and into the civil service and higher education, both by committees which were not royal commissions. He might be aware that there had been a Royal Commission on Tribunals of Inquiry and committees to look into the question of industrial designs and foot-and-mouth disease. He would be unlikely, unless he was professionally involved or had some other special interest, to know that there had been committees on the teaching of Russian, the technology of pressure vessels, the remuneration of milk producers or the organisation of hospital scientific and technical services.

An immediate problem is to decide whether these are all to be regarded as equally committees of inquiry or whether some system of classification is needed. It is obvious, for example, that the range of problems represented by these few committees is considerable. Some are of great social and economic importance, like higher education, and some of a more limited and technical nature, like pressure vessels; some with important legislative implications, like local government structure, and some mainly matters of administrative organisation and procedure, like the hospital scientific and technical services; some concerned with central government's own organisation, like the structure, recruitment and management of the civil service, and some with relations between central government and other organised bodies, like the remuneration of milk producers. Nor are these exhaustive or mutually exclusive categories. Committees like that on foot-and-mouth disease are simultaneously concerned with important social and economic questions, with possible legislation and with government relations with outside interests.

Whether classification by this or by some other means is possible is further discussed in the next chapter. But another implication of adopting a fairly broad definition of committees of inquiry is that it brings into the reckoning a large number of committees, with the consequent practical difficulties of getting and handling the necessary information for detailed analysis. Again, discussion in the next chapter will be concerned with whether, within the broad definition, some limitation of the analysis is possible, for example, by examining only the most important committees. Here, however, it is desirable to indicate some of the limits of the study serving to mark off committees of inquiry from other possible sources of information and advice.

There is in the first place a limitation implied in the fact that these are committees appointed by government. In the most formal cases there will be a Royal Warrant (for royal commissions) or a minute signed by a minister specifying the terms of reference and membership. But whether such a formal document is reproduced in a committee's report or not, an essential characteristic of a committee of inquiry is that it is appointed by and reports to one or more ministers or, in the case of royal commissions, the Sovereign, that is, in effect, the Government as a whole.

The importance of this limitation is that it excludes committees appointed by other public sector bodies such as the nationalised industries or the Arts Council. At the same time, there are perhaps inevitably doubtful or borderline cases. The University Grants Committee, for example, has from time to time appointed committees to look into such questions as library facilities or Latin-American studies. These would be excluded by the limitation. On the other hand, the question arises whether there is so very much difference in function between such committees and, say, committees appointed by standing advisory bodies. The latter are of course themselves appointed by and report to ministers, but may on their own initiative appoint committees to examine matters which are certainly within their general terms of reference but not specifically commissioned by a minister, and such committees may function in a similar manner to committees of inquiry.[1]

Another limitation which gives rise to borderline cases is that we are concerned only with committees to which people from outside government are appointed. Put negatively, this means that they are not committees composed entirely of ministers or civil servants. Occasionally, the reports of official committees are published, and are in some sense committees of inquiry,[2] but there is clearly a difference between the kind of advice which a minister gets from a committee of officials and one which he gets from a committee composed of people not in government service. Put more positively, one can say that a committee of inquiry must contain at least one member who is neither an official nor a minister.

Sometimes committees (usually termed working-parties) are set up

[1] An example is the report on cannabis by a subcommittee of the Advisory Committee on Drug Dependence (see below, p. 151).

[2] See, for example, *A National Minimum Wage: An Inquiry* (HMSO, 1969).

consisting of officials of both central and local government. By a slight extension of the limitation, these are excluded. Rather more difficult are committees consisting of officials but with an independent chairman.[1] These are included in the study even though in status they appear to be mid-way between committees of officials and independent committees of inquiry.

This difficulty can be seen in a slightly different way by considering another type of investigation which can be excluded, that is investigations by a single person. Governments sometimes ask a single individual to investigate a problem and report. Such investigations clearly differ in one important way from committees in that any conclusions represent an individual and not a collective decision. This device is not used very often, but where it is the investigator may well be asssisted by a group of departmental officials, perhaps called assessors or perhaps less formally. Thus when Lord Mountbatten was asked to inquire into certain escapes from prison and to make recommendations for the improvement of prison security he was assisted by three named assessors.[2] On the other hand when Lady Sharp, a former Permanent Secretary of the Ministry of Housing and Local Government, was asked by the Minister of Transport to undertake an inquiry into manpower requirements for urban transport planning she was assisted by an advisory group of twenty-two people, some nominated by local authority associations and professional bodies and some appointed in a personal capacity.[3] As her report makes clear,[4] there is a formal difference between such an inquiry and a committee of officials with an independent chairman in that in the former case the advisers have no direct responsibility for the report and its recommendations. In practical terms, however, the difference may not be so very great.

Borderline difficulties of this kind are, however, only a part of a much wider problem of the relationship between committees of inquiry and other means of investigation and advice, which is discussed at length later in this study. All that need be said at this stage is that in examining committees of inquiry appointed by government all three nouns need to be emphasised. We are looking at *committees*, in the conventional sense of bodies of three or more people, rather than investigations by individuals, on the assumption that there is a special significance in the way

[1] See, for example, the report of the Committee to Examine the Economic Situation of Northern Ireland (Cmnd 1835, 1962).
[2] Report of the Inquiry into Prison Escapes and Security (Cmnd 3175, 1966).
[3] *Transport Planning : The Men for the Job* (HMSO, 1970), para. 10 and Annex A.
[4] Ibid., para. 10.

in which three or more people sitting round a table discuss and resolve problems. We are concerned with *inquiry* as the distinguishing function of certain committees, although precisely what this means is not free from ambiguity and will be further discussed in the next chapter. And our interest is in *government* committees because we are concerned with the way in which government policies are formulated.[1]

SCOPE OF THE STUDY

It follows from the last point in particular that the kind of problems on which governments seek outside assistance will often be ones which have arisen either in the application of particular legislative provisions or through the practical operation of the administrative machine. Investigations are sought and are directed to the possibility of correcting or improving the existing situation whether by legislation or other means, and there is an underlying implication that having invited this particular form of investigation government will give serious attention to the report and recommendations to which it gives rise. Serious attention does not mean automatic acceptance but it does imply that committee reports carry some weight in the complex processes of formulation of policy. The basic theme of the present study is to try to establish what kind of approach is likely to illuminate those processes best so far as the part played by committees of inquiry is concerned.

The main practical problem is the scale of such an undertaking. Not only is the number of committees large, but since they range over a large part of government activity they exhibit great diversity in the kind of problems examined, as has already been suggested. For the purposes of the present study, the main attention has been focused on committees appointed during a ten-year period, 1959–68. There is no particular significance in a ten-year period except that it is sufficiently long to provide examples of most of the main issues which arise.[2] The actual dates were chosen largely by reference to the fact that in following up the consequences of committee reports it seemed necessary to allow two to three years after publication before being able to assess even relatively short-term consequences. Since committees frequently take around two

[1] It should be explained that parliamentary select committees are entirely excluded from consideration here, as being a different species of investigatory body whose analysis requires separate treatment.

[2] It should perhaps be made clear that this is in no sense a historical study and is not concerned with such questions as whether the use of committees of inquiry is increasing.

years from appointment to publication of report,[1] the end of 1968 seemed to be the most reasonable end-point to take for the purposes of the study.

On the basis of criteria set out in more detail in Chapter 2 over 170 committees of inquiry were appointed in the period 1959–68. The next question which arises is therefore whether it is necessary to investigate all these committees in detail. The answer must turn on what it is intended to find out and the availability of the necessary information. A large part of the study is concerned with a discussion of these questions.

Two major concerns of a study of committees of inquiry must be with their origins and with their consequences. If there is a distinctive use of such committees which marks them off from other means of influencing the formulation of policy, then it is plausible to suppose that it is possible to define the circumstances in which governments find it necessary or desirable to appoint committees, and to contrast them with the circumstances in which committees are not used. An examination of origins in this way might be concerned with the kind of subjects examined by committees, the sequence of events preceding the appointment of committees and the motives of government in making such appointments. Given the number and range of committees it cannot be assumed that such analyses will be simple affairs; committees may serve one of a number of purposes, or may simultaneously serve more than one purpose. Hence, as Chapter 3 discusses, there is a two-fold problem: to devise a framework of analysis applicable to the origins of committees, and to obtain reliable information about individual committees so that each can be positively assigned to a particular category.

Governments choose the terms of reference and the membership of committees. On the other hand, they have no control over (although they may seek to influence) the way in which committees interpret their terms of reference and set about investigating the questions referred to them. These three elements, terms of reference, membership and methods of operation, largely determine the kind of report which a committee produces. They are therefore worth studying both in themselves and because of their relationship to the underlying concern with origins and consequences. It is, for example, important to know both what kind of people serve on committees and how far the choice of particular members of particular committees reflects the motives of government in appointing that committee. Similarly, the way in which a committee approaches its task has implications both for the likelihood of its recom-

---

[1] There are of course large variations in the time taken from a few months to (in at least one case) six and a half years, but the great majority of committees appointed in 1968 had reported by the end of 1970.

mendations being accepted and for other possible influences which its report may have. But again, as Chapters 4 and 5 discuss, there are problems both of getting adequate information for individual committees and of relating the information to a more general analysis.

From the point at which a committee's report has been published by Her Majesty's Stationery Office its arguments and recommendations are not only the subject of examination by civil servants and ministers but can provide the focus of general public debate. The consequences of committee reports can therefore be viewed either narrowly or broadly, according to whether one looks simply at whether their recommendations are accepted by the Government or at their possibly longer-term influence on public opinion. In practice, however, as is clear from Chapter 6, it is not always easy to determine whether or rather how far a particular committee's recommendations have in fact been accepted and far more difficult to be sure of the reasons for acceptance or rejection. This has important implications for an assessment in practical terms of the part played by committees of inquiry both in their immediate impact on the formulation of policy and in having a wider influence.

Essentially this main part of the study (Chapters 2 to 6) is concerned to explore the subject through examination of individual committees of inquiry. Such an approach presents some theoretical and many practical problems. In particular, it does not easily lend itself to establishing clearly the distinctive contribution of committees of inquiry and the extent to which policies are evolved by other means. A possible means of examining these questions more effectively is to widen the approach and consider a number of policy issues or policy areas in some of which committees of inquiry have been extensively used and in others either not at all or rarely. The object would be to try to determine the factors which are of most importance for the use of committees. Chapter 7 outlines, with examples, the form which such an approach would take.

Although a comprehensive analysis of the role and practical effectiveness of committees of inquiry presents great, and perhaps insuperable, difficulties, much can be inferred even from a limited study of this nature. The final chapter indicates both that there is inadequate evidence for some of the generalisations which have been applied to committees of inquiry, and that to view them in instrumental terms offers the best chance of enabling a positive assessment to be made.

CHAPTER 2

TYPES OF COMMITTEE

WHAT COMMITTEES OF INQUIRY ARE

Two basic questions are discussed in this chapter. The first is what committees of inquiry are and the second is whether it is possible to classify them in a meaningful way. The first question appears to be a straightforward matter of definition. But the difficulties it raises and the reasons for these difficulties are of great significance, particularly when viewed against the fact that most studies in the past have tended to confine themselves to royal commissions and major departmental and inter-departmental committees.

The essential approach is in terms of the function performed by committees, but that function is difficult to define at all precisely. Wheare, for example, distinguished between 'committees to inquire' and 'committees to advise'. Admitting that committees to inquire are also usually committees to advise he nevertheless proposed a narrow definition of the latter based on the characteristic that their members offer their advice from the resources of their own special knowledge and experience, and that inquiry played 'no significant or substantial part' in their work. In contrast, not only was inquiry of at least equal importance to the making of recommendations for committees to inquire but the latter were also expected to take evidence and produce a report bearing some relation to that evidence and 'making an authoritative contribution to the public discussion and consideration of the subject'.[1]

The difficulties, as Wheare's discussion indicates, are, first, that of determining what constitutes investigation or inquiry, and, secondly, of relating inquiry to other characteristics of committees.

Inquiry means, at the very least, investigation of the facts of a situation. In 1964 the Secretary of State for Scotland appointed a committee 'to investigate the cause of the primary infection in the recent

---

[1] K. C. Wheare, *Government by Committee* (Oxford University Press, 1955), pp. 43, 68–9.

outbreak of typhoid fever in Aberdeen and the means by which it was disseminated, and to report'.[1] This was certainly a committee, and it certainly had inquiry as a main task. It has parallels with inquiries into railway or colliery accidents, with tribunals of inquiry, with courts of inquiry into industrial disputes and with investigations of maladministration like those into the Court Lees Approved School,[2] or into allegations of ill-treatment at Ely Hospital.[3] All these seek to establish the facts of a particular situation, and, in most cases, whether and if so why something went wrong.

Yet, paradoxically, although all these may seem to be pure forms of inquiry they do not perform the expected function of committees of inquiry. Royal commissions and departmental (or interdepartmental) committees of inquiry, which are often regarded as the only or at least the principal forms of committees of inquiry, differ in one significant way from the examples of inquiries given in the previous paragraph. They are concerned with investigating not the facts of specific events but the facts of a general problem or situation. And it is this distinction which causes most of the difficulties about definition and the classification of individual committees.

Take, for example, the terms of reference of the departmental Committee on Allotments, appointed by the Minister of Land and Natural Resources in 1965 'to review general policy on allotments in the light of present-day conditions in England and Wales and to recommend what legislative and other changes, if any, are needed'.[4] There is nothing in these terms of reference, as there was in the Aberdeen Typhoid Committee, about investigation; what the committee is asked to do is 'review policy' and 'recommend changes'. It is what is implied in carrying out these activities which is important for the definition of committees of inquiry. In order to be in a position to review general policy in the light of present-day conditions the committee needed at least to find out what that policy was; how it was being operated, what difficulties had arisen in operating it and what were the causes of those difficulties. All these are matters for investigation, but they require different methods and techniques of investigation from those required for uncovering the causes of an individual event.

It is easy to see, therefore, why an attempt to define a certain sort of committee by its function, namely inquiry, should inevitably be drawn into the questions of methods and procedure. It is not just inquiry that

[1] Cmnd 2542, 1964.
[2] Cmnd 3367, 1967.
[3] Cmnd 3975, 1969.
[4] Cmnd 4166, 1969.

is important, but inquiry which seeks to elucidate some general problem rather than the facts of a particular event. For this purpose the opinions of interested organisations and individuals both about the nature of the problem and about ways in which it might be resolved are important elements in what is to be investigated and may indeed themselves largely determine the problem. By contrast a purely fact-finding inquiry must largely proceed by the questioning of individuals about what happened and relies on the skills of the investigators in uncovering facts and in assessing which are relevant to interpreting the sequence of cause and effect. The object in fact is quite simply to discover the truth; committees of inquiry are appointed to do more than this. Certainly they need to find out the facts, but they have to do two other things as well – to analyse the situation, which involves much more than discovering what caused a particular event, and to suggest possible remedies. These three elements – investigation, appraisal, advice – help to give committees of inquiry their distinguishing characteristics. They also complicate the problem of definition and assignment and this is best seen by contrast with committees whose main purpose is simply to give advice.

Just as committees investigating individual events may be thought of as 'pure' committees of inquiry, so the numerous standing bodies set up to advise government departments provide many examples of 'pure' advisory committees, bodies of experts formulating recommendations for action in a particular field usually by means of written and often unpublished reports whose value lies in the fact that they result from discussions with a committee by people with particular experience and knowledge of the questions remitted to them.[1]

Between pure inquiry and pure advice, there are numerous committees which in varying degrees carry out the functions of investigation, appraisal and advice. Are there distinctions to be drawn between them, and, if so, by what criteria? What, indeed, is the importance of distinguishing between inquiry and advice?

The latter question is a key to this whole study. The assumption has been made that, in terms of their effects on policy-making, advisory committees differ from committees of inquiry, and that governments seek advice, pure and simple, on matters on which they lack sufficient expert knowledge, so that there is a presumption that they will accept the advice given, whereas this is by no means necessarily so in the case of committees of inquiry. This is, however, only an assumption and to

---

[1] Cf. PEP Study Group, *Advisory Committees in British Government* (Allen & Unwin, 1960), pp. 14–16, 97.

test it involves having both a practical way of distinguishing the two types of committee and a means of making comparisons between them.

INQUIRY AND ADVICE

It is natural to start with Wheare's common-sense approach and to distinguish advisory committees from committees of inquiry according to whether advice or inquiry is the predominant function in a particular case. There are several possible ways in which this might be done:

1 Status e.g. *ad hoc* or standing
2 Nomenclature
3 Terms of reference
4 Membership
5 Mode of operation

It is tempting to suppose that one distinction between committees of inquiry and advisory committees is that the former are of a more temporary nature than the latter. Certainly there seems to be a distinction between royal commissions and departmental committees appointed to investigate a particular problem and then ceasing to exist, and standing committees appointed to give advice on a continuing basis. At most, however, this is only an approximation to a distinction. There are royal commissions appointed on a continuing basis,[1] just as there are *ad hoc* bodies to give advice.[2] A further difficulty is that many standing advisory bodies produce reports in which investigation and appraisal appear to be at least as important as advice. When, for example, the Advisory Committee on Drug Dependence appointed a subcommittee 'to examine the question of misuse of cannabis and lysergic acid diethylamide (LSD) in the United Kingdom, and problems arising . . .' it expected and got a review of the 'available evidence on the pharmacological, clinical, pathological, social and legal aspects of those drugs based on considerable investigation by the subcommittee'.[3] In other words, although the presumption is that committees of inquiry tend to be *ad hoc* bodies, this cannot be used as a criterion for distinguishing them from advisory committees.

The situation is somewhat similar with nomenclature. Most committees are simply called committees but some are known as working-

---

[1] A recent example is the Royal Commission on Environmental Pollution set up in 1970.

[2] E.g. the Working-Party on Grit and Dust Emissions (HMSO, 1967); the Committee on the Queen's Award to Industry (HMSO, 1965).

[3] *Cannabis* (HMSO, 1969).

parties, steering-groups, advisory panels and so on. Again, it is tempting to suppose that these correspond to different functions, and again this assumption is only partially borne out by the facts. Whatever the reason for the introduction of the term 'working-party', for example, as applied to a committee rather than a detachment of soldiers,[1] it seems to be applied to at least three types of committee: (a) a body intended to devise a practical scheme; (b) an advisory committee; (c) a committee of inquiry. The Working-Party on Air Freight [2] is an example of the first, charged with examining cargo-handling facilities and methods in the United Kingdom; the working-party set up by the Ministry of Defence in November 1969 to advise on the potential hazards arising from the transport of nerve agents by road from Nancekuke to Porton [3] is an example of the second; the Working-Party on the Hospital Pharmaceutical Service is an example of the third.[4]

These examples illustrate not only that it is not sufficient to use the title of a committee as a criterion for classification, but that to decide whether inquiry is a major function of a committee may be difficult and involve judging on the basis not only of what task the committee is given to do but of how it actually sets about that task. In May 1966, for example, the Secretary of State for Scotland appointed a Working-Party on Suggestions and Complaints in Hospitals. This appeared to be a straightforward working-party of the first type identified above. It had no formal terms of reference but was appointed as the result of the report of a committee of the Scottish Health Services Council on the administrative practice of hospital boards which had drawn attention to deficiencies in existing arrangements and recommended that a working-party should be appointed to devise a procedure which could be recognised and applied by all hospital boards.

In practice, however, as the working-party's report reveals, there was a difference of opinion among the members about how they should go about their task, some wanting simply to go ahead as quickly as possible and devise a procedure enabling as many complaints as possible to be dealt with at hospital level. Against this the majority argued that this was based on an over-simplified view of the existing situation 'and on assumptions of which we had no objective proof; . . . and that our recommendations would be more acceptable if based on fact'.[5] They

[1] See on this Wheare, op. cit., p. 253.
[2] HMSO, 1963.
[3] HMSO, 1970.
[4] HMSO, 1970.
[5] *Suggestions and Complaints in Hospitals*, report of the Working-Party (HMSO, 1969), para. 8.

therefore proceeded not only to invite information from various bodies and organisations but to issue a general press invitation to the public, to canvass views on possible procedures from hospital authorities and other organisations and to get the Research and Intelligence Unit of the Scottish Home and Health Department to carry out an inquiry among patients in hospitals, since they felt that otherwise they would not get adequate information on patients' views.[1] In other words, a body which was intended simply to give advice on procedures on the basis of discussions among its members, in practice operated through the three characteristic modes of a committee of inquiry of investigation, appraisal and advice.[2]

This kind of difficulty in deciding how far inquiry is an important element in a committee's task is not confined simply to a few relatively unimportant working-parties. There are a great many committees where it is difficult to make this assessment except by examining the whole context in which a committee operates – its terms of reference, membership, purpose and general approach. Sometimes the nomenclature or terms of reference indicate one sort of committee whereas external circumstances indicate another.

This may happen, for example, when a committee of inquiry recommends further examination of certain questions remitted to it. Thus the committee appointed by the Secretary of State for Scotland in 1959 under the Chairmanship of Lord Reid to examine the case for introducing registration of title to land in Scotland suggested that two small expert committees should be set up to examine conveyancing legislation and, if the Government agreed to a scheme of registration, to work out the details of such a scheme. The first of these committees, under the Chairmanship of Professor J. M. Halliday, was appointed in 1964 and reported in 1966.[3] The second, under the Chairmanship of Professor G. L. F. Henry, was appointed in 1965, 'to prepare, in the light of the report by Lord Reid's Committee [Cmnd 2032] a detailed scheme for the introduction and operation of registration of title to land in Scotland

---

[1] Ibid., paras 9–15; the results of the survey were published separately, as being of general interest for the hospital service (para. 16).

[2] It is of interest that when Sir Keith Joseph later felt impelled to do something about the same problem in England and Wales he (and the Secretary of State for Wales) decided to appoint an independent and authoritative committee with a QC as Chairman (H. C. Deb. 810, 3 February 1971, WA 408). The Scottish example also illustrates how dangerous it is to generalise about working-parties as the Working-Party on Midwives (1949) did when it claimed that a working-party does not take formal evidence in the same way as a royal commission or departmental committee (quoted in Wheare, op. cit. p. 45, n. 1).

[3] Cmnd 3118, 1966.

with a view to the preparation of a Registration of Title Bill'.[1] The Henry Committee, from the circumstances of its origin, its terms of reference and method of operation,[2] functioned basically as a working-party charged with drawing up a practical scheme and its report consists largely of an elaboration of two chapters of the Reid Report in terms of a draft bill and regulations. It is more like the reports of, say, the Criminal Law Revision Committee than of the Reid Committee. It is not a committee of inquiry.

There is more doubt about the Halliday Committee on Conveyancing. On the one hand, it was a small, expert committee concerned with the details rather than the substance of legislation and operating more on the basis of the expert knowledge of its members than on that of formal evidence.[3] On the other hand, it had wider terms of reference than the Henry Committee and was concerned with more than just the technicalities of conveyancing, since its recommendations raised questions about the existing system of land tenure in Scotland. It is a marginal case, in much the same way as are many reports of standing advisory committees which also carry out some inquiries. Fairly detailed knowledge of the circumstances of each is needed to determine whether they fall into the inquiry or advisory category: examples are the reports on antibiotics in milk in Great Britain (HMSO, 1963) by the Milk and Milk Products Technical Advisory Committee; on the appointed factory doctor service (HMSO, 1966) by the Industrial Health Advisory Committee or on the needs of new communities (HMSO, 1967) by the Central Housing Advisory Committee.

HYBRID COMMITTEES

Perhaps inevitably, it is not difficult to find examples of committees which combine more than one function. There are, for example, committees which are specifically asked to examine the facts of an individual incident and at the same time to draw any necessary conclusions for general policy. Thus the Devlin Committee appointed by the Minister of Labour in 1964 was to examine not only the causes of the current dispute in the docks but also generally causes of dissension in

---

[1] Cmnd 4137, 1969.

[2] E.g. it did not take evidence in a formal sense but got advice and opinions from certain people (ibid., para. 3).

[3] It does not seem specifically to have invited evidence, but twenty-six organisations and individuals tendered suggestions for reform, and the Committee had discussions with fifteen of them (Cmnd 3118, para. 2 and Appendix A).

the industry.[1] Each of these committees has to be examined individually to judge whether it justifies classification as a committee of inquiry.

More puzzling are certain developments in the former Ministry of Transport in the 1960s. Mr Marples's response, not long after he took office in 1959, to the growing problem of traffic in towns was to initiate studies in his Ministry into the long-term problems involved. These were to be carried out by a working- (or study-) group headed by Mr Colin Buchanan, at that time a member of the Planning Inspectorate of the Ministry of Housing and Local Government, but also the author of *Mixed Blessing*, a study of the motor-car and its social impact. Although the working-group was somewhat unusually constituted,[2] its status was reasonably clear as a body of officials charged with carrying out studies and research with a view to putting forward proposals in relation to the long-term problems of traffic in towns. As a body of officials this working-group could not be regarded as a committee of inquiry.

At the same time, however, Mr Marples also appointed a steering-group of six independent members under the Chairmanship of Sir Geoffrey Crowther, whose job it was both to guide the Buchanan Group and to draw conclusions for public policy from its work. The question is whether the work of the steering- and working-groups together constitute a committee of inquiry in fact if not in name.

Mr Marples explicitly differentiated the work of the steering-group from that of the usual type of committee whose members 'take evidence at length, and months are consumed in producing an elaborate report'. His 'new method' had resulted in an enormous field being covered in a short time: 'The time of the Steering Group, all of whom were eminent men, was not wasted. They used it to the best advantage.'[3] Viewed in terms of function, the work of the Buchanan and Crowther groups together contained the three elements of investigation, appraisal and advice. Moreover, it can hardly be denied that the investigations carried out by the Buchanan Group formed an important part of the whole work, even if they happened to be carried out by a group of officials. Yet, Mr Marples, although he put emphasis on the method of working, seemed to be implying a more pragmatic view – that what mattered was the end-result and that, at any rate in the field of traffic in towns, the important thing was to get, as quickly as possible, some well thought out ideas on how to deal with the problems. The traditional method of

---

[1] Cmnd 2523, 1964; Cmnd 2734, 1965.

[2] According to Mr Marples, after reading *Mixed Blessing* he invited Mr Buchanan to lead the group but gave him an entirely free hand to select his own team (H. C. Deb. 689, 10 February 1964, col. 34).

[3] Ibid., col. 35.

getting evidence from interested bodies and individuals was, he implied, a waste of time.

The Buchanan Report thus indicates a further problem: whether not only the importance of investigation in a committee's work but also its methods of investigation are to be taken as a distinguishing criterion, as indeed Wheare [1] implies. The question is important not simply because of conundrums presented by rather unusual investigations like that of Buchanan-Crowther, but because it is much harder to distinguish committees of inquiry from advisory committees if, in addition to assessing the importance of investigation, one also has to take into account methods of investigation.

There are, for example, many reports of committees of the Department of Health and Social Security and the Scottish Home and Health Department to advise on different aspects of the national health service. The majority of these result from the intricate network of standing advisory machinery established under the National Health Service Act, 1946, as the means whereby the Minister could be kept in touch with professional, and especially medical, opinion.[2] Investigation forms some part of the practical operation of most of these committees, and that investigation often includes taking evidence from organisations and individuals, as well as collecting data by questionnaire or other means, and making visits, all of which also form part of the traditional method of working of committees of inquiry.[3] How important do these methods have to be to make one decide that inquiry rather than advice is the main function of these committees?

It is often almost a matter of chance, as the example of the Working-Party on Suggestions and Complaints in Scottish Hospitals showed, whether a particular committee, whether *ad hoc* or standing, chooses to make inquiries an important part of its work or to rely, as did the Working-Party on Grit and Dust Emissions, on discussions amongst the members themselves, that is, their own knowledge and experience as the basis of the advice they offer. If only the latter can be confidently assigned to the advisory category then we are left, as we started, with two relatively small groups of 'pure' inquiry and 'pure' advisory committees with a large undifferentiated mass of inquiry/advisory committees in the middle which we have no firm rules for distinguishing from one another.

---

[1] See p. 24 above.

[2] See National Health Service Act, 1946, S.2 and National Health Service (Scotland) Act, 1947, S.2.

[3] See, for example, *The Field of Work of the Family Doctor* (HMSO, 1963); *The Functions of the District General Hospital* (HMSO, 1968).

There are, of course, other means by which one can attempt to distinguish committees – by their membership, for example, and how they are appointed.[1] But they all raise problems similar to the ones which have been discussed. Common sense would nevertheless say that this whole discussion seems to be making a mountain out of a molehill, and that, although there may be difficulties in certain cases, we can all recognise typical committees of inquiry, like the royal commissions on local government or the Fulton Committee on the Civil Service. Or, as Wheare more elegantly puts it, 'there are . . . many . . . mixed or borderline cases. But the existence of borderline cases does not of itself invalidate a classification'.[2] This is true, but when suggested criteria leave too many committees in a borderline area and are difficult to apply in practice it seems time to re-examine the criteria.

TRADITION AND IMPORTANCE

This can be done by considering why it is that we feel no hesitation about assigning the Redcliffe-Maud Commission or the Fulton or Seebohm committees to the category of committees of inquiry. There are essentially two reasons: tradition and the importance of the subject assigned to the committee.

By tradition I mean the fact that the nineteenth-century royal commission evolved a certain approach to the investigation of problems which still colours our view of the committee of inquiry. Investigation, appraisal and advice were indeed the major elements in those inquiries into the health of towns or the condition of the working classes or the civil service whose volumes fill the shelves of any collection of nineteenth-century parliamentary papers. Investigation meant very largely the receipt of memoranda by the commission and close examination of witnesses at oral hearings, together with visits 'to see for themselves'.

Although they may now sometimes use much more extended means of getting information, royal commissions still largely operate by these means which therefore tend to be the norm against which we judge whether a committee is a committee of inquiry. The difficulty is that, with changing social and economic conditions and with the great extension in the range and character of government activities, committees may be set up in a whole range of circumstances and for purposes which were largely unknown to government 100 years ago. Correspond-

---

[1] PEP Study Group, *Advisory Committees in British Government*, for example, points out that the majority of members of standing advisory committees are appointed by nomination or suggestion from outside bodies (p. 38).

[2] Op. cit., p. 45.

ingly, as the discussion of the Buchanan Report showed, new types of committee, or at least new ways of using committees, have been developed.

The question of tradition links up with the second reason for feeling confident about assigning certain committees to the inquiry category, namely, the importance of the subject matter. Importance here has two meanings. A subject can be important because it is likely to affect a great many people and to have consequences outside a narrow, limited, field; or because, although it appears to be relatively narrow or even trivial, it has become politically contentious. Many of the nineteenth-century inquiries were important in this sense, and it is noticeable how often modern committees of inquiry which indisputably fall into that category, do so for this reason and indeed in some cases, like that of the Fulton Committee on the Civil Service, are in fact covering ground similar to that of nineteenth-century commissions.

Most committees, whether *ad hoc* or standing, whose reports are published do not deal with subjects which are important in either of these two senses. The main reason is that with the great extension of government activity in this century the range of matters which now involve questions of government policy has greatly increased. Correspondingly there has been an increase in the need felt by governments for outside information and advice. To the extent that this need has been met by the appointment of committees, it is hardly surprising that such committees should exhibit a much greater range both of subject matter and of modes of operation than their nineteenth-century predecessors.

A committee of inquiry is then a body which investigates by means particularly, but not exclusively, of the examination of evidence a general problem or set of problems which are relevant to the determination of government policy. Such a definition clearly is a very broad one and permits the inclusion of many committees which fall outside the traditional categories. In education, for example, it allows for the inclusion of a committee considering 'the place, if any, of finger spelling and signing in the education of the deaf',[1] or one whose task is 'to investigate the possibility of improving and extending the teaching of Russian',[2] just as much as a more traditional kind of committee asked 'to review the pattern of full-time higher education in Great Britain and ... to advise Her Majesty's Government on what principles its long-term development should be based. ...'[3]

It may be as well to summarise the discussion at this point. Among

---

[1] *The Education of Deaf Children* (HMSO, 1968).
[2] *The Teaching of Russian* (HMSO, 1962).
[3] *Higher Education* (Cmnd 2154, 1963).

independent committees appointed by the Government, that is, committees consisting wholly or partly of people who are not officials of either central or local government, three broad categories can be distinguished according to the functions which they serve. The first group consists of committees whose sole or main purpose is investigation of particular events; the third group consists of committees whose sole or main purpose is to give advice based on the knowledge and experience of its members. In between is the second group which combines inquiry into general issues with advice; it is this second group which forms the subject of the present study and to which the label 'committees of inquiry' is therefore attached.

It is important to be clear what purpose these distinctions between different kinds of committee serve. They are not in the first place intended to indicate the relative importance of independent committees. The fact that the first group is concerned with individual incidents, for example, does not mean that they are necessarily less important for public policy. Indeed, it is very often the implications for public policy which attract considerable public attention to these individual fact-finding investigations: the tribunal of inquiry into the Aberfan disaster;[1] the investigation into the collapse of the Ronan Point block of flats;[2] and the series of inquiries in the 1960s into allegations of ill-treatment of patients in hospitals[3] are all examples of this kind. Yet it remains true that there is a significant difference both in purpose and in practical operation between investigating an individual event and investigating a general problem. The main significance for the present study is that in the former case general questions of policy or procedure emerge only by implication, whereas in the latter they are the *raison d'être* of the investigation.

Again, committees which exist to offer advice largely on the basis of the experience and knowledge of their members rather than as a result of investigation may make a significant contribution to the development of public policy. The reports of the Criminal Law Revision Committee, for example, or the Food Additives and Contaminants Committee may well have had significant consequences for the way in which changes in the criminal law have been made or for the development of controls on the use of chemicals in foods. It is, however, true that the great

[1] H. C. Deb. 553, 1967; a tribunal of inquiry is, as its name indicates, not strictly a committee.

[2] HMSO, 1968.

[3] See especially the inquiries following publication of the book *Sans Everything* (Cmnd 3687, 1968); allegations of ill-treatment at Whittingham Hospital (Cmnd 4861, 1972); and at Ely Hospital (Cmnd 3975, 1969).

majority of these purely advisory committees are concerned with individual issues rather than general questions – with recommending food standards for cheese, or dust control for potteries – and this naturally follows from the fact that their members are generally experts in a particular field.

To exclude these two groups and concentrate on the middle group of general investigatory-advisory committees as committees of inquiry cuts across purely formal categories of classification such as by status (e.g. *ad hoc* or standing; statutorily-appointed or non-statutory), or by nomenclature (e.g. royal commissions as a separate group). The justification is that none of these categories in practice enables one to distinguish clearly those committees which share a common function. Those who have written on royal commissions, for example, are isolating a group of committees which, as has been recently pointed out,[1] may have little in common and may not differ significantly from committees with other titles.

But the functional approach adopted here raises certain difficulties, of which the main one is the sheer number and range of committees which it covers. Hence for practical reasons there are attractions in trying to limit the number of committees dealt with, or at least to concentrate attention on certain kinds of committee within the broad general range. A possible means of doing this is to select those committees of inquiry which because they deal with important subjects come closest to the traditional idea of a committee of inquiry.

SELECTION BY IMPORTANCE

Selection on these lines could be justified on the grounds that, since we are interested in the policy-making process, what really matters is to examine those committees which are significant in policy-making terms. This really raises two questions: (*a*) can it be done satisfactorily? and, more importantly, (*b*) is it right to restrict the study of committees of inquiry in this way?

One of the points which emerged from the discussion earlier in this chapter, and can be confirmed from the list in the Appendix, is that practically any subject which does or might involve action by the Government may be examined by a committee of inquiry. One distinction which might be drawn is between committees examining subjects where possible legislative changes are involved, and those in which

---

[1] Cf. Richard A. Chapman (ed.), *The Role of Commissions in Policy-Making* (Allen & Unwin, 1973), pp. 174–5.

administrative practices and procedures are under scrutiny. Clearly for some purposes this is a useful distinction to draw, but at best it is only an approximation to the kind of distinction proposed in the previous paragraph. It would, for example, put into the category of committees significant for policy-making some which clearly belong there, like the Jenkins Committee on Company Law [1] or the Kilbrandon Committee on the Marriage Law of Scotland.[2] And it would exclude committees concerned with purely organisational and practical questions such as the role of special hospitals [3] or highway maintenance.[4]

The difficulty is that there are many committees where in itself this criterion does not appear to offer a very satisfactory means of distinguishing significant from less significant committees. In 1967, for example, the Minister of Housing and Local Government appointed a committee to examine the arrangements for dealing with footpaths and bridleways which, as its report makes clear, was largely concerned with reviewing the existing legal provisions.[5] Early the following year the same minister appointed a committee which was to report on the best methods of carrying out the provisions of the Town and Country Planning Act, 1968, relating to public participation in the making of development plans.[6] The first committee clearly falls in the significant category on the criterion proposed just as clearly as the second does not, and yet it seems distinctly arbitrary to regard the first as more significant than the second if one views these committees in a wider context. The issue of public participation, for example, carries implications for social policy, and is likely to prove politically far more significant than footpaths policy.[7]

Nor are these isolated examples. A classification which puts committees on field monuments,[8] or the assessment of disablement [9] in the significant category but treats as less significant in policy-making terms committees on the training of pilots [10] or delays in commissioning power

[1] Cmnd 1749, 1962.
[2] Cmnd 4011, 1969.
[3] *Special Hospitals*, report of the Working-Party (HMSO, 1961).
[4] Report of the Committee on Highway Maintenance (HMSO, 1970).
[5] Report of the Footpaths Committee (HMSO, 1968).
[6] *People and Planning*, report of the Committee on Public Participation in Planning (HMSO, 1969).
[7] See, for example, J. B. Cullingworth, *The Social Content of Planning*, Vol. 2 of *Problems of an Urban Society* (Allen & Unwin, 1973) especially his final chapter, 'Planning in a Democratic Society', which stresses the political importance of pressures for citizen-participation in planning.
[8] Cmnd 3904, 1969.
[9] Cmnd 2847, 1968.
[10] Report of the Committee on Pilot Training (HMSO, 1963).

stations [1] is not entirely satisfactory. What is needed is a judgement of the relative importance of different committees based on a variety of factors of which the type of subject examined, the political circumstances of their origins and the implications in a broad sense for public policy are probably the most important. Such an assessment is more easily done when examining committees which bear on one particular area of policy e.g. education, than it is when looking at such vastly different areas as those covered by the committees cited earlier in this paragraph since at least in principle one can say in a defined area which committees are more important.

The important point, however, is that a large degree of subjective judgement is necessarily involved in trying to classify committees in this way; nor can it be got round, as has been ingeniously proposed, [2] by selecting for study only committees whose reports have been published as Command papers. For although use of the Command prefix is supposed to indicate the importance, and particularly the political importance, of a report,[3] in practice its use varies considerably from department to department.[4] To deal only with Command reports is to substitute the subjective judgement of officials for one's own judgement of importance.

It may be asked whether this really matters. Given the fact that there is no completely satisfactory means of classification in this field, then, it might be argued, subjective assessment or use of the Command prefix gives at least a rough and ready means of distinguishing major inquiries like the Royal Commission on Trade Unions and Employers' Associations or the Committee on the Civil Service from minor inquiries like that into the marine search and rescue organisation or that into the prison medical service.

The answer to this question really depends on the object in mind in examining committees of inquiry. If it could be assumed that important

[1] Cmnd 3960, 1969.

[2] See T. J. Cartwright, *Royal Commissions and Departmental Committees in Britain* (University of London Press, 1974).

[3] Current use of the Command prefix is governed by a Treasury circular to departments of 1921; a Command paper should either be the subject of early legislation or otherwise essential to MPs in carrying out their responsibilities (see P. and G. Ford, *A Breviate of Parliamentary Papers, 1917–1939* (Oxford University Press, 1951), p. xi).

[4] For example, important committee reports of the former Ministry of Transport like those on rural bus services (1961) and carriers' licensing (1965) were not issued as Command papers whereas relatively minor reports of the Home Office (e.g. licensing planning, Cmnd 2709, 1965) or the Ministry of Agriculture, Fisheries and Food (e.g. herbage seed supplies, Cmnd 3748, 1968) are frequently included in this series.

committees of inquiry were representative of all committees of inquiry, then a study of the former would indeed not only give us all the information which was needed but would also be more interesting. Unfortunately, not only can this assumption not be made, but it is in fact one of the questions which a study of committees of inquiry is designed to answer. It might, for example, be argued that important committees of inquiry operate in different ways and have different consequences from other committees of inquiry in that governments are less likely simply to accept and act upon reports dealing with complex and highly controversial subjects like the intermediate areas or higher education than they are with more limited and technical reports like those on hospital building maintenance or the selection and training of supervisors. To examine whether this is so or not requires consideration of the circumstances in which different kinds of committees of inquiry are appointed in order to draw comparisons between them, which would be impossible if the study were simply confined to important committees.

In other words, a study of committees of inquiry must at least start by acknowledging the very broad limits of the subject matter. Whether, and if so how, the practical problems of handling such a large and diverse subject can be satisfactorily resolved must inevitably underlie much of the subsequent discussion in this book. This question is very relevant to the problems of classification.

CLASSIFICATION OF COMMITTEES OF INQUIRY

One question suggested by this discussion is whether committees of inquiry can be classified according to the subject area with which they are concerned. The object of such a classification would be to try to make comparisons between committees dealing with different subject areas.

So far as the use of committees is concerned, it might seem relatively easy and useful to classify them according to the departments which sponsor them. There are certain problems in this approach, especially where a committee is sponsored by more than one department, like the Seebohm Committee [1] which had no less than four sponsoring departments (Home Office, Department of Education and Science, Ministry of Health and Ministry of Housing and Local Government). However, even allowing for these problems, it is by no means certain that departmental sponsorship is a useful guide for comparative purposes, except to the extent that one might wish to examine whether different depart-

[1] Committee on Local Authority and Allied Personal Social Services (Cmnd 3703, 1968).

mental traditions accounted at least in part for the different use of committees of inquiry.

The reason is the well-known one that government departments differ widely both in the extent and nature of the subjects they deal with and in their administrative responsibilities. They may be responsible for a single subject (like the former Ministries of Education and Health) or a group of subjects (like the Home Office or the former Board of Trade); they may be concerned with directly running a service (like the former Ministry of National Insurance) or with running it indirectly (like Education), or their duties may be largely regulatory (like the Board of Trade); or they may have a mixture of sometimes confusing purposes (like the former Ministry of Transport). Furthermore, as the examples indicate, departmental sponsorship may become even less useful for comparative purposes when previously quite separate departments, like Transport and Housing and Local Government, are merged into a single larger department.

CLASSIFICATION BY POLICY AREAS

Since this study is concerned with the use of committees of inquiry in relation to policy-making, a better approach to classification is in terms of policy areas. Such policy areas are not to be thought of as necessarily sharply-defined subjects, since the activities of government do not fall so neatly into compartments. There are, it is true, some policy areas which both approximate to subjects in this sense and correspond largely to the sphere of activity of major departments; examples are education and agriculture. But there are also subjects which are less easily defined and have much less relevance to departmental boundaries, like law reform or government relations with private industry or local government.

Policy areas are, therefore, in practice to be defined in pragmatic terms according to one's interest in particular aspects of government activity. Such definitions are not completely arbitrary, but on the other hand they cannot be entirely logical and schematic without introducing a wholly artificial and unrealistic note into the whole discussion. It follows that no scheme of classification will be valid for all purposes, although there are likely to be significant areas of overlap between different schemes. The Appendix to this study (pages 213 to 225) is an example of one attempt to distinguish policy areas and to allocate committees appointed between 1959 and 1968 to them. The following discussion draws on the Appendix material to illustrate the problems and difficulties.

It follows from what has been said above that the easiest areas for the allocation of committees are those, like education, which both conceptually and in practice are reasonably well defined. There are difficulties even here, of course. Should committees on medical education or agricultural education be assigned to the education category or to health services and agriculture? The answer depends on a judgement of where the main interest of the committee lies, and although this may not always be easy to decide it is in principle no more difficult a question than that for any kind of classification.

More difficult questions arise once one moves away from these relatively self-contained subjects. One can, for example, identify an important area of government policy as relations with industry. It is relatively easy to identify specific subjects, such as 'support for private industry' where the questions which arise are whether, and if so how, government should give support; the committees on the shipbuilding and aircraft industries fit neatly enough into this category. It is also relatively easy to identify areas where government has become more extensively involved with a particular industry like agriculture.

But there are other kinds of relationships which government may have with industry, and there are some kinds of industry which are important for other reasons. As regards the first point, the committees on the pressure vessel industry or on the means of authenticating engineering products are examples of government having little direct involvement with the industries concerned but seeking to help them resolve their own problems. Although, therefore, it is quite logical in one sense to include committees on shipbuilding and pressure vessels in the same category of government relations with specific industries, from another point of view these two could be regarded as exemplifying distinct subjects of interest.

Transport illustrates the second point raised in the preceding paragraph. From one point of view, transport is an industry, or rather series of industries, though of a distinctive kind. Committees like that on carriers' licensing are concerned with government relations with the road haulage industry, this time from the point of view of the extent of government regulation which is thought desirable. Yet a committee like that on traffic signs is concerned with transport in a much broader sense. Certainly, in part it is concerned with the effects of possible changes in policy on bodies such as the road haulage industry, but equally it is concerned with relations with the local authorities and the police and with the general public as road users.

One could of course meet these points to some extent by a more complex classification, for example, by having basic 'subject areas' as one axis and the particular aspect of government policy as a second axis (e.g. regulatory, financial support, etc.). Not only would this complicate the problem of assigning particular committees to particular categories and lead to a large number of different 'boxes' of classification; it would not adequately resolve other problems which arise.

There are, for example, a large number of committees whose task is to examine some set of statutory provisions and to consider whether any changes in them are desirable. Hence there seems to be a need for a category of 'law reform' in a classification of policy areas. But 'law reform' can in this sense cover anything from relatively limited questions like the use of positive covenants affecting land, which is of little general public concern, to more specific questions affecting definite though still limited interests, like industrial designs, rather more general concerns affecting important interests, like company law, and broad areas of general public interest, like the law on Sunday observance.

To put all these together in a single category would imply that the main focus of interest was what they had in common, namely, that they were all in some sense attempts to determine the adequacy of existing provisions of Acts of Parliament. In practice, it is surely more likely that one would want to examine the significance of the committees on industrial designs or company law in the context of their effect on these particular areas rather than as examples of law reform. On the other hand, the question of positive covenants is one which is much more concerned with legal technicalities and is therefore more likely to be of interest from a law reform point of view. There is another problem again with Sunday observance. It was not simply concerned with legal technicalities, nor on the other hand did it have a very specific policy-content, since, in general, governments do not claim responsibility for regulating how people should spend Sunday, as opposed to dealing with specific questions as they arise. The committee in fact falls into an area of general social policy, an admittedly ill-defined area but one which is important in terms of public interest and concern.

The differing nature of policy areas is also illustrated from the fourth main category distinguished in the Appendix, central and local government. The characteristic feature of this category is that the emphasis is on the organisation of public services and on the recruitment, training, etc. of public servants. This comes out most clearly in the case of such 'general' committees as the Fulton Committee on the Civil Service or the two royal commissions on local government. Yet it is often difficult to draw the line between this category and that of specific subject-categories. A committee like that on local authority and allied personal social services is both about the provision of a certain kind of service and about the internal organisation of local authorities; just as the Royal

Commission on the Police was concerned both with the constitutional position of the police and with the organisation and recruitment of police forces.

However one draws the boundaries for classification purposes there are thus likely to be awkward demarcation lines as well as examples of committees which seem to belong to two or more categories. It is hardly surprising that the largest category in the Appendix is headed 'Miscellaneous', although this category in fact covers two distinct groups of committees, those which fall into a subject group which is, however, too small to be separately distinguished, like the Committee on Broadcasting; and those which belong simultaneously to several different categories, like the Committee on the Remuneration of Ministers and Members of Parliament, or that on trawler safety.

Not only are there difficulties in drawing up a suitable system of classification of policy areas and in assigning committees to it; it may also be necessary sometimes to use more than one system of classification. Transport, for example, may, as indicated in the Appendix, form a subcategory of an industry group. But for certain purposes one may be interested in government policy towards the nationalised industries. For this purpose it would be necessary to reclassify the industry group into subcategories of 'public sector' and 'private sector' industries.

It might seem that the ambiguities and difficulties of drawing up a classification made the attempt to do so hardly worth while. Yet even within the broad limitations which have been discussed the classification in the Appendix is not entirely meaningless. It does, for example, suggest considerable variation in the use of committees even between areas in which government has direct responsibilities, that is, leaving aside those considerable areas in which a major question is whether, and how far, government should take action, such as relations with private industry or general social policy. In view of this, the remainder of this chapter will examine briefly six policy areas of major government activity and will consider whether the varying use of committees of inquiry gives any indication of the circumstances which are or are not favourable to their use.

SELECTED POLICY AREAS

The six areas chosen for discussion are:

1 Defence;
2 Overseas affairs;
3 Education;

4   Housing;
5   National health service;
6   Social security.

An obvious starting point is the fact that certain areas of government activity give rise to few if any committees of inquiry. Prominent among them are defence matters and overseas affairs. The main reasons are clearly connected with the manner in which government administration is conducted in these two areas. Many questions of defence policy are just as much matters of public concern and controversy as many matters of domestic policy. If it is right to have a royal commission to review the constitutional position of the police and the arrangements for their control and administration, then equally the position of the armed forces might seem a suitable subject for a committee of inquiry; and if policy on foot-and-mouth disease is a fit subject for a committee of inquiry, then equally policy on equipping the services with atomic weapons seems, on the face of it, to be a suitable subject.

Some defence subjects are examined by committees of inquiry. Examples outside the period covered by this study are the Donaldson Committee on Boy Entrants and Young Servicemen,[1] or the Nugent Committee (1971–3) which reviewed the holding of land for defence purposes; [2] and there are fairly frequently investigations into individual incidents, not necessarily by committees, like the one carried out by Mr Roderick Bowen, QC, in 1966, into the methods used for dealing with suspected terrorists in Aden,[3] or, more recently, the tribunal of inquiry into the shooting incident in Londonderry on 30 January 1972 in which thirteen civilians were killed.[4]

In relation, however, to the importance of defence policy not only to the security of the country, but in financial and economic terms, too, relatively little investigation is carried out by independent government-appointed committees.[5] One reason is clearly that governments are reluctant to have too much outside investigation of matters which are regarded as secret, as much defence information is. But even more fundamental is the difference between the way in which defence policy

[1] Cmnd 4509, November 1970.
[2] HMSO, 1973.
[3] Cmnd 3165, December 1966.
[4] H. C. 220, 1972.
[5] Though governments may, and frequently must, appoint advisory committees to assist them, whose reports, and indeed very existence, may not be known until long afterwards. (Cf. the account by C. P. Snow of the pre-war Committee for the Scientific Study of Air Defence, in *Science and Government*, Oxford University Press, 1961.)

is evolved and carried out, on the one hand, and say, agricultural or education policy on the other.

Agriculture and education involve relationships between government and people outside who are actually carrying on the business either of agriculture (farmers and farm-workers) or education (teachers and pupils). Clearly it involves a good deal more than this, but this is a minimum, basic fact of the situation.

The business of defence, on the other hand, is itself a government activity carried on by agents of the Government, that is, the armed forces. Much of the evolution of defence policy is consequently part of the internal activity of government. There are many specialists outside the Government, experts in this or that aspect of defence policy, and there is of course a very strong public interest in defence policy, but there are no organised bodies of people actively involved in the work of defence to compare with the unions, associations and organised pressure bodies of many different kinds which are so marked a feature of the domestic non-defence policy scene.

Similarly, the whole question of relations with other countries, which since 1968 has been the responsibility of the combined Foreign and Commonwealth Office, is regarded primarily as one for the Government itself to deal with, with advice from outside no doubt, but not requiring, in its substantive aspects, the kind of investigation and advice which a committee of inquiry provides. It is significant that the two committees of inquiry directly affecting the Foreign Office in the years 1959–68 were both concerned with organisational problems and not with foreign policy as such; [1] and that the few committees of inquiry affecting the former Colonial and Commonwealth Offices were largely concerned with technical advice and assistance. [2]

The question is not whether there ought to be more investigation of defence and foreign policy matters but rather what use government makes of committees of inquiry and for what reason. This question cannot simply be confined to listing the areas of government in which committees of inquiry are or are not commonly used. But to seek explanation necessarily involves not only trying to elucidate the significant differences between the policy-making process in different areas of government but also to some extent looking to the circumstances in

[1] Representational Service Overseas (Cmnd 2276, 1964); Overseas Representation (Cmnd 4107, 1969).

[2] E.g. Technical Assistance for Overseas Geology and Mining (Cmnd 2351, 1964): some committees came close to being committees of inquiry on substantive matters of policy, e.g. the Advisory Commission on the Review of the Constitution of Rhodesia and Nyasaland (Cmnd 1148, 1960).

which committees of inquiry are appointed – which is to anticipate the discussion in the next chapter.

Education by contrast is a subject which provides a good deal of activity for committees of inquiry, but it is not easy to see why this should be so without going into detailed discussion of the origin of individual committees. Given the importance of education politically there are obviously many controversial questions for decision, but this alone does not imply frequent use of committees of inquiry. Government relations with the nationalised industries, for example, is also an area of political and economic importance and one which gives rise to highly controversial questions. Yet in the period covered by this survey there were scarcely any committees of inquiry concerned with the nationalised industries, and those that existed were mainly related to civil air transport.

If this suggests that committees of inquiry are perhaps more likely to be found dealing with issues of social rather than economic importance, one can point on the one hand to the fact that other social issues like the policy and operation of the social security system are not commonly the subject of committees of inquiry; and on the other, to the fact that government policy for a number of major industries, which for various reasons have got into difficulties, has been the subject of committees of inquiry in recent years, among them the Geddes Committee of Inquiry into the Shipbuilding Industry,[1] the Plowden Committee on the Aircraft Industry [2] and the Rochdale Committee on Shipping.[3]

The difficulty which these illustrations point to is simply that there is no single or simple explanation of why committees of inquiry are more frequently used in some areas of government than others. We are not of course concerned with the purely chance factors which may make a particular subject or area prominent at a particular time and not at others. That is a matter for examination of the reasons for the appointment of a particular committee at a particular time.

The point can be illustrated by a brief and inevitably rather superficial comparison of the two halves of what since 1968 has been the 'giant' Department of Health and Social Security.

The former Ministry of Health, responsible for the administration of the national health service, either through its appointed agents, the regional hospital boards, boards of governors, hospital management committees and executive councils or through elected local authorities, made extensive use of both *ad hoc* and standing committees largely for

[1] Cmnd 2937, March 1966.
[2] Cmnd 2853, December 1965.
[3] Cmnd 4337, May 1970.

the purpose of getting advice from the professions most intimately con-cerned with the day-to-day running of the service – doctors, dentists, nurses, pharmacists and so on. Some of those committees, whether *ad hoc* or standing, were committees of inquiry, others more in the nature of expert or advisory committees. Committees of inquiry were typically concerned with organisational questions like the Committee on Senior Nursing Staff Structure[1] or the Working-Party on the Hospital Pharmaceutical Service.[2] But some were concerned with broader questions like the relationship of the pharmaceutical industry with the national health service.[3]

By contrast, the remaining responsibilities of the DHSS, and especially what used to be called the national insurance scheme, are rarely the subject of examination by committees of inquiry. Outside advice is provided by the National Insurance Advisory Committee and the Industrial Injuries Advisory Committee, and some of the investigations carried out by these bodies are of a sufficiently broad nature to be classed as committees of inquiry. But in the ten years covered by this survey no *ad hoc* committee of inquiry was appointed to examine a national insurance topic, with the partial exception of the Committee on the Assessment of Disablement which was, however, largely an expert committee with very limited terms of reference.[4]

Or again one may contrast government policy in the education field with that in housing. Both are politically and professionally contro-versial areas. There is extensive use of committees of inquiry into education matters, ranging from broad investigations like those into higher education[5] or primary education[6] to much more limited topics like the work and training of educational psychologists[7] or the teaching of Russian.[8] By contrast few committees are appointed to look into housing matters and fewer still to make the far-reaching investigations characteristic of the recent situation in education.[9]

DIFFICULTIES OF CLASSIFICATION

It is clear then even from this brief discussion that there is no single or

[1] HMSO, 1966.
[2] HMSO, 1970.
[3] Cmnd 3410, September 1967.
[4] Cmnd 2847, December 1965.
[5] Cmnd 2154, October 1963.
[6] HMSO, 1967.
[7] HMSO, 1968.
[8] HMSO, 1962.
[9] See also below pp. 199–200.

simple answer to the question why Committees of inquiry are more commonly found in some areas of government than others. Some of the important factors can be identified, such as the aims of government activity in different areas, the extent to which government is directly involved in the provision of a service or the nature of government's relations with outside interests. But to elucidate satisfactorily the use of committees of inquiry in different areas of government seems to require a very extensive investigation indeed. It seems to imply nothing less than an examination of the way in which policy-making evolves in different areas of government and of the part played by committees of inquiry in those individual policy-making contexts. The complexity of factors involved and the sheer size of such an undertaking rule it out as a practical task covering the entire field of government activity.

This chapter began with two questions: how to define committees of inquiry and how to classify them. The first question proved to be soluble only by the adoption of a very broad definition which brings in a large number of committees covering a wide range of subjects. This in turn makes it difficult to resolve the second question in a satisfactory way. Some very broad differences in the use of committees of inquiry in different areas of government can indeed be seen and some of the factors making for these differences are indicated, but the problem remains that to carry the analysis further requires much more detailed investigation.

The basic difficulty is that to make significant generalisations about committees of inquiry implies first that they form a homogeneous group or at least can be subdivided into a series of homogeneous groups. Yet in practice there are not (or not yet) adequate criteria for determining whether committees performing the same general function should be treated as a single category or several different categories. In theory an examination of the use of a sufficient number of committees in sufficient depth should help to resolve these questions. In practice it seems doubtful whether this is feasible.

Alternative more limited approaches are possible. One would be to follow up the kind of approach suggested in relation to the national health service and social security, that is to select specific areas of government policy and to examine what committees had been appointed and what part they had played in the development of policy. To be worth while, each of these would be a major study in itself. Or the case-study approach could be adopted, of looking in depth at a limited number of committees in isolation, chosen because they appeared to represent something of the variety of committees in subject matter and importance. Or possibly these two methods in combination might be used. It is impossible to take the discussion further without considering first other aspects of committees of inquiry in the following chapters. What is clear from the discussion in this chapter is the difficulty of devising a satisfactory classification in practice.

THE PURPOSES WHICH COMMITTEES SERVE

THE PROBLEM

On 9 December 1964 the Minister of Aviation, Mr Roy Jenkins, announced in the House of Commons the terms of reference and members of a committee to examine 'the future place and organisation of the aircraft industry in relation to the general economy of the country. . . .' Mr Angus Maude, for the Opposition, immediately asked what the Minister expected the Committee to find out 'which his Ministry, with its considerable expertise and its access to expert sources, does not already know or can very easily find out'. Mr Jenkins replied merely that he would hesitate to say what he expected the Committee to say after it had deliberated.[1]

Perhaps the commonest criticism of committees of inquiry is that they are a form of delaying-tactic, serving to enable the Government to put off a decision on some awkward problem. Such criticisms are frequently made both by Oppositions and by those who are anxious for a decision on the particular question referred to a committee of inquiry. The argument implicit in Mr Maude's question is that facts and opinions are already known or can be discovered by less formal and time-consuming means, and the important thing is for the Government to decide on its policy with the least possible delay.

Governments, on the other hand, rarely attempt to justify the appointment of a committee in very specific terms. Sometimes it is said that a committee is desirable because of strong differences of opinion among those affected by the subject in question, as happened when a committee was appointed to examine a proposal to import Charollais cattle on an experimental basis.[2] More commonly, if pressed, a minister may refer in general terms to the desirability of having difficult problems thoroughly examined, to the fact that changing circumstances may require changes in policies or practices, or simply to the fact that

[1] H. C. Deb. 703, 9 December 1964, 1548–51.
[2] H. C. Deb. 607, 15 June 1959, 9–10.

a long time has elapsed since a particular question was last examined by an independent committee. Thus Mr Henry Brooke, the Home Secretary, when accused of delaying tactics in appointing a committee on jury service in 1962 pointed both to the complexities of the problem and to the fact that the previous inquiry had been made forty-nine years earlier; [1] and Mr Maudling, the President of the Board of Trade, announcing the appointment of a committee to examine company law in 1959, gave as the main reason the fact that ideas and practices had changed since the war and it was desirable to see what implications these had for changes in the law. [2]

Most commonly, however, either no reason at all is given for the appointment of a committee, or else reference is made to the particular event or circumstance immediately preceding the appointment. [3] Committee reports themselves also frequently do not discuss the reasons for their appointment, although they often imply them. Sometimes, however, they have historical introductions giving the background to the inquiry, including a record of previous investigations. [4]

In considering the purposes which committees of inquiry serve, the basic question to be examined is why governments choose to use this particular device, and this question involves looking both at the circumstances in which committees are used and at the motives of governments in appointing them. An essential element in this examination is the extent to which accurate information is obtainable for answering these questions. It is also important to bear in mind the choices open to governments. Appointing a committee is one way of responding to a problem situation, but there are other choices at least theoretically possible: to do nothing, or to announce a preferred policy, for example. And there are situations where a government is specifically pressed to hold an inquiry and refuses without at the same time conceding any changes in policy. [5]

Several theoretical considerations are relevant to the question of the

[1] H. C. Deb. 667, 15 November 1962, 535–6.
[2] H. C. Deb. 614, 26 November, 1959, 569–73.
[3] There may of course be several reasons given; Mr Brooke's announcement about the Committee on Jury Service, for example, was in response to a question about representations he had received for increasing the number of women who served on juries.
[4] A notable recent example was the Committee on Allotments, whose report contained a long historical chapter (Cmnd 4166, October 1969).
[5] See, for example, Mr Harold Wilson's refusal to set up a royal commission on poverty on the grounds that government policy was already adequate to deal with the problems (H. C. Deb. 796, 17 February 1970, 209–11; 799, 16 April 1970, 1570–3).

purposes which committees serve. The rationale behind their appointment is that they serve in some way to provide a better means of dealing with a problem which has arisen, better, that is, than the alternatives open to the Government. But in what precisely does this 'better means' consist? One characteristic feature of committees of inquiry, for example, is that they enable a problem to be looked at in depth over a period of time by a group of people who are not directly involved in government. One question which arises, therefore, is whether an important reason for the use of committees of inquiry is that this is seen to be a positive advantage in the resolution of at least certain kinds of problem. Ministers and senior civil servants, it could be argued, are generally too much concerned with immediate and urgent issues to be able to devote time to the investigation and discussion of rather longer-term issues which nevertheless require for their resolution detailed and patient investigation. The implication is that the Government in these cases is entrusting to outsiders a task which it would like to carry out but which it is not well suited to doing.

This, however, raises further questions. Investigation and advice by outsiders leading to a published report is likely in any case to have a different quality from investigation by those working within government. A further question, therefore, is whether, in addition, governments see advantages in the fact that an independent, outside view expressed in a public document may carry more weight with public opinion and help to focus the policy issues better than some purely internal investigation. This view has affinities with that put forward by Sir Geoffrey Vickers, who sees the importance of committees of inquiry not so much in what they recommend as in the ways in which they form or change our appreciation of a situation.[1]

Simply to raise these questions is to indicate that an answer to the question why governments use committees of inquiry is likely to be a complex one, not least because we are concerned both with motives and with the choice of means and these can be looked at from different viewpoints. To a minister and his civil servants being pressed to take a certain course of action it may seem by no means obvious that that course is the right one, and certainly not without further investigation. To those pressing for action, setting up a committee may appear simply as cowardice and unwillingness to take necessary decisions. To outside observers it may often appear very difficult to decide when a prudent refusal to make too hasty a decision becomes unwillingness to take a necessary but politically unpopular decision.

[1] Sir Geoffrey Vickers, *The Art of Judgement* (Chapman & Hall, 1965), p. 50.

The criticism of use of committees of inquiry as a delaying tactic is also not quite so straightforward as it appears. If the criticism means that a particular committee has been appointed purely in order to avoid a necessary decision, there are nevertheless certain risks in doing so. The committee will ultimately produce a report which will be published and which may produce arguments and encourage debate even more unacceptable to the Government than the original pressures which the committee was designed to head off. It is true that by careful choice of the terms of reference and members, governments may to some extent hope to avoid getting unwelcome answers from a committee, but this cannot be by any means guaranteed.

Moreover, delay simply to put off an awkward question should, at least in theory, be distinguished from delay which enables a problem to be resolved through recommendation by a committee of a course of action which can be endorsed both by the Government and by at any rate a substantial body of outside opinion. There may of course be significant differences of view in relation to a particular problem about how far such a delay is really necessary as opposed, say, to the Government's deciding on a course of action without the benefit of a committee's advice, but it can hardly be denied that the use of committees in these circumstances indicates a difference of attitude as compared with a situation where government is simply trying to avoid having to come to a decision.

This brief introduction needs to be amplified by examining in more detail the origins of some individual committees. It should be emphasised that although information has been sought to make these accounts of origins as accurate as possible, the main aim has been to illustrate the problems, and especially the practical problems, of assessing the purposes which committees serve.

ORIGINS OF PARTICULAR COMMITTEES

Jury service

The Committee on Jury Service (1963–5) has already been mentioned. It was concerned only with 'the qualifications for, exemptions from, and conditions of jury service'. In other words, considering the controversial nature of the jury system itself, it was concerned with relatively limited questions. There were both immediate and longer-term reasons for the appointment of a committee at that time. There had long been criticism of the fact that liability for jury service was based on property qualifications originally laid down in 1825. Not only did the operation of the system give rise to anomalies in twentieth-century conditions (e.g. it effectively excluded large numbers of women), but there was a fairly general feeling that a qualification based on property was in any case inappropriate to the social conditions of the mid-twentieth century.

The immediate circumstances giving rise to the committee included a certain amount of agitation about the anomalies of the system particularly as they affected women, mainly from some women's organisations and from some Labour backbenchers.[1] But although these provided the immediate occasion of the appointment of the committee, the more interesting question is why the Government found it necessary to set up a committee at all, given that there was little dispute that the system needed changing.

There were two reasons for the appointment of a committee in preference to the Government's simply deciding on a change of policy. There was first the tradition against making changes in the administration of justice without first having some kind of formal inquiry.[2] This tradition was reinforced by the feeling that since the jury represented the lay element in the administration of justice it was right that any change in the system should be the subject of public scrutiny. Secondly, there was the question of what should replace the property qualification. The obvious candidate was the electoral roll, but there was argument about whether some additional or separate qualification might be necessary, on the grounds that some at least of the cases going before jurors (e.g. some fraud cases) were too complex for voters of limited education and experience to deal with satisfactorily.

The main element in this particular case, then, was the desire of the government to have an independent review which would both demonstrate the desirability of a change and put forward a practical scheme to achieve it. It is possible to argue both from the appointment of the committee and from events following its report [3] that the committee merely served to put off a decision which the Government could perfectly well have made in 1963; but it could equally well be argued that it would have been wrong to change a long-standing legal practice without having the arguments thoroughly examined by a committee and set out and published. This question, like the more fundamental question of

[1] E.g. Sir Barnett Janner and Mrs Judith Hart (see H. C. Deb. 656, 20 March 1962, 210–20; 672, 19 February 1963, 249–258).

[2] Cf. the remarks made by a Conservative backbencher lawyer Mr Charles Doughty on an attempt by Mrs Hart to bring in a Bill on the subject (H. C. Deb. 656, 20 March 1962, 214).

[3] The Government accepted the report in August 1965, but legislation was not passed until 1972.

whether there ought to have been an inquiry, not simply into jury service but into the working of the jury system itself,[1] leads directly into a discussion of the ways in which law reform is carried out. This important issue will be examined later, but here it can at least be said that the committee on jury service exemplifies the classic dispute between reformers and government. To Sir Barnett Janner it was as 'plain as a pikestaff' that the law was ridiculous even without an inquiry, whereas to Mr Brooke the reformers were underestimating the complexities of changing the law and the need to look at the whole subject very carefully before doing so. One man's unnecessary delay is another man's essential prudence.

Civil air transport

By way of contrast we may consider the (Edwards) Committee of Inquiry into Civil Air Transport (1967–9). In announcing the Committee the President of the Board of Trade (Mr Douglas Jay) referred first to the 'feeling of uncertainty' about the future of the industry expressed in criticism of the licensing system and, secondly, to the fact that he wanted independent advice before making changes particularly as 'there has been no independent inquiry since the war and the time has come to take stock'.[2] The terms of reference were in fact drawn widely to include 'the economic and financial situation and prospects of the British civil air transport industry' as well as the methods of regulating competition and licensing.

The reasons for the appointment of a committee at that particular time have to be looked at in the wider context of the history of governmental relations with the airline companies, and, in particular, the decision of the Conservative Government in the late 1950s to allow private airlines a much larger share in civil air transport and the setting up in 1960 of the Air Transport Licensing Board to further that end and regulate competition between the state and private airlines. This was followed in 1962 by a pledge by the Labour Party that they would put an end to the 'undermining' of the public air corporations.[3] Thus the relationship between the public and private sectors in air transport and the means of regulating that relationship were certainly important factors in the appointment of the Committee.

This, however, is merely the bare bones of the story. Granted that a problem had arisen in that arrangements instituted in 1960 had not, in the view of the Labour Government, proved satisfactory, three other

[1] See H. C. Deb. 733, 4 August 1966, 660–1.
[2] H. C. Deb. 751, 26 July 1967, 641–3.
[3] See David Corbett, *Politics and the Airlines* (Allen & Unwin, 1965), p. 160.

questions require to be answered. Why have a wider inquiry? Why set up a committee? Why particularly in 1967? The attempt to answer these questions poses certain problems which are relevant to the wider discussion of the uses of committees of inquiry.

In a recent work an academic economist has argued that because world air travel is growing rapidly and because of the problems of rapid technological developments there is a need for airline operators to adopt a flexible policy to meet changing circumstances, and for the institutional arrangements to be brought up to date fairly often, and he sees in the fact that these conditions were not being met in the early 1960s the reasons for the Government's decision to set up the Edwards Committee.[1]

There are thus a number of specific issues behind the appointment of the Edwards Committee which imply and lead into the more general issue which their terms of reference required them to examine. There is, first, the issue which figured most prominently in parliamentary debates, the ideological issue between the two main parties couched in the language of free enterprise and competition versus state control and management. At an early stage in the life of the Labour Government, the Minister of Aviation (Mr Roy Jenkins) announced two decisions affecting the relations between the public air corporations and the independent airlines. On 25 November 1964 he announced that BEA and BOAC would in future be allowed to tender for long-term contracts for carrying troops and defence equipment, which had hitherto been the province solely of the independent airlines.[2] Of more importance was his statement on 17 February 1965 laying down 'guidelines' which indicated the Government's view of the objectives of air licensing policy; these included the undesirability of having more than one British carrier operating on the same international route, and refusal to allow independent airlines operating limited frequency services on United Kingdom routes to have unrestricted or extended frequency services.[3]

In spite of the fact that Mr Jenkins claimed that these statements did not represent a change of policy, the Conservative Opposition saw them as an attempt to protect the air corporations at the expense of the independent airlines. In a debate (on an Opposition supply motion) the Opposition spokesman (Mr Angus Maude) gave an undertaking to restore opportunities to the independent airlines, but he also said that a future Conservative government might well want to take 'a broad

[1] A. W. J. Thomson and L. C. Hunter, *The Nationalised Transport Industries* (Heinemann, 1973), p. 36.
[2] H. C. Deb. 702, 25 November 1964, 1287–91.
[3] H. C. Deb. 706, 17 February 1965, 1186–92.

searching' look at the whole system of licensing and appeal and at the relations of independents and corporations on scheduled routes. It was left to Mr Edward Heath, in winding up for the Opposition, to make the strongest attack on Mr Jenkins, especially on the grounds that if he wanted to change the policy laid down in the 1960 Act he should have brought forward new legislation.[1]

Behind and as it were merging into this issue of party politics was the practical question of the right machinery for regulating the relationship between the air corporations and the independent airlines. Mr Maude's implied hint that the 1960 Act might not after all be the final answer was taken up much more strongly by others. Mr Stonehouse for the Ministry of Aviation in the same debate claimed that policy had been uncertain and in a muddle since 1960, and later the Edwards Committee endorsed the view that the Air Transport Licensing Board had not been able to evolve a coherent policy within which the industry could make firm plans.[2]

The initial policy of the Labour Government to attempt to work within the framework of existing legislation gradually gave way to the view that new legislation might well be the only way to deal with the situation. Four months before he announced the appointment of the Edwards Committee, Mr Douglas Jay, President of the Board of Trade (which had by then taken over the responsibility for civil aviation), spoke of his careful and continuing study of these difficult problems, of the possibility of changes being made, but of the need to carry on on the existing basis until precise conclusions had been reached.[3] By the time he was almost ready to announce the committee he was saying more definitely that he did not regard the existing legislation as satisfactory.[4]

Thus the question of the licensing system provided the focus for continuing examination of civil aviation policy. If there had been no more to it than a question of machinery, Mr Jenkins's statement of objectives, combined perhaps with some modification of the machinery, might have been enough and might have done away with the need for a committee. But the difficulties of the licensing system were only a symptom of the bigger problems which had to be resolved – what general policy should there be for civil aviation, what should be the structure of the industry to help achieve this, as well as what administrative arrangements should be made. Once the stage of considering these wider issues had been reached, a committee of inquiry became a distinct possibility,

[1] H. C. Deb. 707, 1 March 1965, 935–1064.
[2] See Cmnd 4018, esp. paras 639–40, 652.
[3] H. C. Deb. 743, 15 March 1967, 494–5.
[4] H. C. Deb. 750, 19 July 1967, 2123–4.

not because the Government had no ideas of its own to bring forward but because a committee would be able to expose the problems and analyse them at length, as well as putting forward specific proposals. Furthermore a committee could also take into account other important issues such as the financial performance and (in the case of the private sector) viability of the airlines and the quality of management and its relation to efficiency.

This does not necessarily mean that the decision to appoint a committee evolved in a neat and orderly way. Discussion of issues like civil aviation policy arises just as much out of the continuous process of day-to-day administration, such as how to decide a particular appeal to the Minister arising from a decision of the Air Transport Licensing Board, as out of a conscious attempt to define policy in the abstract. Nevertheless, it seems possible to distil from this complex situation the important stages in the appointment of the Edwards Committee: the desire to achieve certain political ends frustrated by unsuitable administrative machinery but leading to a realisation that much wider issues were involved; the complexity of these issues leading to uncertainty about the best course to follow; the decision to appoint a committee.

If we ask what purpose the Edwards Committee served and whether the Government could have decided to do without it, it seems clear that the answer to the second question is 'yes'. In one sense the appointment of a committee served to delay a decision and to continue a period of uncertainty for the industry which, because of the election of June 1970, in fact lasted until the Civil Aviation Act of 1971. On the other hand, the Government hoped both to get from the Committee acceptable and workable solutions to the problems and to be able to demonstrate the complexities and difficulties arising from the particular circumstances of the industry – or, as the Edwards Committee put it, 'there are certain problems in transport that are excruciatingly difficult even in theory let alone in practice'.[1] The critical question is not whether the Government could have acted without a committee but whether a committee enabled the problem to be dealt with in the long run in a more satisfactory way.

Educational psychologists

The future of the airlines might be expected to arouse political controversy. Jury service also, in its more limited sphere, has a general public interest. The field of work of educational psychologists employed by local education authorities, their qualifications and training, does not on

[1] Cmnd 4018, para. 10.

the other hand appear to be a subject likely to be of much interest and concern outside a narrow circle of people. A working-party on this subject was set up by Mr Crosland, Secretary of State for Education and Science, in February 1965 and made its report three years later.

The broad general background to the appointment of the Working-Party was the situation which had developed since the last investigation, into the problems of maladjusted children, by the Underwood Committee in 1955. That Committee had recommended an expansion in the child guidance service, which had, however, not been fully achieved partly because not enough trained psychologists had been coming forward, and partly because of wastage among those working in the service. A more specific precursor to the 1965 working-party was a pamphlet issued in 1963 by the British Psychological Society alleging, among other things, the inadequate salaries of educational psychologists as a reason for the relatively disappointing growth of the service.[1] Much of the pressure for action to be taken came from the local authority associations which were particularly concerned about the difficulties experienced by local authorities in obtaining staff.

The appointment of the Working-Party by the Department of Education and Science was thus largely a response to these pressures. The situation was a not uncommon one in relation to the appointment of committees. There was general agreement that something should be done to strengthen the child guidance and school psychological services, but precisely how it was to be done needed examination. The advantage of a committee was that it could both examine the possibilities and also provide in a public document the necessary arguments and statistical data for its recommendations as a contribution to any decisions which might ultimately be taken on the future of the service. It is true that there was nothing in the terms of reference of the Working-Party to prevent it from coming to the conclusion that the service was adequate. It was highly unlikely that they would do so given the fact that the members all had a background in the subject and that the evidence was largely of deficiencies in the service and possible remedies.

The situation needs also to be set against the general background of the education service. If more and better-paid educational psychologists were to be required it was largely for local education authorities both to acknowledge this as a desirable aim, and to take the necessary steps to make it a reality. As *The Times Educational Supplement* pointed out

[1] See the article by Phillip Williams, a member of the Committee, on the School Psychological Service in *New Society* (4 February 1965), pp. 17–20.

when the Committee reported, the crucial questions of where the extra money was to come from and what priority educational psychology was to have among the many competing claims on educational resources had still to be resolved.[1]

Traffic signs

In December 1961, Mr Ernest Marples, Minister of Transport, and Mr John Maclay, Secretary of State for Scotland, jointly appointed a committee 'to review traffic signs on all-purpose roads, as distinct from motorways, including roads in urban areas, and to recommend what changes should be made'.[2]

Unlike the other committees so far considered in this chapter, the Committee on Traffic Signs was concerned with a problem which simultaneously had a high technical content and had a very direct and immediate implication for the general public. There were also distinct financial implications in making changes in the existing system.

The general background to the Committee is easily explained. Britain's traffic signs had been devised in 1933 and last examined by a departmental committee in 1944. Since then the amount of traffic as well as the conditions under which it operated had changed enormously. It was therefore reasonable to consider whether the existing system of traffic signs was still appropriate in the changed circumstances.

This was the *raison d'être* of the Committee but in itself it does not indicate precisely why the Government decided to appoint a committee in 1961 nor what its exact purpose was. Criticism had been voiced of the existing signs in Parliament and the press and by the motoring organisations – that they were too small, often poorly sited, difficult to pick out at night, etc. These criticisms served to keep the question active in the Ministry. The problem of what, if anything, to do about it was also kept more clearly in focus by the existence of an alternative, the system in use in most European countries and adopted by a United Nations conference in Geneva in 1949. As more and more drivers encountered this system on their journeys to the Continent so more and more asked whether the European system should not be introduced here.[3]

The particular date, 1961, when the Committee was appointed is related to a further development. When the first motorways were built in the late 1950s the question of what traffic signs should be provided on them was remitted to an advisory committee whose final report was

[1] *The Times Educational Supplement* (27 September 1968).
[2] The Committee reported in 1963.
[3] Cf. H. C. Deb. 631, 30 November 1960, WA 53.

dated December 1960.[1] The committee's advice was adopted and the success of these new signs was one of the factors emphasised by the Ministry as drawing attention to the need for revision of ordinary traffic signs.[2]

It might seem, therefore, that a relatively simple decision had to be made by the Department on whether to change the existing system in favour of the internationally agreed system. But, in the first place, a great many interests were involved, including the police, motoring organisations, planners and treasurers; and, in the second place, this is just the kind of issue on which people tend to hold strong, personal views.

There was therefore an advantage from the Department's point of view in having the whole question examined by an independent committee whose recommendations would be more likely to win a favourable reception whan would a simple announcement of a decision by the Minister. Essentially, therefore, the job of the Worboys Committee on Traffic Signs was to prepare the way for a change to a new system. What the Committee recommended is what the Department wanted to do anyway. The Committee's function was therefore largely educative.

Medical education

The Royal Commission on Medical Education, 1965–8, was, according to the *British Medical Journal*, 'born in somewhat obscure circumstances in 1965'; the journal went on to hint darkly that 'the manner of its origin remains to cast a shadow over its destiny'.[3] What the *British Medical Journal* seemed to be suggesting was that the Royal Commission was merely a piece of political window dressing. It is worth trying to see how far this was so.

It was common ground between the profession and the political parties in the 1960s that largely because of serious errors in forecasting demand Britain faced a shortage of doctors. Shortly before the 1964 General Election, Labour's spokesman on health affairs and subsequent Minister of Health, Mr Kenneth Robinson, pledged that a new Labour Government would establish at least four new medical schools.[4] Eleven months later the Prime Minister announced the appointment of a royal

[1] The Report, *Traffic Signs for Motorways*, an attractively designed booklet was not published until 1962 which suggests that it was intended to form part of the educative process for new signs generally.

[2] *Roads in England and Wales*, 1961–2 (H. C. 279), para. 48.

[3] *British Medical Journal* (13 April 1968), p. 66.

[4] H. C. Deb. 699, 27 July 1964, 1018: Labour's 1964 election manifesto was more cautious in promising to establish new medical schools but without specifying the number.

commission to review the whole question of medical education including 'the pattern, number, nature or location of the institutions providing medical education'.

Thus a fairly immediate issue, that of increasing the output of doctors from the medical schools, was merged into more general and longer-term questions of the kind of training doctors should receive and the form of organisation and administration appropriate for the medical schools.

These longer-term questions, especially about the nature of medical education, were, however, ones which had been a matter of increasing concern and debate, particularly in view of the rapid changes and developments taking place in medical science. The departments most closely concerned (Education and Science, and Health) were therefore moving to the view that a full-scale inquiry was desirable. In a sense the Labour Party's specific commitment to building new medical schools served to focus the need for such an inquiry, since without it it was by no means clear whether, and if so how many, new medical schools were needed.[1]

Thus, there was not really anything very obscure about the origins of the Royal Commission. An acknowledged and growing problem was brought to the fore by a political event, but even without the latter a committee of inquiry would amost certainly have been needed.

Turnover taxation

The Committee on Turnover Taxation appointed by Mr Maudling, the Chancellor of the Exchequer, in April 1963 had several unusual features. Probably the most important from the point of view of the present discussion is the fact that Mr Maudling gave fairly explicit reasons for the appointment of the Committee. He pointed out that many people advocated an added-value tax of the kind which was common on the Continent, on the grounds that it provided a built-in incentive for exports. He went on: 'Whatever case there may be on other grounds for broadening the base of indirect taxation, I have never been convinced that the substitution of an added-value tax, either for profits tax or for purchase tax, would provide, in practice, an effective incentive to exports.'

However, many people did believe this and 'neither I, nor my advisers, would claim for Whitehall a monopoly of knowledge in these matters'. Since much would depend on how businessmen would react

[1] The Royal Commission in fact proposed and the Government accepted, before it made its report, that a new school should be established at Southampton, but it was not until late in 1970 that the (Conservative) Government accepted the need for the establishment of a second school at Leicester.

to a different system of this kind and this was a matter of considerable controversy he had asked Mr Gordon Richardson to conduct an inquiry which 'will enable the full facts of this controversy, which I do not think are yet widely known, to be made available for public discussion and for the formulation of policy'.[1]

Value-added tax was, and, it need hardly be said, remains, a highly controversial subject. As with all taxes, controversy tends to focus on three areas, the economic effects, the relative burdens and fairness for different groups of people, and the cost and complexity of administration. The importance of the first of these considerations for VAT was that if it could be shown that it could make a positive contribution to the growth of exports, the case for its introduction would be immeasurably strengthened. This indeed was the argument put forward by the Labour Opposition in 1961 in urging the Government to consider the feasibility of a turnover tax as an encouragement to exporters.[2]

That Mr Maudling should at the outset have expressed considerable scepticism about the effects of a value-added tax on the stimulation of exports strongly suggests that he and the Treasury did not expect that a committee would come to a different conclusion. The expectations of ministers in appointing committees are often implicit in the circumstances in which this happens and in the manner of appointment; they are rarely made so explicitly. Ministers indeed are usually careful to avoid any expression of opinion, contenting themselves with general statements such as 'the time has come for a thorough review' or 'it is desirable that the whole question should be examined impartially'. Mr Maudling also went on explicitly to draw attention to one advantage of appointing a committee, that of presenting the facts of the situation for public debate.

It is, of course, true that the mere fact of setting up a committee does not in itself guarantee that the hoped-for or expected conclusions will emerge in the committee's report. On the other hand, governments can influence both in drawing up the terms of reference, and, as is considered in a later chapter, in appointing members of committees, the kind of inquiry which is carried out.[3]

[1] These statements were made in the course of a Budget Speech: see H. C. Deb. 675, 2 April 1963, 467.

[2] See the speech by Mr Harold Wilson (H. C. Deb. 645, 26 July 1961, 452–3).

[3] Mr Harold Wilson, Leader of the Opposition, complained that a 'full' and 'high-powered' committee with tax experts and representatives of industry ought to have been appointed instead of the three-man committee consisting of a merchant banker, an accountant and an economist (H. C. Deb. 675, 2 April 1963, 513).

The terms of reference of the Richardson Committee were not confined simply to the question of the effect on exports. The Committee was to consider the practical effects of introducing a turnover tax having regard to a number of broad issues.[1] Although, therefore, the Government had publicly expressed scepticism about one of the main arguments used in favour of such a tax, its main purpose in appointing the Committee was to give public airing to the whole question without commitment to any particular solution.

Pressure vessels

By contrast with the Committee on Turnover Taxation, the Committee of Inquiry of Pressure Vessels was not specifically asked to make inquiries but simply 'to recommend ways of improving pressure vessel technology, including standards, design and manufacture'.

The subject matter of this committee also differs from that of all the other committees so far considered in this chapter, in that there was no direct government involvement. It might be thought that the improvement of pressure vessel technology was essentially a matter for the industry itself, with government interest and concern limited to advice and encouragement. It was not, after all, an industry in which public ownership was an issue, nor one dependent on government support in the very different ways in which the aircraft and shipbuilding industries, both the subject of committees of inquiry in the 1960s, have become dependent.

Mr Wedgwood Benn, the Minister of Technology, in announcing the appointment of the Committee in December 1966, referred to difficulties which had arisen in formulating standards for pressure vessels and said that he had appointed an 'expert and independent' committee 'at the request of the British Standards Institution' and after consultation with the CBI and other interested bodies.[2] Standards were indeed at the root of the reasons for the appointment of this Committee. The manufacturers were in dispute with the insurance companies over whether the standards fixed by the BSI concerning safety were too stringent and therefore affected the industry's competitiveness in

[1] The full terms of reference were: 'To inquire into the practical effects of the introduction of a form of turnover tax, either in addition to existing taxation, or in substitution either for the purchase tax or the profits tax or both. In conducting the inquiry regard should be had to (a) the development of the economy and the promotion of exports; (b) the fair distribution of the burden of taxation; (c) the maintenance of the revenue; and (d) efficiency in tax collection and administration.

[2] H. C. Deb. 737, 9 December 1966, WA 378–9.

export markets. This was a dispute which the BSI could not resolve and which carried wider implications than simply the question of standards. Government was involved to the extent that the BSI was supported by government funds, but perhaps more to the point was the importance of the pressure vessel industry in a technologically advanced economy. Government was therefore interested in a healthy, competitive industry. Basically, therefore, the Government's role in the appointment of the Committee was that of an honest broker wanting to find a solution acceptable to all sides of the industry. The attitude was illustrated by government reaction to the Committee's recommendation, that a pressure vessel authority should be established, where it was made clear that it would be left to the industry to decide whether it wanted such a body.[1]

Foot-and-mouth disease

In October 1967 there was recorded the first outbreak of foot-and-mouth disease in what proved to be the worst recorded epidemic of the disease in this country. The following February the Minister of Agriculture, Fisheries and Food, Mr Fred Peart, appointed a committee under the Chairmanship of the Duke of Northumberland 'to review the policy and arrangements for dealing with foot-and-mouth disease in Great Britain and to make recommendations'.

In this he was following a tradition of fifty years. Three times, from 1922 onwards, after a major outbreak of the disease, departmental committees had been appointed usually to examine the causes and make recommendations.

The reason for the tradition is obvious. The policy of slaughter of affected herds causes both hardship to individual farmers and expense to the Exchequer which has to pay compensation. Since that policy has not been sufficient to prevent serious outbreaks from time to time, it is natural that the policy should be re-examined on the occasions when serious outbreaks do occur, and possible alternatives, especially the use of vaccination, examined. Re-examination of policy could of course be carried out simply by the Ministry consulting as necessary with the farming and other interests. However, the advantage of a committee in this kind of situation is that it is open in the sense that it receives formal evidence from anyone who cares to provide it and that it publishes a report setting out its analysis and the reasons for its particular recommendations. A policy which carries such heavy implications as the slaughter policy for foot-and-mouth disease might therefore be thought

---

[1] See H. C. Deb. 794, 19 January 1970, WA 17–18.

to be more acceptable if it has been endorsed by an independent committee; alternatively, if the Committee recommends a different policy the arguments will be set out for public discussion.

The Department and the Minister believed the slaughter policy to be the right one and therefore hoped that the Committee would endorse it.[1] If so, it would reassure the farmers and the public that all reasonable steps were being taken to deal with the disease.

HOW FAR IS GENERALISATION POSSIBLE?

The eight examples of committee origins described above seem to offer a large range of possible circumstances and motives for the appointment of committees. The exercise could be repeated with a further eight or eighty committees but, the criticism might be, however interesting or illuminating this might be for the particular committees concerned it would tell us little or nothing by way of generalisation about the purposes which committees serve, except to show that they can serve a great variety of purposes. Apart from the fact that this latter point may be of some interest in itself, the object of examining these eight committees has been to see whether anything revealing or significant can be said about committees in general from a selection deliberately chosen to represent some of the varied possibilities which can arise; and, secondly, to comment on some of the difficulties and problems which arise and the implications which they have for more extensive generalisations.

It is possible to distinguish three questions in relation to the purposes which committees serve – real versus ostensible motives, the relative importance of different motives, and the circumstances which give rise to committees. In most cases the three need to be considered together rather than in isolation. Even where a committee appears to have a straightforward origin, as with the Northumberland Committee on Foot-and-Mouth Disease, it is not enough simply to assume a connection between the immediate origins of the Committee, in this case an outbreak of the disease, and its ostensible purpose, that is to re-examine existing policy. Re-examination of policy scarcely ever, if at all, takes place out of the blue. There will almost certainly be in any given situation pressures for a change in policy, weak or strong, internal or external, which have to be accommodated in the perpetual process of policy-

---

[1] As Mr Peart implied in an interview on radio in the autumn of 1972 when a further outbreak of foot-and-mouth disease seemed to threaten (although in fact it was later diagnosed as swine vesicular disease). Of course, endorsement of the general lines of policy did not necessarily mean endorsement of all aspects of it, as indeed proved to be the case with the Northumberland Committee.

making. To put it at its most extreme, the Northumberland Committee *might* have been appointed because there was a strong feeling in the Department that existing policy should be changed and the outbreak in 1967 merely provided the occasion for this opposition to existing policy to be most strongly voiced; the Committee might then have been appointed either to head off this opposition or as a concession to it depending on what view one takes of the kind of committee which was appointed.

If there are or can be doubts of this kind in relation to a relatively straightforward committee like that on foot-and-mouth disease, many more questions can be raised about a committee with more complex origins, like the Edwards Committee on Civil Air Transport. Here both specific and general reasons were put forward by the Minister for having an inquiry at that particular time, and other reasons have been indicated from the history of events in the early 1960s. But were these the only reasons for the committee? Whether they were or not, what was the relative strength of them, and was there in fact a primary reason or motive?

Such questions are of great importance in trying to elucidate what really happened in a particular case. Unfortunately, there can rarely, if ever, be conclusive answers to the questions. At some point one has to judge the answers on the available evidence. The question is, therefore, how far it is reasonable to pursue the evidence in order to have an adequate basis to judge.

At this point, too, the nature of the evidence is also relevant. Public statements, whether by ministers, committees, interested parties or 'outsiders', are obvious sources of information but, like all such sources, have to be interpreted, that is to say, they cannot necessarily be taken simply at their face value. Moreover, the true reasons for the appointment of a particular committee may well remain as a result a matter of considerable argument. This is hardly surprising, given that we are concerned with trying to distil out of a mass of day-to-day discussion and debate, first, the precise point in time at which a decision to appoint a committee was taken, secondly, the main factors affecting that decision, and thirdly, the motives and intentions of those making the decision. All these three questions inevitably involve both factual knowledge and inference, and the process of arriving at a conclusion from the available evidence is a familiar one in any historical inquiry.

The real difficulty is in applying the process to contemporary or near-contemporary events where there is a two-fold problem: first, the inaccessibility in most cases of certain documentary evidence, namely that recorded on departmental files in the form of correspondence, reports of private meetings and discussions, memoranda to ministers, cabinet committees, etc.; secondly, the possible relevance of unrecorded and private conversation and discussion. Beyond this is the practical problem, which recurs throughout the whole study, of the sheer number of committees and the extent to which it is practicable to examine origins in detail – a point which will be considered further later in this chapter.

THE DONOVAN COMMISSION

To illustrate the first two points in the previous paragraph, however, it is useful to examine two accounts of the (Donovan) Royal Commission on Trade Unions and Employers' Associations set up by the Labour Government in 1965. It is characteristic of the great bulk of committees of inquiry which are set up that there is little public discussion of why they are set up. Most comment is reserved for the reports of committees and the proposals for action which they make. This is certainly true of the eight committees considered earlier in this chapter. But some committees, largely because of their political implications, attract more attention, and this is certainly true of the Donovan Commission which has been examined by Peter Jenkins as part of a wider account of the origins of the Labour Government's policy towards the trade unions [1] and by Robert Kilroy-Silk as one of five case-studies of committees.[2]

The Commission themselves did not, except by implication and in the most general terms, indicate why a royal commission should have been appointed in 1965. They referred to the 'transformation of the social and economic life of the country' since the previous Royal Commission of 1903, and to more recent changes which had seemed to represent a departure from the general principle of non-intervention by the State in industrial relations, as in the Contracts of Employment Act, 1963, and they concluded that they were doing their work at a 'time when the basic principles of our system of industrial relations are in question'.[3]

More explicitly, Kilroy-Silk refers to the 'fairly widespread dissatisfaction' with trade unions and industrial relations and the demand for reforms expressed in books published in the early 1960s.[4] The specific issue which brought matters to a head, however, was the judgement in the Rookes v. Barnard case which made unions threatening strike action

---

[1] Peter Jenkins, *The Battle of Downing Street* (Charles Knight, 1970).
[2] Robert Kilroy-Silk, 'The Donovan Royal Commission on Trade Unions', in Richard A. Chapman (ed.), *The Role of Commissions in Policy-Making* (Allen & Unwin, 1973).
[3] Cmnd 3623 (June 1968), paras 16, 45.
[4] Op. cit., p. 42.

liable to legal action from which they had hitherto believed themselves immune under the Trade Disputes Act, 1906. The TUC simply wanted the law amended to restore the position to what it had been thought to be before Rookes *v.* Barnard; the Conservative Government in its last months in office in 1964 thought that this question should be linked to the wider issue of trade union law and proposed a committee to be appointed after the forthcoming election.

This much is public knowledge, but what of the decision by the Labour Government elected in October 1964 to appoint a royal commission in spite of the fact that they appeared to be committed simply to an amendment of the existing law, as the TUC wanted? [1] Kilroy-Silk says that the Government 'appear to have decided' on a royal commission and got the TUC to acquiesce in making a reversal of the Rookes *v.* Barnard judgement dependent on the setting up of a royal commission. He regards that case as a 'godsend' for the Labour Government; the demand for an investigation was 'almost irresistible', but was politically difficult for a Labour Government; so the case 'provided the excuse for a Commission, and the Commission provided the excuse for procrastination. The Government could claim to be doing something when, in fact, it was doing nothing. Or rather it had managed to pass what to it was a politically dangerous issue on to other shoulders.' [2]

Peter Jenkins, from his standpoint as a political journalist, gives a rather more personal interpretation of events. Harold Wilson did not want an inquiry but George Woodcock offered it because ever since he had become general secretary of the TUC in 1960 'he had been looking for a catalyst for trade union reform'. Convinced of the need for strengthening the TUC at the expense of individual unions and for a reform of the structure of the movement he wanted an inquiry which would help to educate the unions, the public and the Government in this direction. Hence it was essential that he himself should be a member of the Commission. Ray Gunter, on the other hand, Labour's Minister of Labour, was looking for answers to practical questions about problems like productivity and restrictive practices and did not therefore want partisan people like Woodcock as members. The quarrel between Gunter and Woodcock ended in a compromise, and the Royal Commission had the useful purpose from the Government's point of view 'of doing something about an awkward problem without actually doing it now'.[3]

[1] Mr Wilson's speech to the TUC in September 1964 (quoted by Kilroy-Silk, p. 43) said as much.

[2] Op. cit., p. 44.

[3] Jenkins, op. cit., pp. 12–15.

Both commentators therefore agree in attributing to the Government a desire to meet or appear to be meeting certain public doubts and criticisms without, however, actually going so far as to disturb the status quo too much. They differ considerably in their interpretation of how precisely the decision to set up a royal commission was arrived at and these differences are largely attributable to the different sources of information which they have used. Even so, a great deal remains unexplained. If the Jenkins account is true, how far did Mr Gunter's view represent the departmental appraisal of the situation? If the Kilroy-Silk view is correct whose view was it that the case for an inquiry was so strong? And in either case how can we be sure that the desire to postpone an awkward issue was so dominant a motive in the Government's thinking?

These questions are not raised just to throw doubt on the interpretations offered by Jenkins and Kilroy-Silk, nor in a spirit of idle academic inquiry. They go to the root of the whole question of how committees of inquiry are used and why.[1] Yet the point of the question is to demonstrate that there can be no finality about such discussions. And if this is so it has implications also for the assumption that a general assessment of the origins of and reasons for committees of inquiry is possible.

Such an assumption depends essentially on being able to identify with reasonable accuracy the main factors in the appointment of a fairly wide-ranging selection of committees and, preferably, to follow up some of these committees in more detail. This is the real importance of the eight committees considered earlier in this chapter. They are important not so much for the light they throw on the circumstances in which each arose as for the clues they offer to the difficulty of explaining those circumstances and for the inferences, if any, which can be applied more widely to other committees.

How valid then, first of all, are the interpretations offered of these eight committees? For the reasons already given on the Donovan Commission these interpretations are not put forward as being final and complete accounts of the circumstances and motives which led to the appointment of the committees. At the same time they offer reasonable explanations of the facts so far as they are known. Moreover, the great majority of committees are not, like the Donovan Commission, concerned with highly contentious political issues. Controversy certainly is at the root of the appointment of committees, but as the previous chapter showed the controversy is far more likely to touch on relations

[1] Kilroy-Silk, for example, argues that if the Government had been genuinely interested in getting a disinterested report they ought to have set up a different kind of inquiry (op. cit., p. 46).

between government policy and affected outside interests than it is on issues which divide the political parties. Although, therefore, circumstances and motives may be more or less complex in any particular case, on the whole the more complex cases are likely to be in a minority.

Validity of interpretation depends, however, not only on identification of the factors leading to the appointment of committees but also on assessing their relative importance. Here there is more room for argument if only because even if all the facts are known two people may well differ significantly in their interpretation of relative importance and arrive at different conclusions. It is here perhaps that the greatest difficulties arise because so much depends on knowledge of and relationship of a committee to its context. It may well be, for example, that the most satisfactory account of the Edwards Committee on Civil Air Transport would need to relate it not simply to the more or less immediate circumstances of its origin but to the whole history, at least since 1945, of the evolution of civil aviation policy. Nevertheless it can still be agreed that although the fullest and truest interpretation of some individual committees might require a whole book to be written, this does not mean that briefer explanations are wholly misleading, merely that one should be cautious about putting too much weight on discussion of one committee.

For the important thing, surely, is to identify the kinds of factors and combinations of factors which appear to be operating. To expect more from a general survey of committees of inquiry is unrealistic, so that although it would be surprising if the interpretation of individual committees in detail could not be faulted there ought to be reasonable agreement that certain factors are or are not to be generally found. In looking at the eight committees, therefore, one is looking both for those factors and for possible parallels with other committees not so far mentioned, i.e. for the uniqueness or otherwise of these eight.

FACTORS IN THE ORIGIN OF COMMITTEES

One may start by listing the general elements, some or all of which seem to be present in all these committees:

1 An identifiable problem;
2 An immediate precipitating factor;
3 Specific proposals for dealing with (1);
4 A publicity or educational element.

Of these, the first seems the most obviously necessary. There are, it is true, rare occasions when committees are appointed not because some specific identifiable problem has arisen but to review a whole area of government, like the Plowden Committee set up 'to consider primary education in all its aspects. . . .'[1] In practically all the eight cases examined here, however, there is no difficulty in identifying the problem, whether it is the consequences of introducing turnover taxation or how to deal with foot-and-mouth disease.

There is usually, but not always, an immediate precipitating factor. It need not always be so dramatic as an outbreak of foot-and-mouth disease. There may be a relatively long period when a particular problem has been under discussion and some incident then provides the occasion for holding an inquiry.

In many cases specific proposals for dealing with a problem help to define what the problem is. Proposals for replacing purchase tax by an added-value tax, or for adopting the continental system of road signs themselves help to formulate the problem. Of equal importance for the present analysis is the way in which governments react to the proposals. They may be reluctant to accept them without further inquiry, or they may regard them favourably but see practical difficulties in introducing them, or they may be fairly neutrally disposed towards them.

These government reactions are closely linked to the fourth element of publicity or education. A course of action to which the Government has no firm commitment may benefit from examination by a committee in the sense that whatever specific conclusions a committee reaches the whole problem will be exposed to public comment and discussion. Governments may or may not find it easier to decide what to do after a committee has reported, but at least the discussion may change its tone if not its content as a result of having a committee.

Looked at in the light of these four elements it is clear that most of the eight committees fall into a middle area of discussion. They are not dealing with problems for which the Government already has a solution in which it is urgently committed. Nor on the other hand are they dealing with problems which the Government has no intention of doing anything about; none of these, in other words, is a committee just for form's sake. It is here that we see the importance of the argument that committees serve merely as a delaying tactic whereas, it is often argued, governments ought to decide their policy on the strength of the well-known arguments and proposals which have already been put forward or, alternatively, if further information is needed, to get it without

---

[1] This was, however, exceptional in being a statutorily-constituted standing committee: see Maurice Kogan, 'The Plowden Committee on Primary Education' in Chapman (ed.), op. cit., pp. 81–4.

going through the elaborate and formal procedures of appointing a committee.

As the discussion in the earlier part of this chapter and the eight examples of committees showed, matters are rarely, if ever, quite so simple as that. Committees, after all, like other elements in policy-making, are concerned with change and the ways in which changes are brought about in a democratic system. The matters which committees are charged with investigating may rarely be directly concerned with major issues of policy, and are more often matters of administration and procedure. This being so, it is hardly surprising if governments faced with conflicting pressures and always aware of the need to order priorities and concentrate on the urgent questions find the committee an attractive device for helping to resolve an issue.

This may sometimes amount to a fairly straightforward attempt to dispose of an argument by demonstrating that it is not as strong as its advocates maintain. The Committee on Turnover Taxation illustrates this situation in relation to the argument about the effect of such a tax on exports, although this in fact was only part of the reason for the appointment of the committee. A commoner situation is one where the department and the minister, although sceptical of a proposal, acknowledge the force of pressure and opinion in its favour and the element of doubt about whether some change is desirable. A committee is, therefore, set up not certainly to promote change but with a reluctant feeling that perhaps it may be necessary after all to do something rather than simply argue for the status quo.

A classic case was the Brambell Committee set up in June 1964 to examine the welfare of animals kept under systems of intensive livestock husbandry. It followed a lengthy period of agitation culminating in a widely publicised book *Animal Machines* by Ruth Harrison which was published in 1964. During this period the Minister (Mr Christopher Soames) argued that existing legislation was adequate to deal with cases of cruelty to animals, and that intensive rearing systems were not really a problem since animals would not thrive if they were suffering. It was in keeping with this approach that when he finally appointed a committee it was described as an expert inquiry by a technical committee.[1]

Scepticism and unwillingness to change represent what might be called negative attitudes in the genesis of committees. But there can also be neutral or positive attitudes. By a neutral attitude I mean one which, while hoping for support for current policies, recognizes that changes,

[1] Cf. H. C. Deb. 667, 19 November 1962, 794–6; and 693, 20 April 1964, WA 129–30; and the Committee's report, Cmnd 2836, December 1965.

or at least modifications, may be needed. The Northumberland Committee on Foot-and-Mouth Disease perhaps belongs here, although it is obviously difficult to draw a sharp dividing-line between this kind of committee and one where there is reluctance to make changes of policy.

Again, the Worboys Committee on Traffic Signs illustrates the difficulty of drawing a dividing-line between a neutral attitude and a more positive attitude, that is, one which favours change. It was suggested earlier that the Worboys Committee was appointed in part at least as a means of preparing the way for changes which the Department recognised as desirable. At the same time of course it is necessary to recognise the influence of factors such as criticism of the existing system on departmental attitudes and therefore as at last an indirect contribution to the appointment of the Committee. The Summerfield Working-Party on Educational Psychologists again reflects a more positive attitude in the sense that the main motive behind it was the feeling that something needed to be done to strengthen the service.

The positive attitude is also evident in the other three committees considered in the earlier part of this chapter (the Edwards Committee on Civil Air Transport, the Todd Royal Commission on Medical Education and the Nicholls Committee on Pressure Vessels). What is also evident in the majority of these committees is the relatively small party political element in their appointment. Questions like foot-and-mouth disease or turnover taxation are certainly political issues but they are not issues which are strongly divisive politically. Another way of putting the point is to say that all these committees, with the possible exception of the Edwards Committee, could and in some cases certainly would have been appointed whichever government was in power.

RELATIONSHIP OF ORIGINS TO OTHER FACTORS

The main question raised by this discussion is what general inferences, if any, can be drawn about the purposes which committees serve. At first sight, this seems to be a question of classification. Assuming that enough information can be gained about enough committees, then each one could be assigned to a category. The categories could be more or less refined, broadly in accordance with the negative, neutral or positive attitudes described earlier or with these three categories subdivided e.g. according to whether attitudes were entirely negative, or qualified negative and so on.

But even if this laborious task could be carried out over a sufficiently large number of committees, in itself it would provide information of only limited value. To know that 50 per cent of committees (or whatever figure it turned out to be) were inspired mainly by a mildly positive desire to bring about some change in current policies and practices would be of some interest, but in view of the very disparate subject-matter of committees, it would not shed a great deal of light on the role of committees in policy-making.

The basic difficulty is one which was touched upon in the previous chapter. The primary interest in the reasons for the appointment of a particular committee is the desire to throw more light on the way in which specific policies have evolved. Thus interest in the origins of the Edwards Committee on Civil Air Transport is closely related to the evolution of government policies in this highly controversial field. The appointment of the Committee is viewed largely in this context rather than in the context of the use of committees in general. The choice therefore seems to be between studying a limited number of policy issues to see whether any generalisations or comparisons are possible about the ways in which committees are used in policy-making or studying a larger number, although inevitably still limited for practical reasons, of individual committees in some depth. The first would put each committee firmly in its policy-making context but would leave fairly limited opportunities for generalisation. The second raises the question of how far the origins of and reasons for committees can be considered in isolation, as well as the extent to which generalisation would be possible.

It is obvious that, as indicated in the earlier discussion in this chapter, there is a close connection between the origins of committees and their membership, and membership and origins in turn are very relevant to the ways in which committees operate. There is thus a case for saying that at least part of the study of committees of inquiry should be examination in some detail of a number of committees, following them through from origins to report and beyond. This too seems to involve many problems; for example, although it would give a great deal of interesting information about those individual committees, would it necessarily provide a useful basis for generalisations, or rather how many committees would have to be studied and in what depth for this to be possible?

Thus the problems of investigating the purposes which committees serve lie at several different levels. There is the basic practical problem of discovering the origins of particular committees and the motives for their appointment. This can never be finally or conclusively settled in most cases mainly because of the elusiveness of the interpretation of motives, but a good deal can be done nevertheless to illuminate the questions involved. A more difficult problem is to devise a means for handling data about a number of committees in such a way as to be able to draw meaningful conclusions about the use of committees. There are a number of possible approaches to this problem, each of which has drawbacks. At this stage it is hardly possible to do more than suggest tentatively that if progress is to be made it may lie in combining more than one approach, examining specific policy issues, as well as particular subject areas of government and making studies in depth of individual committees. Whether such an approach is the right one and if so whether it is feasible are questions which will need to be considered after other aspects of committees of inquiry have been examined.

CHAPTER 4

MEMBERSHIP OF COMMITTEES

The previous chapter was mainly concerned with interpretation of known facts and with inferences about motives. The membership of committees seems, by contrast, to provide much more in the way of hard facts and quantifiable information; the size of committees, the kind of people who are appointed as chairmen, the extent to which 'experts' and 'laymen' are found as members of committees – all these are questions which permit, in theory at least, definite and precise answers. Moreover, the choice of a chairman and other members of a committee is clearly a matter of great importance from the point of view of the way in which the committee approaches its task and the kind of report which it produces, as well as in indicating the motives behind its appointment. Hence, it is not surprising that the question of membership figures prominently in the literature on the subject and forms the central focus of discussion in K. C. Wheare's general study of *Government by Committee.*

It is first necessary, however, to make clear from what point of view the question of membership is to be examined. It is generally discussed from the point of view of the *effectiveness* of committees. For example, is a small committee likely to give better results than a large one; is the use of judicial chairmen always the best way of ensuring a thorough analysis of a problem; how far should committees be composed of experts and how far of laymen? These are the kind of questions often posed and they imply a view of how committees ought to be constituted. If it can be shown that the achievement of certain ends is more likely to be brought about by the appointment of a certain kind of committee, then surely, the argument implies, governments ought to choose committee members accordingly.

This is, however, only one possible way of looking at the question. It may be characterised as the viewpoint of the detached but interested observer, one who sees the main point of a committee as being to examine a problem in as rational and dispassionate a manner as possible and to put forward reasonable and practical proposals for dealing with it. Thus Sir Kenneth Wheare remarks on the value of having judges as chairmen of committees to inquire because of their 'combination of impartiality and skill in dealing with a variety of technical matters'.[1] Such an approach often carries implications for the way in which inquiries ought to be conducted. The virtues of judges as chairmen, for example, are best realised if it is held that the way to establish the truth of a situation is to sift evidence by the kind of process which is to be found in a court of law. It is not, however, always or necessarily the case that this is the best way, and to the extent that it is not it may be that qualities other than those of a judge are needed in a chairman.

There are, however, at least two other ways of looking at the question of membership of committees. There is, first, the point of view of those with a positive interest in the problem under examination by a committee. They may simply believe that a particular change or reform is desirable or necessary, or they may equally be strongly opposed to a change or, as is perhaps the most common situation, they may combine both approaches since they may well hold that although one kind of change is to be welcomed, change in another direction would be wrong. Sometimes interest in this sense will be confined to interested parties, or those with a vested interest in the subject, but is here used in a wider sense to include those who are partisans. When, for example, a committee was set up to examine the law on Sunday observance, known and fairly predictable views could be expected from the Lord's Day Observance Society and representatives of the entertainment interests; but many members of the public might also be expected to have fairly strong views for or against relaxing the law. And the same is true of many other questions, particularly those with a strong social context (marriage and divorce, licensing laws, experiments on animals, etc.).

People who are interested in this sense obviously have certain expectations that the committee will at least look seriously on their point of view. Membership of committees is liable to be scrutinised and criticisms voiced, if for any reason it seems possible that this will not happen. The criticism is usually to suggest that certain points of view may not get a fair hearing or be adequately assessed because the committee lacks that particular kind of expertise or is unduly weighted by other interests. Thus, it was suggested (by a sociologist) that the Royal Commission on Local Government in Greater London (1957–60) ought to have had a social scientist among its members in order that it could give proper attention to the social as opposed to the technical effects of local govern-

[1] K. C. Wheare, *Government by Committee* (Oxford University Press, 1955), p. 85.

ment reorganisation.[1] Similarly, the Seebohm Committee on Local Authority and Allied Personal Social Services (1965–8) was criticised for not having doctors in its membership.[2] In both cases the critics feared or believed that the committee's report would as a result of its composition arrive at the wrong recommendations.

Finally, one may look at the membership from the point of view of those who have to make the choice, the civil servants and ministers. Here, as the last chapter showed, the choice is not made easy, when, as frequently happens, the decision to appoint a committee arises as a result of conflicting pressures and motives. They may simultaneously be trying to get reasonable answers, as the disinterested observers want, and trying to satisfy the partisans, and trying to avoid unwelcome proposals. It is not surprising that the resulting choice of members is frequently a compromise.

These are not the only questions which have been raised about the membership of committees, of course. It has often been remarked how the same names tend to recur as chairmen and members of committees.[3] More broadly, there is a tendency for committee members to be drawn from a fairly narrow range of people; a high proportion of them will be found in *Who's Who*, as lawyers, industrialists, professors, retired civil servants and so on. The question is raised whether it is necessary, or desirable, to draw membership from such a narrow field of choice.

Intelligent discussion of these questions depends first on an accurate statement of the facts about the membership of committees and secondly on an interpretation of those facts particularly in relation to the purposes of committees. The right thing to do about membership is best considered once we know what happens, and why.

SIZE OF COMMITTEE

Examination of the committees listed in the Appendix shows that half of them have between six and ten members and two-thirds have between six and twelve members. In itself this is not very revealing information. One might of course take it further by examining a number of committees in detail to try to discover how the particular number was arrived at in each case. Even if this could be done with any accuracy in the

[1] Marjorie McIntosh, 'The Report of the Royal Commission on Local Government in Greater London', *British Journal of Sociology* (September 1961).

[2] See on this N. M. Thomas, 'The Seebohm Committee on Personal Social Services', in Richard A. Chapman (ed.), *The Role of Commissions in Policy-Making* (Allen & Unwin, 1973), pp. 151–2.

[3] Cf. Wheare, op. cit., pp. 87–8.

absence of access to the official files, it would be very slow and laborious work.

Some light may, however, be thrown on the subject by considering the probable factors which lie behind the choice of small or large committees. In other words, if we assume that the aim is generally speaking to make a committee, in the words of the old advertisement 'not too big and not too small', and that this is the overriding consideration leading to the majority of committees coming in the six to twelve range, examination of committees with less than six or more than twelve members may give some indication of the special factors which condition the size of committees in these cases.

The first thing to be said is that large committees are commoner than small. There are a certain number of five-member committees but three- and four-member committees are rare; thirteen- and fourteen-member committees, on the other hand, are fairly common and there is a scattering of others up to twenty members, with a few even larger than this.

Taking three-member committees first, it seems likely that a major factor in their appointment is the desire for a quick answer. It is assumed that smaller committees are more likely to reach speedy conclusions. Perhaps the clearest example is the committee appointed by the Foreign Secretary (Mr Michael Stewart) in August 1968 to review overseas representation. Its very lengthy terms of reference began, 'to review urgently the functions and scale of the British representational effort overseas . . .' and ended '. . . and to aim to report within six months in order that the benefit of any savings may accrue as rapidly as possible.'[1]

Again, the 'D' Notice Inquiry by a committee of privy councillors in 1967 clearly needed to be conducted with speed in view of the possible implication of any change in the system, and in fact was completed in less than three months.[2] But a further factor in limiting membership may have been the desire to confine investigation of security matters to as few people as possible. An earlier investigation into security procedures in the public services, for example, following the celebrated Portland Spy Case was carried out by a committee of five with the same chairman (Lord Radcliffe) as the 'D' Notice investigation; this too was a relatively swift inquiry.[3]

Of quite a different character was the Committee on the Means of

---

[1] The Committee took ten months to report, which in the circumstances was remarkably quick; for example, they visited thirty-four overseas missions in addition to holding meetings in London (Cmnd 4107).

[2] See report, Cmnd 3309, June 1967.

[3] It was completed in less than six months; see Cmnd 1681, April 1962.

Authenticating the Quality of Engineering Products and Materials set up by the Minister of Technology (Mr Wedgwood Benn) in June 1968. Speed was not a major question here; what the Minister (and the CBI) wanted was a stimulus to voluntary action in making better arrangements for supervising quality control etc. and for the certification of products. Probably the main reason for having a small committee was the desire to impress on industry the importance of the subject which could be more effectively done through a small high-powered committee.[1]

Small committees are also often associated with examination of subordinate questions. For example, the Fulton Committee on the Civil Service (1966-8) recommended that there should be an inquiry into the Method II system of selection of recruits, and this was subsequently carried out by a committee of five.[2]

Similarly, a small committee of five was appointed by the Secretary of State for Scotland in June 1964 to examine conveyancing legislation and practice in Scotland with a view to amending legislation or introducing new legislation following the report of an earlier committee which had examined the whole question of whether registration of title to land should be introduced in Scotland.[3]

Very large committees are nearly always ones which have representation of all the main interests concerned. In November 1961 the Secretary of State for Scotland (Mr Michael Noble) appointed a committee to examine the arrangements for the award (and withdrawal) of certificates of competency to teach in Scotland. Behind this innocent-sounding inquiry was the difficult and controversial question of whether the teaching profession should have greater control over entry to the profession. The committee had 22 members with an independent judicial chairman (Lord Wheatley), and representatives of various teachers' organisations, 4 local authority elected members representing the local authority association, 3 directors of education, 2 administrative civil servants from the Scottish Education Department, 1 principal of a college of education and 3 independent members. Such a committee tends to become a negotiating body as well as a committee of inquiry as

[1] The committee arose out of the discussions of a joint Ministry of Technology/CBI working-party and was chaired by Sir Eric Mensforth, President of the Institution of Production Engineers; it spent a good deal of time on publicising its activities, including the circulation of 2,000 copies of the draft report for comment and criticism (see report of committee, HMSO 1971).

[2] Cmnd 4156, 1969.

[3] See Cmnd 3118, December 1966; the (Reid) Committee on the Registration of Title to Land was appointed in 1959 and reported in 1963 (Cmnd 2032).

was emphasised by the fact that it did not find it necessary to get oral evidence from some of the main interested bodies since they were represented on the committee.[1] In this it resembles some of the large advisory committees which operate mainly or exclusively by giving advice without taking evidence.[2]

There are other large committees, however, where the reason for the size of the committee is not obvious and has to be sought in the circumstances of its origin. In May 1963, for example, the Home Secretary (Mr Henry Brooke as he then was) appointed a committee 'to consider the present control over experiments on living animals, and to consider whether, and if so what, changes are desirable in the law or its administration'. It had a very mixed membership of fourteen, including not only experts like a veterinary surgeon and a professor of surgery, but also two MPs, a retired admiral, a retired librarian, and a methodist minister, with an eminent solicitor (Sir Sydney Littlewood) as chairman. The appointment of the Committee had a lengthy background in an RSPCA campaign for amendment of the legislation and discussions in the Home Secretary's Standing Advisory Committee on the Administration of the Cruelty to Animals Act. But the subject is a characteristically Home Office one in that a relatively minor piece of government regulation (going back to 1876) with a scientific and expert basis arouses a good deal of emotional reaction. All the evidence, both before the Committee and afterwards, suggests that it was an area in which neither the Department nor the Government was very anxious to make fundamental changes. The size of the Committee was mainly due to an attempt to balance the known interests with as many 'neutrals' – a situation which was unlikely to result in the recommendation of any sweeping changes.

In practice, then, it is scarcely possible to evaluate the size of committees in isolation. Whatever theoretical merits there may be in having small committees to get speedy answers or large committees to ensure that the interests affected are fully involved in discussion of the problem, it is rarely possible for the choice to be a simple one. Moreover, as has been indicated, questions about the size of committees inevitably involve looking at first the purposes for which a committee is wanted, and secondly, the kind of members appointed. Before taking the discussion further, therefore, this latter question also needs to be examined.

[1] Cmnd 2066, June 1963, esp. para. 2.
[2] For example, the Working-Party on the Lighting of Motor Vehicles (HMSO, 1967), whose job was to advise the Minister on whether to exercise the power to make regulations on the use of headlamps at night, had thirty-eight members.

LAWYERS ON COMMITTEES

In his discussion of committees to inquire, Sir Kenneth Wheare devoted much attention to the place of the expert and the layman on such committees, and suggested that in most cases a layman (especially a lawyer) was often a good choice for chairman, although he pointed out that many chairmen fell into an intermediate category of general practitioners, that is, with some knowledge of the particular area under review although not necessarily expert knowledge.[1]

In practice lawyers are probably the largest group of people to be found as members of committees, mainly as experts, but, particularly in the case of chairmen, often as laymen. There are several reasons for this: one is that, as was pointed out in Chapter 2, there is a large group of committees concerned more with the technicalities of the law than its substantive content. To these committees it is normal to appoint lawyers, sometimes with one or two laymen. In January 1966, for example, the Lord Chancellor appointed a committee 'to consider the jurisdiction and procedure of the Courts in actions for personal injuries. . . .' The Chairman was Lord Justice Winn, the Vice-Chairman was also a judge and the other five members included two QCs, a Master of the High Court, and two other lawyers.[2] On the other hand, the Royal Commission on Assizes and Quarter Sessions, which was concerned with legal administration, yet had much wider implications for general public policy, had an independent Chairman (Lord Beeching) and three of its other eight members were also not directly concerned with the law.[3]

The second reason for the predominance of lawyers is that many committees are concerned with matters which are closely governed by legislative provisions, and, therefore, the lawyer who works in this particular field is an expert and knowledgeable about such matters as the effect of particular statutory provisions. Thus the Jenkins Committee on Company Law which was appointed in December 1959 had among its fourteen members a QC, a solicitor who was President of the Law Society, and a Professor of Commercial Law of London University.[4] Similarly the Committee on the Patent System (1967–70) had three

[1] Wheare, op. cit., pp. 81–8.

[2] Cmnd 3691, July 1968.

[3] Cmnd 4153, September 1969. These three consisted of two industrialists and a trade union official.

[4] Cmnd 1749, June 1962. The chairman was also a lawyer (see below).

lawyers among its ten members.[1] These then are lawyers on inquiries concerned particularly with the law on technical matters.

The third reason for having lawyers on committees is the one referred to by Wheare and applies particularly to chairmen, that is, the particular kind of approach which they bring to investigation. Quite apart from the committees concerned with legal administration, therefore, which nearly always have a lawyer (and usually a judge) as chairman, other committees may have legal chairmen, as indeed was the case with the Committee on Company Law, already referred to, whose Chairman was Lord Jenkins.

EXPERT KNOWLEDGE AND PERSONAL QUALITIES

So far as chairmen are concerned, however, the predominance of lawyers is probably far less marked now than it once was. For committees concerned with broad matters of policy rather than with narrow technical inquiries, where it is usual to have an independent chairman, businessmen/industrialists or professors are now commonly appointed. Thus the Committee on Rural Bus Services (1959–61) had an academic chairman,[2] as did the Committee on Statutory Smallholdings (1963–7),[3] and that on Football (1966–8).[4] On the other hand, the Committee on Carriers' Licensing (1963–8) had a businessman as chairman,[5] as did the Committee on Social Studies (1963–5),[6] the Committee on Noise (1960–3),[7] the Committee on the Fire Service (1967–70),[8] and the Committee on the Pharmaceutical Industry (1965–7).[9]

It is, however, frequently not enough to categorise chairmen and other members of committees simply in terms of their occupation. Expert knowledge, particular kinds of approach to problems, status and personal qualities may all play a part in the selection of individuals. Wheare points out that members of the House of Lords are frequently chosen to be chairmen of committees, but it would be difficult to say

[1] Cmnd 4407, July 1970.

[2] Professor D. T. Jack, Professor of Economics, Durham University (HMSO, 1961).

[3] Professor M. J. Wise, Professor of Geography, London University (Cmnd 2936, 1966; and Cmd 3303, 1967).

[4] D. N. Chester, Warden of Nuffield College, Oxford (HMSO, 1968).

[5] Lord Geddes, a Director of the P. & O. Steam Navigation Co. and other companies (HMSO, 1968).

[6] Lord Heyworth, Chairman of Unilever (Cmnd 2660, 1965).

[7] Sir Alan Wilson, Deputy Chairman of Courtaulds (Cmnd 1780, 1962: Cmnd 2056, 1963).

[8] Sir Ronald Holroyd, Deputy Chairman of ICI (Cmnd 4371, 1970).

[9] Lord Sainsbury, Chairman of J. Sainsbury (Cmnd 3410, 1967).

with precision what part the prestige and status of having a lord as chairman weighed in the choice of particular individuals, as against, for example, the fact that they had particular qualities or particular professional or other expertise (which of course may also be why they had received peerages). And given that there are many committees with non-lords as chairmen it seems that one should at least look at a number of committees in more detail before making generalisations.

Again, it is often claimed that committees are chosen to give a balance of interests.[1] It would be easy to cite examples of such committees, but equally it would be easy to cite other examples where the members appear to be a collection of individuals whose interests are very remote from the topic under discussion. Of course, interests can in this sense be of two kinds – a direct interest in the subject matter, as teachers' organisations had in the certification of teachers in Scotland, or a more general interest as when a trade unionist can be said to have an interest in company law and may be appointed to balance the employer's interest. But a committee such as that on overseas representation can hardly be said to consist of a balance of interests in any but the most general sense. It had an eminent industrialist as chairman, and the other two members were a retired ambassador and an economist and foreign affairs expert.[2]

The problem, in the case of membership of committees (and this applies to their size as well as to the particular persons who are chosen), is whether it is possible to devise any meaningful classification of committees related particularly to the purposes for which they are appointed. To examine this, it will be necessary to look at some further examples in more detail.

SOME EXAMPLES OF COMMITTEE MEMBERSHIP

In February 1965 the President of the Board of Trade (Mr Douglas Jay) appointed a Committee of Inquiry into the Shipbuilding Industry; the terms of reference laid stress on the examination of organisation and methods of production to make the industry competitive in world markets, and the Committee were to recommend 'what action should be taken by employers, trade unions and Government' to bring about

[1] E.g. R. J. S. Baker, *Administrative Theory and Public Administration* (Hutchinson, 1972), p. 102; cf. Chapman (ed.), op. cit., p. 178.

[2] Sir Val Duncan, Sir Frank Roberts and Mr Andrew Shonfield (the latter is not easily classified, having been a journalist with *The Financial Times* and *The Observer* before joining the Royal Institute of International Affairs in 1961, of which he is now Director).

necessary changes.[1] The general background to this inquiry was the industry's declining share of the world market and, from about 1960 onwards, a decline in orders too. This was not the first report on the industry. In March 1961 a subcommittee of the Minister's [2] Shipbuilding Advisory Committee had published a report on future prospects for the industry, and later that same year a report commissioned by the Government from a firm of chartered accountants (Peat, Marwick, Mitchell) confirmed that price was the main factor in inducing British shipowners to order ships abroad.[3]

These reports and the state of the industry led the Government to introduce a shipbuilding credit scheme in 1963 as an inducement to shipowners to order from British yards. But the Labour Minister of Technology (Mr Wedgwood Benn) later claimed that when Labour came to power in the autumn of 1964 they realised that what was needed was a major reorganisation of the industry and for this reason had appointed the Geddes Committee.[4]

The Committee consisted of seven members, of whom the Chairman, Mr Reay Geddes, and two other members were industrialists in no way connected with shipbuilding; there were two professors, one a scientist and the other an economist, an accountant and a trade union official, again unconnected with the industry. The Minister of State at the Board of Trade (Mr Roy Mason) described the inquiry as the first 'objective appraisal by a technical team of experts who have nothing to do with the industry itself'.[5]

It is obvious that this was intended to be an independent committee in the sense that none of the members had any direct familiarity with the problems of the shipbuilding industry. To call it 'a technical team of experts' is, however, a rather different matter. The nature of the inquiry was more akin to a broadly-based management consultancy operation, but the question of how to reorganise an industry can hardly be termed a matter simply of technical expertise. Rather the intention seems to have been to rely on the experience of those with knowledge of industrial problems together with more specific skills (e.g. the accountant and the economist). This was the prime aim and particular individuals were picked with this in mind.

By contrast, the six people on the Committee on Social Studies

[1] Cmnd 2937, March 1966.

[2] At that time the Minister of Transport was responsible for shipbuilding.

[3] See H. C. Deb. 649, 22 November 1961, 1347–50.

[4] H. C. Deb. 742, 9 March 1967, 1773 (responsibility for shipbuilding was transferred from the Board of Trade to the Ministry of Technology in November 1966).

[5] H. C. Deb. 707, 4 March 1965, 1508–9.

(1963–5) were chosen mainly for their eminence in the field of investigation of the committee. The independent Chairman was Lord Heyworth, a former Chairman of Unilever, and one of the other members, Dame Mary Smieton, might be called a neutral.[1] The remaining four members were all academics with an active professional interest in research in the social sciences, though chosen to give a balance between different fields of study.[2]

Again, their choice has to be seen against the background of the reasons for the Committee's appointment. Although the Clapham Committee in 1946 had rejected the idea of a specific body for co-ordinating and channelling funds for research in the social sciences, support for such a body had grown in the 1950s and early 1960s. The Government were reluctant to act, generally putting off requests by a 'wait and see' attitude.[3] Clearly, some departments took a sceptical view of the value of such a body,[4] and the Minister chiefly responsible (Lord Hailsham, Minister for Science) put forward the idea of a committee as a means of making progress and in the hope of gaining support, although, as often happens in such cases, the terms of reference were more widely drawn and the Committee was actually appointed by the First Secretary of State (R. A. Butler).[5] Hence the need was for a strong committee but with members who were not identified with the pressure for a social science research council.

[1] She was Permanent Secretary of the Ministry of Education from 1959 until her retirement in 1963 but had spent most of her official career in the Ministry of Labour.

[2] Noel Annan (Provost of King's College Cambridge from 1956, a political scientist), Professor Bradford Hill (statistician), Professor C. F. Carter (economist) and Professor C. H. Wilson (historian).

[3] See, for example, H. L. Deb. 220, 9 December 1959, 192, 209, 260; H. C. Deb. 645, 4 August 1961, 1853–71.

[4] It was claimed by some that departmental opposition was mainly because the results of social science research could prove embarrassing: *New Society*, no. 36 (6 June 1963), p. 4; for a circumstantial account of more hard-headed Treasury objections, see Noel McLachlan, 'Why No Social Research Council?', *New Society*, No. 4, (25 October 1962), pp. 14–15.

[5] The terms of reference were: 'to review the research at present being done in the field of social studies in government departments, universities and other institutions and to advise whether changes are needed in the arrangements for supporting and co-ordinating the research'. Mr Butler's announcement of the Committee was greeted with 'profound disappointment' by the Opposition after years of agitation and discussion, and the Government was accused of inability to make up its mind (H. C. Deb. 678, 30 May 1963, 1513–15). By a political irony, it was a Labour Government which in 1965 received the report of the Committee (Cmnd 2660) which recommended the setting up of a Social Science Research Council.

In strong contrast to a committee like the Heyworth Committee on Social Studies are committees, often with large membership, where, as was suggested earlier, representation of interests and the element of negotiation are as prominent, if not more so, as the element of inquiry. The sixteen members of the Committee on the Education of Deaf Children (1964–8) for example, included educationists, teachers of the deaf, a psychiatrist, a professor of audiology and a professor of psychology under the chairmanship of a retired professor of education. They were required only 'to consider the place, if any, of finger spelling and signing in the education of the deaf'; but this disputed subject had considerable implication for the education of the deaf.[1]

The report of the Committee claims that the members sat as individuals not as representatives of organisations, but in a case like this it is difficult to know where to draw the line between choosing individual experts and choosing representatives of interested organisations. Obviously there is a formal distinction in the sense that, with some large (especially advisory) bodies, organisations are invited to nominate representatives, but, as was seen in the case of the Scottish Teachers' Committee, large committees can in effect represent interests in a less formal way but without committing those interests to agreeing with committee recommendations.

In a similar way, the galaxy of eminent medical talent on the Royal Commission on Medical Education (1965–8) might be said to be both expert in the field of medical education and representative of different interests and points of view within the profession rather than of any organised interests. Apart from the professors of medicine, surgery, psychiatry, radiology and other medical specialities most of the other members of the Committee were at least indirectly concerned with medical education, like the Chairman, Lord Todd, Professor of Organic Chemistry at Cambridge, but also, since 1963, Master of Christ's College; Sir Edward Collingwood, Chairman of Newcastle Regional Hospital Board and Vice-Chairman of the Central Health Services Council; E. M. Wright, Principal and Vice-Chancellor of Aberdeen University, and a former Professor of Mathematics there; and Professor E. G. Young, Professor of Biochemistry at Cambridge and Master of Darwin College. Perhaps only two or three members could be regarded as not having a direct interest or as being concerned with the

---

[1] So much so that the Secretary of State (Mr Short) was able to point to the existence of this Committee as well as those on educational psychologists and visually handicapped children as reasons for not referring the education of handicapped children to the Central Advisory Council (H. C. Deb. 770, 17 October 1968, 563–4).

public interest, among them Professor R. M. Titmuss, Professor of Social Administration at LSE,[1] Mrs Elizabeth Chilver, Principal of Bedford College, London and J. R. N. Barber, a Director of the Ford Motor Company.

Little criticism was voiced of the membership of the Royal Commission on Medical Education.[2] Criticism, is, however, frequently made of the membership of committees concerned with questions which arouse more general public interest, largely on the grounds that the choice makes it impossible or unlikely that the committee will produce the kind of report which the critic desires. Thus the membership of the Donovan Royal Commission on Trade Unions and Employers' Associations (1965–8) has been criticised because it was too heavily weighted with members, like Mr George Woodcock and Professor Clegg, dedicated to the status quo and was unlikely to produce a 'cool and disinterested report'.[3] The Seebohm Committee on Local Authority and Allied Personal Social Services (1965–8) similarly was criticised for being weighted towards the vested interests of the social workers.[4]

The criticisms emphasise the close connection between the membership of committees and the purposes which they are designed to serve. In the case of the Donovan Royal Commission, for example, differences of view between Mr Ray Gunter, the Minister of Labour, and Mr George Woodcock, the General Secretary of the TUC, on the purposes which an inquiry might serve were probably the main factor leading to a compromise over the choice of membership in which a balance of affected interests was sought with some neutral members.[5] Thus there were, apart from the judicial chairman, two trade unionists (Mr Woodcock and Lord Collison), two businessmen (Sir George Pollock and Mr John Thomson), a chairman of a nationalised industry and former Minister of Labour (Lord Rubens), two academic experts (Professors Hugh Clegg and Otto Kahn-Freund), an industrial journalist (E. L. Wigham) and two people quite unconnected with the subject (Lord Tangley, a solicitor and company director, and Miss Mary Green, a headmistress).

Representation of interests, shading into and sometimes hard to dis-

[1] Of course, this is not to imply that Professor Titmuss was a neutral, either in a professional or a political sense (see below).

[2] There was, however, some criticism that it did not have any members familiar with the problems of the London Teaching Hospitals.

[3] Robert Kilroy-Silk, 'The Donovan Royal Commission on Trade Unions', in Chapman (ed.), op. cit., pp. 45–6.

[4] See the criticism cited by N. M. Thomas, ibid., p. 132.

[5] See on this Peter Jenkins, *The Battle of Downing Street* (Charles Knight, 1970), pp. 12–15.

tinguish from the appointment of members with expert knowledge, is naturally more noticeable the more technical the subject under discussion. This is particularly so with advisory committees like the Working-Party on Grit and Dust Emissions (1964–7), which with its narrow terms of reference ('to consider ways and means of measuring grit and dust emissions . . .') consisted entirely of technically-qualified people many of them officials of central or local government. But the same situation is found with committees of inquiry like the Working-Party on the Hospital Pharmaceutical Service (1968–70) which consisted entirely of pharmacists, doctors and others concerned with the operation and administration of the service, under an independent Chairman, Sir Noel Hall, Principal of Brasenose College, Oxford.

One may also compare with these and with one another the Committee on Higher Education (1961–3) and the Committee on Noise (1960–1963). Of the twelve members of the former, including the chairman, almost all had a direct, professional concern with the subject which was a definite though wide-ranging one, concerned with principles and organisation. But the Committee on Noise was concerned with 'the nature, sources and effects of the problem of noise' and with measures which could be taken to mitigate it. In other words, although the Robbins Committee on Higher Education had demarcation and definition problems, 'higher education' was a concept which was generally understood. The problem of noise on the other hand was one which in general (as opposed to particular manifestations) was so vast and ill-defined, and had been so little examined, that the interests affected were numerous, and experts could equally cover a multitude of subjects from audiology to engineering.

The thirteen members of the Committee on Noise reflected these difficulties; some represented specific interests; some were experts and some intelligent laymen. The Chairman, Sir Alan Wilson, should be counted as an independent; as Deputy Chairman of Courtaulds he could of course be said to have an interest, like any industrialist, in the problem of noise, but this was not a very specific interest.[1] The other members included professors of psychological medicine and aeronautical engineering, an engineer from Rolls-Royce, the director of the Motor Industry Research Association, and the managing director of an aircraft firm; there was also a medical officer of health, a housing manager, a town clerk and a housewife.[2] Perhaps the choice of members

[1] It should also be noted that before he went into industry, Sir Alan was a Cambridge mathematics don, a subject of some relevance to the noise problem.
[2] It is also worth noting that, exceptionally, this committee had assessors from six different departments, and a secretary from a seventh.

as compared with, say, the Working-Party on Grit and Dust Emissions emphasises the contrast between examining a technical subject with wide social and economic implications, and a much narrower technical subject. In the former case, expert knowledge is of many different kinds and in any case much of the work is in identifying problems and assessing their relative importance, a job requiring a rather different approach and rather different qualities in the members taking part than a more narrowly technical inquiry.

PROBLEMS OF ASSESSING MEMBERSHIP

These examples of committee membership, like those in the previous chapter of the reasons for appointing committees, ultimately raise more questions than they solve. To begin with, there is the whole vast question of why a particular individual should be chosen. It is relatively easy to find out what a person does, particularly where, as with most of the individuals in the examples given here, he (or more rarely she) is listed in *Who's Who*. It is not so easy to know, except through personal knowledge, what particular qualities a person has, and even harder often to judge the reasons why a particular individual was chosen for a particular committee.

It is this, in particular, which often makes it difficult to decide how far and, as it were, in what proportions, expert knowledge, degree of representativeness of interests and personal qualities influence choice. And, as was indicated earlier in the discussion of lawyers on committees, it is misleading simply to assume that any one factor is predominant. Again, it is sometimes said that certain kinds of people are regularly to be found on committees – MPs, trade unionists, a woman member, for example.[1] In much the same way it is claimed that a balance of representation is sought of different parts of the country, and in particular that members from Scotland and Wales are appointed where a committee is examining a subject which is of concern to the whole of Great Britain rather than simply England. Again, if a trade unionist is appointed to a committee he will, it is said, be balanced by having also a representative from an employers' organisation.

The difficulty about such assertions is not so much to establish whether they are true as to discover in what circumstances they are true and why. It is easy enough to find examples of committees in which balance of representation in these ways can be seen, but they tend to be

[1] Cf. Chapman (ed.), op. cit., p. 178.

committees examining wide-ranging questions of general public interest, like the Pilkington Committee on Broadcasting of 1960–2 or the (abortive) Royal Commission on the Penal System of 1964–6. Since most committees are not of this kind, it is not surprising that it is difficult to apply these assertions to committees of inquiry in general. Very few committees, for example, have Members of Parliament among their members; [1] rather more have trade union officials and more still have at least one woman. It is, however, difficult to find any consistent pattern in the choice of such members.

For example, MPS might be expected to be appointed to committees which have their origins largely in parliamentary (and especially back-bench) pressures. A classic example is the Committee on the Law on Sunday Observance, set up in 1961 following a series of back-bench motions and bills, which contained no less than four MPS among its eight members and was under the chairmanship of a former minister (Lord Crathorne). A similar example is the Committee on Privacy appointed in 1970. Yet the Committee on Rural Bus Services (1959–61) which also had its origins very largely in back-bench pressure did not have a single MP among its twelve members. On the other hand it is sometimes difficult to know why committees should have MPS among their members. The Committee on Fowl Pest Policy (1960–2), for example, had two MPS among its eight members. It is true that a precipitating factor in the appointment of the Committee was a report of the Estimates Committee drawing attention to the sharply rising cost to the taxpayer of the current policy of dealing with the disease. Yet if that were a decisive factor one would surely have expected the Committee of Inquiry into the Relationship of the Pharmaceutical Industry with the National Health Service (1965–7) to have had MPS among its membership since one factor in its appointment was the long-expressed disquiet of the Public Accounts Committee at the price of medicines and the profits of the drug firms. [2]

It is easier to understand the circumstances in which trade union officials are found on committees of inquiry. One might expect them to be appointed either to broad-ranging inquiries of general public interest or to committees in which there is a specific trade union interest. Among

[1] Cf. the Prime Minister's (Mr Macmillan) reply to a question about the number of committees into social and economic matters appointed in the five years 1958 to 1962; of the two royal commissions and fifty-six committees listed, only five had MPS as members (H. C. Deb. 675, 2 April 1963, 236–42).

[2] See, for example, PAC third report 1961–2 (H. C. 251, paras 23–33: third report 1962–3 (H. C. 275, paras 54–5): and third report 1964–5 (H. C. 265, paras 60–5).

the former, examples would be the Royal Commission on Local Government in England (1966-9) of which Mr Vic Feather was a member, and the Royal Commission on Assizes and Quarter Sessions (1966-9) with Mr Leslie Cannon as a member. Among the latter the committee on Trawler Safety (1968-9) with Mr David Basnett of the General and Municipal Workers' Union [1] and the Committee of Inquiry into the Aircraft Industry (1964-5) with Mr Fred Hayday also of the GMWU are examples. As these last two examples indicate, the trade union interest is generally represented by someone from a union unconnected with the particular subject area under investigation.

Certainly, it is rare for committees investigating particular industries or topics of particular concern to the trade unions (e.g. the intermediate areas, the Truck Acts) not to have a member from a trade union. And the same is true of those rarer occasions when white-collar workers are particularly affected; thus the Fulton Committee on the Civil Service (1966-8) had the General Secretary of the National and Local Government Officers' Association among its members. But there are many other committees where one might expect trade union representatives but none is appointed. The Committee of Inquiry into the Welfare of Animals Kept under Intensive Livestock Husbandry Systems (1964-5) was, for reasons indicated earlier,[2] named as a technical committee, and had no union representatives, although there was clearly a strong union interest in the outcome of the inquiry.

The question of women on committees is fraught with difficulties, largely because, despite a general view to the contrary, the cases where women are appointed *qua* women are not all that common. A large number of committees have no women members, and those which have may well have women in their own right. A former Permanent Secretary to the Ministry of Housing and Local Government (Dame Evelyn Sharp) was hardly appointed to the Royal Commission on Local Government in England simply to represent the woman's viewpoint, although the housewife appointed to the Committee on Noise may well have been. It was entirely natural that the Committee on Senior Nursing Staff Structure (1963-5) should have several nurses among its membership, that a woman gynaecologist should be appointed to the Royal Commission on Medical Education and that the housing manager of Westminster, who happened to be a woman, should be a member of the Committee on Housing in Greater London (1963-5). There may

[1] He has since become a prominent trade union representative on 'general' committees e.g. the abortive Royal Commission on the Penal System (1964-6) and the Royal Commission on the Constitution (1969-73).

[2] See above, p. 73.

have been additional reasons for the appointment of some of those people but it is difficult to regard them as having been appointed simply because it was thought necessary to have a woman on the committee.

As this discussion has showed there can rarely be any simple answer to the question why particular committees were constituted as they were. The simplest case would be a committee composed wholly of representatives of organised interests in which the main questions to arise would be the number of representatives which each organisation should have. Such representative committees are more likely to be advisory rather than committees of inquiry, like the Working-Party on the Lighting of Motor Vehicles. Another relatively simple case would be a committee composed entirely of experts in which the personal knowledge and experience of each individual would be the main factor in his appointment. But again such committees, like the Working-Party on Grit and Dust Emissions, are more likely to be advisory in nature.

It is characteristic of the committee of inquiry that its membership is rarely homogeneous. Even where, like the Royal Commission on Medical Education or the Committee on Social Studies, its membership is largely confined to a single profession it will have one or more independent members, independent in the sense that they have no direct connection with the subject under review. Most committees, as the examples used in this chapter have illustrated, are much more mixed. At one extreme they may be small independent bodies, like the Duncan Committee on Overseas Representation, at the other they may contain a whole variety of interests; expertise and lay membership, like the Committee on Noise. The crucial question is whether one can go further than this, and indicate more specific patterns of relationships between membership and type of committee.

RELATION BETWEEN MEMBERSHIP AND TYPE OF COMMITTEE

The practical difficulties are formidable. Since each committee is to some degree unique it would be necessary to examine a large number of committees and get information on who was appointed, and why, and then to relate this to the kind of investigation carried out by the committee and, most importantly, to the reasons for its appointment. This would involve a great deal of patient work – and guesswork in many cases – since, for the reasons indicated, it must often be a matter for conjecture to assess the reasons for a particular choice. To take one example – what was the reason for choosing Professor Titmuss as a member of the Royal Commission on Medical Education? An eminent and respected academic in his own particular field of social administration, it might be thought that the main reason for choosing him was to bring his expert knowledge to bear on the subject and set it in a wider context. At the same time, one cannot ignore other more personal facts – that he was a supporter of the Labour Party, well known as one of the authors of an earlier plan for national superannuation, and a man with some – though difficult to assess precisely – influence with Labour ministers. How far these facts contributed to his appointment is a matter for speculation of the 'who said what to whom?' variety. It would be as absurd to regard his as a purely political appointment as it would be to assume without qualification that he was only appointed in his professional capacity. Truth, as so often, lies somewhere in between.

The enormous task of sifting through the membership of dozens of committees in this way is clearly impossible. Short of it, most writers on the subject of committees of inquiry, even those doing detailed case-studies of individual committees, tend to fall back on the broad categorisation, based particularly on occupation, which has been used in this chapter. In doing so it is essential to keep in mind the limitations of this approach and the qualifications which have to be made. Above all, the approach has to be in terms of the kinds of question which ministers and civil servants put to themselves if we are to be clear why particular committees were constituted as they were.

What is important is the close connection between the choice of members and the motives or intentions behind the appointment of a committee. Where there is a fairly clear and definite aim and the intention is to get something done there is less likely to be ambiguity about the choice of members than where there are conflicting aims, and no conviction that action is necessary. In the light of the discussion in the previous chapter it is not surprising that it is easier to find examples of the latter category than of the former. The Committee on the Law on Sunday Observance and the Royal Commission on Trade Unions and Employers' Associations in their different ways exhibit the kind of mixed membership which springs from mixed motives. On the whole, it is the committees concerned with the more limited topics, like those on deaf children or pressure vessels or that set up by the Lord Chancellor in 1964 to examine the mechanical recording of court proceedings, which seem to present clearer and more straightforward issues of membership.

It may seem unexciting thus to conclude that fruitful generalisation may not be possible without enormous labour, but the discussion does emphasise that if one is considering how committees of inquiry are used, as opposed to how they ought to be or might be used, the key questions centre on the intentions behind the appointment of committees. Criticisms about ineffectual or unbalanced membership may in fact conceal two quite different arguments. The critics may, on the one hand, be seeking to promote a different view of the purpose of a particular committee. Such criticisms can only be examined later, after we have considered further how committees do in fact operate.

There is, however, a quite different criticism which may be made; that is, accepting the kind of aims and intentions which governments hope to serve by appointing committees, do they in fact select the right kind of people in the right kind of way to achieve them? It was remarked earlier what a high proportion of committee members are to be found in *Who's Who*. This statement needs some amplification. Generally speaking, the broader and more general the subject of inquiry the more likely it is to be composed of people to be found in *Who's Who*. Royal commissions are mostly made up in this way, but committees like that on statutory smallholdings (1963–7) or hospital building maintenance (1968–70) or the demand for agricultural graduates (1962–4) are much less likely to be.

Of course, inclusion in *Who's Who* is only to be taken as an indication of the kind of people to be found on committees – those who have attained a certain standing, particularly in business, politics, the professions, and the arts. Apart from the latter group, who rarely find themselves on committees of inquiry,[1] these are precisely the kind of people who figure prominently among the membership of such committees. It is well known that the Civil Service Department maintains a list of 'the great and the good', and other departments doubtless have their own lists of people suitable for membership.

It is, however, possible to distinguish three main groups of people. First, there are the generalists: those whose names crop up fairly regularly on committees, not usually as experts or representatives of interests in the particular subject of inquiry but as generally useful committee men and particularly chairmen. For example, Sir Edwin Herbert (later Lord Tangley) was Chairman of the Committee on the Electricity Supply Industry in the 1950s, and of the Royal Commission on Local Government in Greater London (1957–60), and a member of the Donovan Royal Commission on Trade Unions and Employers' Associations, among others; Mr (now Lord) Annan was Chairman of the Committee on the teaching of Russian (1960–2) and of the proposed Committee on Broadcasting which the Labour Government intended to set up in 1970 and a member of the Committee on Social Studies and the Committee on the Sale of Works of Art by Public Bodies (1962–4). Sir

---

[1] Occasionally, they may find themselves on a committee concerned with their own subject; the Committee on the National Film School, for example, of 1965–1967 included Sidney Gilliatt and Karel Reisz, among others.

Roy Allen was a member of the committees on the remuneration of milk distributors (1959–62) and decimal currency (1961–3) and Chairman of the Committee on the Impact of Rates on Households (1963–5) to say nothing of his membership of the Air Transport Licensing Board.

Secondly, there are the specialists, men and women, well known in their particular sphere and chosen to sit on committees where they can exercise their particular expertness or knowledge. This is a very numerous class and includes many of the academic members to be found on committees, such as Professor Ewer, Professor of Animal Husbandry at Bristol University, a member of the Committee on the Welfare of Animals (1964–5), and Professor Grimmes, the Archaeologist who was a member of the Committee to Examine the Arrangements for the Protection of Field Monuments (1966–8). Sometimes they may become roving specialists serving on many committees, so that it may be difficult to decide whether to place them in this category or the former. Professor L. C. B. Gower, for example, who was Professor of Commercial Law at London University from 1948 to 1962, was a member of the Committee on Company Law (1952–62), the Committee on the Legal Education of Students from Africa (1959–60) and the Committee on Legal Education (1967–71); he was also a member of the Law Commission for 1965–71.

The third group is also a large one, and consists of the experts and representatives who are to be found not only on committees of inquiry but on the numerous standing bodies and in the consultations and discussions which form so large a part of day-to-day administration in government. They are the nurses on the Committee on Senior Nursing Staff Structure, or the teachers on the Committee on the Teaching Profession in Scotland. They are also the people chosen to represent the man (or woman) in the street on such committees as that on consumer credit (1968–70) or the London taxicab trade (1967–70).

Members of the first and second groups are likely to be in *Who's Who* and on the CSD List; those in the third group are much less likely to be. Yet they are not just names picked out of a hat but for the most part people who become known to the department appointing a committee through its regular contacts with outside organisations.

Obviously, people who serve on committees of inquiry come from a restricted range of people. Whether this is a good or bad thing depends, first, on whether committees are failing to achieve the purposes for which they are designed, and secondly, if so, whether this is because the right kind of membership is not being chosen. These are questions which it is not possible to answer at this stage.

CONCLUSION

Many other questions could be (and have been) raised about the membership of committees of inquiry such as the circumstances in which serving, as opposed to retired, civil servants are appointed as members and, more particularly, as chairmen.[1] But underlying the whole discussion of membership are two basic approaches: first, the attempt to understand the reasons why committees differ in size and membership, and, secondly, the desire to draw practical conclusions and to suggest ways in which the choice of members might lead to the more effective working of committees.

The two approaches are connected to the extent that practical guidance must obviously be related to the varying circumstances and needs of different committees and, more particularly, different sorts of committees. It is clear, for example, that since the choice of members affects a committee's approach to its task, the purpose or purposes which a committee is intended to serve will be very relevant to the choice. Wide-ranging inquiries like those into the problem of noise present greater difficulties to those deciding what kind of members should be appointed, as well as which particular people should be approached, than do more restricted inquiries, like that into the education of deaf children, precisely because in the former case the committee is intended to serve more varied and conflicting aims. With the education of the deaf there would be hardly any dispute that the committee ought to have people with expert knowledge of the problems involved, since the principal aim was to resolve a controversial and mainly practical question. With the problem of noise a major question was whether and if so to what extent expert knowledge needed to be balanced by membership chosen to represent a more general public interest.

These are questions which may be raised in relation to particular committees, and they provide the basis for discussions, like those by Wheare, into the place of experts or laymen on committees of inquiry.

---

[1] This question is also relevant to the distinction between committees of inquiry and advisory committees; as has been pointed out (PEP Study Group, *Advisory Committees in British Government*, Allen & Unwin, 1960, pp. 47–8), civil servants are nearly always members of advisory committees, whereas they are rarely members of committees of inquiry and then usually because questions of civil service organisation or procedure are involved (e.g. the (Trend) Committee on the Organisation of Civil Science, Cmnd 2171, 1963). There are obvious difficulties in having serving civil servants appointed to committees which may be critical of departmental policies.

Then there are the more fundamental questions, like those concerned with the relatively narrow basis of selection of members in general, or with the view that members should be chosen for particular personal qualities.[1] The difficulty is to see how these questions can be satisfactorily investigated, let alone answered, in order to provide more than the most broad generalisations.

If, as is argued throughout this study, the starting-point should be what happens at present, the main difficulty is that readily-available information, such as the occupations of members of particular committees, although of some interest and value, is often only half and sometimes less of the story because of the close interconnection between the choice of members and the reasons for the appointment of a committee. Detailed case-studies of individual committees may take things further and illuminate the connection for those particular committees but, unless they are carried out on a very large scale, can hardly serve as a basis for generalisations about what happens, still less for the assertion of views about the desirability or undesirability of having lawyers or women or trade unionists on committees.

The conclusion must be at this stage, as it was at the end of the previous chapter, that no one single approach in itself is likely to be satisfactory. Detailed case-studies are necessary but so are broader examinations of committees of inquiry whether in the context of particular policy-issues or particular subject areas of government, both for understanding the issues involved in choosing members of committees and for offering practical guidance on those issues.

[1] For example, their ability to direct research and organise evidence; see Alan Beattie, 'Commissions, Committees and Competence', *New Society* (29 July 1965), pp. 10–12.

CHAPTER 5

COMMITTEES IN OPERATION

Two basic ways of examining the methods of operation of committees of inquiry may be distinguished, one narrow and one rather broader.

The first is concerned with examining the sources of information and views which particular committees use. The object is to see how far the methods employed by committees enable them to carry out intelligent investigations of controversial issues with a view to putting forward practical solutions. And to the extent that there are found to be deficiencies in these methods, suggestions are often made for improving the situation either in relation to specific committees, or more generally.

More broadly, methods of operation may be viewed in relation to the whole process by which committees contribute to the policy-making process. Attention is then focused not simply on the means by which they get information and views, but on such questions as the factors influencing them to take a particular view of their task, and the stages by which they reach their conclusions. Such an approach will be concerned with the general constraints under which committees operate (e.g. of time and money) and with the pressures both external (e.g. a strong departmental view on the problem under examination) and internal (e.g. strong differences of view among members of a committee), which may help to explain the shape and content of a committee's report.

Underlying both approaches is the fundamental question of whether and to what extent committees of inquiry are an effective means of investigating the kinds of problem which are entrusted to them. Before saying something on this question, this chapter will be mainly concerned with examining, first, the formal means by which committees set about their tasks, and the problems of analysis to which this gives rise; secondly, the informal means by which they operate. The distinction is intended to correspond very largely to the distinction between the two main approaches outlined above.

It was earlier suggested that committees of inquiry have three main tasks of investigation, appraisal and advice.[1] Correspondingly, they have a need particularly for information to enable them to carry out the first task, and for views and suggestions which are relevant to the second and third. The formal means by which committees operate is largely concerned with what information and views they seek and how they seek it; the informal means is largely concerned with the use they make of such information and views, and the influences operating on them. It is therefore particularly concerned with the internal working of the committee.

FORMAL METHODS

Written evidence

Practically the first task of any committee of inquiry is to invite written evidence. Indeed, it was earlier suggested that one of the criteria for distinguishing committees of inquiry from purely advisory committees is that the former do and the latter do not call for evidence. There is, however, an important distinction to be drawn here. Most committees, whether investigatory or advisory, require basic information about the subject which they are examining. Advisory committees, whether *ad hoc* or standing, do not necessarily have such information when they start work and may seek it from outside sources by various means, some of which correspond to those used by committees of inquiry. Since, however, they operate by means of offering advice on the basis of the expert knowledge and experience of their members, such seeking of information does not amount to obtaining evidence. The characteristic of evidence-taking, and a distinguishing mark of committees of inquiry, is that it involves both factual information and views and opinions of interested parties. It is indeed because some so-called standing advisory committees carry out investigations based on the taking of evidence and the assessment of views and opinions that their reports have been regarded as constituting the reports of committees of inquiry.[2]

This characteristic dual role of evidence needs to be emphasised. Committees differ far more in the extent to which they rely on written evidence as their sole or major source of information than they do in the extent to which they use it as a source of opinions particularly of interested parties. Criticism is indeed increasingly expressed of committees for relying too much on evidence for investigating the facts of a problem and too little on other means. The Widgery Committee on

[1] Above, p. 26.
[2] One example among many is the report of the Advisory Committee on Agricultural Education of the National Advisory Council on Education for Industry and Commerce (HMSO, 1966).

Legal Aid in Criminal Proceedings, for example, was criticised for not seeking information on such matters as the frequency with which legal aid was not granted in cases resulting in imprisonment. More generally the charge has been made that a law reform committee often fails to investigate questions that are central to the area it is supposed to be investigating through not consulting a statistician or sociologist.[1]

These criticisms imply a contrast between committees more or less passively using whatever information happens to be presented to them and those which pursue investigations more actively according to their own view of what is needed. As will be seen later, the position is not quite so clear-cut as this but the criticism does illustrate one controversial aspect of evidence-taking.

The use of evidence to obtain the views of interested parties and others on the nature of the problem and how it might be resolved is less controversial in this sense. How valuable it is is another matter. On some subjects, at least, much evidence is received which is both repetitive and fairly predictable.[2] But although the committee may not receive a great deal of enlightenment in such cases, it does not follow that there is no value in inviting evidence. Apart from the general value to those giving evidence of knowing that their point of view has been put to the committee there are many occasions when it is important to a committee to know the strength of support for arguments for a particular course of action.

In practice, since few committees, apart from royal commissions, publish the evidence which they receive it is often not possible to be sure how much of it is factual and how much the expression of views. At least one committee, the Fulton Committee on the Civil Service (1966–8), has however both published the evidence and classified it according to whether it consisted of 'factual, statistical and explanatory papers' or 'proposals and opinions'.[3]

Even without the actual evidence to go on, there are many indications of variations in the approach of different committees to the question of evidence. In particular we need to consider, first the extent to which committees invite evidence from specific persons and organisations, and, secondly, what indication they give of the sort of evidence they want.

Nearly all committee reports begin with an introductory section setting out their terms of reference, number of meetings held and other

---

[1] Both these criticisms were made by Michael Zander in *What's Wrong with the Law?* (BBC Publications, 1970), pp. 6–7.

[2] An example is the voluminous evidence of individual local authorities to the royal commissions on local government.

[3] See Volumes 4 and 5 of the Committee's report (Cmnd 3638, 1968).

similar information. Frequently, there is reference to a decision at the first meeting of the committee to issue a general press notice inviting evidence. Such notices are almost invariably issued by committees with a wide brief which is likely to be of general public interest, like the Committee on Broadcasting,[1] the Royal Commission on the Police [2] or the Committee on Council Housing,[3] but they are used almost as a matter of routine even by committees with a relatively limited field of investigation.[4]

Whether or not a general press invitation to give evidence or make representations is made, it is almost universal practice for committees to write specifically inviting evidence from organisations known or thought to have an interest in the problem under examination and possibly to selected individuals as well. It is here that possibly the greatest variation occurs between committees both in the extent of their approach, and, more specifically, in the degree to which they indicate whether factual information or opinions are desired and on what topics.

Again the basic information is usually in committee reports in the form of a list of bodies and individuals from whom written evidence was received. Often, there is no more than that, and this is only to be expected where the subject of investigation is a relatively limited one. The Working-Party on the Problems arising from the Cyclical Pattern of Machine Tool Orders, for example, got written evidence from the Machine Tool Trades Association and five individual companies, presumably in order mainly to have their views on what the Committee described as 'an already over-publicised problem'.[5] But even committees investigating more general problems, such as the Committee on Death Certification and Coroners [6] or the Committee on the Patent System [7] give no indication that they invited those giving evidence to concentrate on specific issues. Nor for that matter did the Fulton Committee on the Civil Service.

On the other hand, some committees specify, often in considerable detail, the kinds of information on which they particularly want evidence although without excluding other evidence coming within their terms of reference. Thus the Dainton Committee on National Libraries 'asked

[1] Cmnd 1753, 1962, para. 4.
[2] Cmnd 1222, 1960, para. 5.
[3] *Council Housing : Purposes, Procedures and Priorities* (HMSO, 1969).
[4] E.g. the Committee on Footpaths (1968) and the Committee on Local Authority Records in Scotland (1967).
[5] Report of the Working-Party (HMSO, 1966), para. 53.
[6] Cmnd 4810, 1971, para. 2.
[7] Cmnd 4407, 1970.

particularly for factual information concerning the adequacy and use of existing national library facilities, and for estimates of the pattern of future demands for these services'.[1] And the Committee on Fowl Pest Policy invited those giving evidence to suggest ways of improving present procedure.[2] The Robbins Committee on Higher Education went further in drawing up a note on their terms of reference for the benefit of those submitting evidence in which they listed at some length questions on the present system which needed in their view to be investigated (e.g. how adequate are the opportunities for potentially qualified students?) and topics for discussion on future needs (e.g. is there an optimum size of institution?).[3]

Simply to cite these examples, however, gives little indication of the true differences between committees. There is to begin with the basic difficulty that committees differ a great deal in what they put into their reports and these differences are not necessarily related to the nature of the subject examined. Some committees, like the Robbins Committee, go into considerable detail about their formal methods of operation, while others, like the Committee on Shipping,[4] say very little. These differences may of course be an indication of different attitudes to their work by different committees; they may, for example, indicate how much or how little importance they attach to evidence as compared with other sources of information and ideas. But it cannot necessarily be assumed, for example, that because a committee does not specify in its report what evidence it asked for it did not try to channel the evidence along certain paths.

A further difficulty concerns the relationship between evidence and other means employed by committees especially to get factual information. The Dainton Committee's request, for example, is closely linked to the seeking of information by questionnaire, which is discussed later. And it is sometimes hard to draw the line between what is invited evidence and what is purely background information, such as that normally provided by the sponsoring government department at the start of a committee's work.

What is certain is that written evidence is for most committees a major and often very bulky part of the material which they have to consider. There are frequent references in committee reports to the 'great mass' or 'considerable volume' of evidence received. Where the evidence is published the volume can be physically measured as in the two volumes

[1] Cmnd 4028, 1969, para. 2.
[2] Cmnd 1664, 1962, para. 219.
[3] Cmnd 2154, 1963, Addendum to Annex (pp. 313–15).
[4] Cmnd 4337, 1970.

containing 275 memoranda published by the Pilkington Committee on Broadcasting [1] or the 1,800 closely-printed pages of the Fulton Committee's evidence.

Much the greater part of this evidence comes from bodies (and to some extent individuals) with a direct interest in the subject under examination – from government departments, civil service staff associations and ex-civil servants in the case of the Fulton Committee, and from local authorities and their associations in the case of the two royal commissions on local government. Most of the other evidence comes from bodies with a general interest, like the CBI or the TUC which frequently give evidence to major committees, or from bodies which are interested in one or two specific points. For example, the Stock Exchange gave evidence to the Fulton Committee, but their very short note was simply a mild complaint that government departments sometimes seemed to take a long time reaching a decision; and Plaid Cymru gave evidence to the Pilkington Committee on Broadcasting purely on the question of adequate representation of Welsh interests.

Some evidence, usually in the form of letters rather than memoranda, also comes from members of the general public in response to the general press invitation which many committees issue. The volume of such evidence is, hardly surprisingly, not usually very great, even where the subject is one of considerable public interest and concern, given the effort and difficulty involved in trying to put a coherent and convincing argument on paper. Thus the committee set up to examine 'the con-conditions in which livestock are kept under systems of intensive husbandry', a matter on which a good deal of public concern had been expressed, received 250 letters from members of the public, which in the circumstances was a reasonably high figure,[2] although other committees sometimes express disappointment at such a level of response.[3] The Pilkington Committee said it had a large number of submissions from members of the public, though without specifying how many, but the Committee on Consumer Protection with its 1,918 letters must surely have achieved about as high a response as a committee is likely to get simply from a general invitation.[4]

---

[1] Cmnd 1819 and 1819–I, 1962. These, however, represented only part of the evidence submitted.

[2] Cmnd 2836, 1965.

[3] The Committee on Privacy, for example (1970–2), with a wide-ranging subjcet for inquiry, went out of its way to get evidence from the general public but found the 214 letters which it received (113 of them outside its terms of reference) a poor response (Cmnd 5012, paras. 6–7).

[4] Cmnd 1781, 1962, p. ii.

Oral evidence

Committees, however, do not simply wade through the mounds of memoranda which they have invited. Most of them also invite some of those who have submitted written evidence (and sometimes people who have not, as well) to appear before the committee and answer questions put to them by members. It is true that occasionally these oral hearings are dispensed with, as when the Committee on the Teaching Profession in Scotland did so on the grounds that it was sufficiently representative of the interests concerned not to need to take oral evidence from those bodies.[1] The great majority of committees, however, not only take oral evidence but often spend an astonishing amount of time doing so. The Committee on Industrial Designs, for example, held forty-eight meetings, at twenty-two of which it took oral evidence;[2] and the Committee on the Probation Service took oral evidence on thirty-three of the fifty-four days on which it met.[3]

Even so, oral hearings represent a highly selective approach by a committee to the evidence. Only relatively few people can be questioned by the time-consuming process of oral hearings and inevitably those who are selected tend to be those most closely involved in the committee's subject of inquiry. If the subject is of relatively limited scope and attracts comparatively few written submissions, the committee may it is true decide to interview practically all those giving written evidence, as happened with the Committee on Registration of Title to Land in Scotland which gave oral hearings to eighteen of the twenty-three organisations and individuals who put in written evidence.[4] More typical, though, even of committees with relatively restricted subjects is the Committee on the Truck Acts which received thirty-eight submissions but gave oral hearings to only three organisations.[5]

It is almost universal practice for committees to list in their reports the organisations and individuals from whom they have received evidence, carefully distinguishing those who were questioned orally by the committee from those who provided only written evidence. It is, however, very rare, except in the case of royal commissions, for any record of oral hearings of committees to be published and even the internal private papers of the committee will normally consist only of a record in the form of minutes rather than a verbatim account of the

[1] Cmnd 2066, 1963, para. 2.
[2] Cmnd 1808, 1962, para. 2.
[3] Cmnd 1650, 1962, para. 3.
[4] Cmnd 2032, 1963, Appendix A.
[5] Report of the Committee on the Truck Acts (HMSO, 1961), Appendix I.

proceedings. Royal commissions indeed have traditionally been distinguished from other kinds of committees of inquiry because of the formal, public nature of their oral questioning of witnesses and subsequent publication of the 'minutes of evidence' which in fact are verbatim records of these public sessions. This tradition is still carried on and results in the publication of a vast quantity of printed information,[1] although there are signs that less formal (and less expensive) means of making this information available may be adopted in future.[2] Some others, for example the Fulton Committee on the Civil Service, have indicated in their reports that they deliberately chose to make their oral hearings private in order to allow for freer discussion,[3] but for the most part it is assumed rather than explicitly stated that committees meet in private. Clearly, as with the publication of written evidence, there are practical reasons why, given the large number of committees of inquiry, publication of oral evidence might not be justifiable, even apart from the kind of argument advanced by the Fulton Committee. It must simply be noted here, however, that one consequence is that although it is easy to discover whom a particular committee thought it worthwhile to talk to, it is very much harder to find out what they talked to them about.

To sum up the question of evidence; it would be extremely difficult to see any consistent pattern in the approach of different committees to the range and intensity of evidence sought. Nor is this surprising, given the wide differences in the subjects investigated by committees and their membership. All committees are expected to take evidence, but what evidence they take is largely left to them. In other words, further discussion really belongs to the later section of this chapter concerned with the different ways in which committees view their task in practice.

One reason for leaving the question somewhat open at this stage has already been hinted at, namely, that the use of evidence cannot be sharply

---

[1] For example, the Donovan Royal Commission on Trade Unions and Employers' Associations published a verbatim record of oral hearings on sixty-eight days during which over 11,000 questions were asked; among the few committees, other than royal commissions, to publish records of oral hearings in recent years were the Jenkins Committee on Company Law and the Robbins Committee on higher education.

[2] The Royal Commission on Assizes and Quarter Sessions, for example, arranged for a complete set of transcripts of its oral hearings to be deposited at the Public Record Office, along with a complete set of written evidence (Cmnd 4153, 1969, Appendix 1); on the other hand the Commission on the Constitution appointed in 1969 has followed the more traditional method of publishing Minutes of Evidence as it goes along.

[3] Cf. Cmnd 3638, 1968, App. L, para. 13.

separated from the use of other sources. This is particularly true of sources of information. Evidence, as has been seen, can produce information, as well as opinions, but it will not necessarily produce all the relevant information which a committee needs. Various possibilities are open to committees in seeking additional information.

Questionnaires, surveys, research

One of the commonest means by which committees traditionally call for specific information is by means of questionnaires. One of the more celebrated (or notorious) committees to do this in recent years was that appointed in 1965 by the Minister of Land and Natural Resources 'to review general policy on allotments. . . .' In view of the 'storm of protest by correspondence, telephone, in the press and on television' which these questionnaires provoked the Committee felt it necessary to explain and justify their procedure at some length. Having reviewed existing data which were available they concluded that many important questions still remained unanswered and that to get the comprehensive information which they judged to be necessary required them to ask every allotment authority, together with a random sample of 16,000 allotment holders and 200 local associations, a very detailed series of questions on subjects ranging from the amount of allotment provision (in acres per 1,000 population) at different dates to the estimated annual value of the produce from each allotment. It was the number and detail of questions which provoked the storm, many local authorities objecting that they were out of all proportion to the importance of the inquiry.[1]

Local authorities, perhaps not surprisingly, are favourite recipients of questionnaires from committees since quite a number of committees are appointed to examine matters administered, in whole or part, by local authorities, such as education (e.g. the Committee on the Teaching of Russian, 1960–2, and the Working-party on Psychologists in Education Services, 1965–8), planning (e.g. the Committee on Public Participation in Planning, 1968–9) and smallholdings (Committee on Statutory Smallholdings, 1963–6). But commercial firms (e.g. the Committee on Decimal Currency, 1961–3, and the Committee on Consumer Credit, 1968–71) also come in for their share of questionnaires. And their use has been extended in some cases to users of services; the Committee on Criminal Statistics, for example, had a questionnaire inserted in the 1963 edition of the *Criminal Statistics,*[2] and the Committee on the

---

[1] Cmnd 4166, 1969, paras 95–100, Appendix III and Appendix VI.
[2] Cmnd 3448, 1967, para. 13: this produced eighty-one replies.

London Taxicab Trade had questionnaires left in taxis so that users could record their views.[1]

These last two examples, however, also show how questionnaires can be used to gather not only factual information but also views about how satisfactory existing arrangements are and what can be done to improve them. Nevertheless, the most widespread use of questionnaires is to get factual information, and although the questions are rarely so numerous and detailed (or so controversial) as those asked by the Committee on Allotments, a considerable amount of work can be involved for the bodies and organisations concerned in meeting these requests.

The use of questionnaires is, however, only the first and simplest stage by which a committee may positively seek information (and views) which it might otherwise lack. The preparation and analysis of questionnaires are usually undertaken by the committee's sponsoring department, and that department may be asked also to carry out further work, as the Ministry of Health, for example, was asked to carry out a census of nursing staff by the Committee on Senior Nursing Staff Structure (1963–6).[2] Outside consultants may be commissioned to carry out specific investigations: the Committee on Shipping asked two firms to do studies, first, of the financial position of a wide cross-section of shipping companies and, secondly, of the management structure of certain companies.[3] Sample surveys may be commissioned to test public opinion, as the Committee on Death Certification and Coroners commissioned two surveys, first on what the public thought about coroners, and, secondly, on the reaction of relatives when a death was reported to a coroner.[4] Finally, a very recent development, research may be commissioned into one or more aspects of the committee's field of inquiry as the Royal Commission on Local Government in England commissioned and published ten separate research studies into subjects as diverse as local government in south-east England and the relationship between size of authority and performance.

Committees differ widely in the extent to which they use any of these various means to obtain information and views. Sometimes these differences can be related to the nature of the subject which is under investigation. It is hardly surprising, for example, that the Committee on the Organisation of the Scientific Civil Service (1964–5), did not find it necessary to conduct a public opinion survey or that the Committee on

---

[1] Cmnd 4483, 1970, para. 5: the response rate was 'disappointing' but the results 'very interesting'.

[2] Report of Committee (HMSO, 1966), para. 7.

[3] Cmnd 4337, 1970, p. xvi, para. 7.

[4] Cmnd 4810, 1971, para. 9.

the Law of Succession in Relation to Illegitimate Persons (1964–6) did not consider appointing outside consultants to help them. One would expect committees investigating problems of considerable economic significance like the Committee on Decimal Currency (1961–3) to need a good deal of data requiring at least the use of questionnaires, just as one would expect committees investigating important social problems such as the education of 13- to 16-year-olds of average ability,[1] to consider at least the desirability of carrying out surveys.

In practice, however, the differences between committees are very much broader than this. The Committee on Company Law, with wide-ranging terms of reference, undertook no specific inquiries of its own and relied on the evidence which it received.[2] The equally wide-ranging inquiry into consumer credit not only made use of question-naires to companies and local authorities, but commissioned surveys from a market research organisation particularly into the borrowing patterns of consumers.[3] The Committee which looked into fatstock and carcase meat marketing and distribution found that little information was available about the industry but contented itself with trying to get some basic statistical and financial information through the industry's trade association and government departments; and pointed out that further studies were needed to fill gaps in the available information.[4] The Committee on the London Taxicab Trade equally found itself short of facts and drew up a detailed programme of research which had to be cut down through shortage of funds; nevertheless, it carried out sample surveys, commissioned studies from consultants and devoted a chapter of its report to the research findings.[5]

Again, to explore these differences further requires examination of the reasons influencing a committee to take a particular view of its task. One influence may, however, be mentioned here since it is of general significance. A number of committees in recent years have drawn up at an early stage a full programme of research which frequently includes all the various means outlined above for obtaining information and views. They may appoint a research director and they may have augmented staffs to enable the research material to be handled and perhaps to undertake part of the programme themselves.

The first committee to operate on this kind of scale was the Robbins

[1] See *Half Our Future*, a report of the Central Advisory Council for Education (England) (HMSO, 1963), esp. paras 29–31 and Part Three.
[2] Cmnd 1749, 1962, para. 8.
[3] Cmnd 4596, 1971, introductory letter.
[4] Cmnd 2282, 1964, paras 7–14.
[5] Cmnd 4483, 1970, paras 3–6.

Committee on Higher Education which reported in 1963.[1] Their 'most ambitious undertaking' was the commissioning of six major sample surveys, but they also undertook several lesser inquiries, got a good deal of specially provided statistical information from government departments, drew on a number of academic studies some of which specially provided them with information, and obtained material from other countries; the appendixes to their report containing much of this information fill six large volumes.[2] Quite apart from the value and influence of this material on the Committee's recommendations, the fact that it was done has in turn helped to make other committees more aware of the possibilities of doing research. Committees since Robbins which have conducted extensive investigations whether through the use of their own staff or by commissioning outside bodies include the Maud Committee on the Management of Local Government, the two royal commissions on local government, the Fulton Committee on the Civil Service and the Donovan Royal Commission on Trade Unions and Employers' Associations.

The significance of this development needs, however, to be kept in perspective. The great majority of committees, whether before or after Robbins, still rely mainly on evidence with in some cases limited fact-finding surveys by questionnaires to provide them with the information which they need. No doubt some, like the Committee on the London Taxicab Trade, or the Committee on the Law on Sunday Observance,[3] contemplate doing more than they actually carry out; no doubt, too, there has been some extension of the use of sample surveys in such diverse situations as that of the Working-party on Suggestions and Complaints in Scottish Hospitals (1966–9) (for the views of patients) or that of the Committee on the Age of Majority (1965–7) (for the views of young people). But it is still true that these remain the exception rather than the rule for committees of inquiry.

Visits
One further general source of information for committees should also be mentioned, that is, the paying of visits. This is one of the traditional aspects of committees of inquiry and often now includes brief trips to

[1] There are isolated examples of earlier committees using extended research, notably the Royal Commission on Population of 1944–9, but for practical purposes this may be regarded as a recent development.

[2] Cmnd 2154, 1963, Annex (pp. 297–312).

[3] The Committee considered trying to get the views of the man in the street by means of a sample survey but thought that the subject was too complicated and in any case the results would not be ready in time (Cmnd 2528, 1964, para. 47).

other countries. Although in one sense such visits largely form part of the informal aspect of committees' work, the fact that they have taken place is duly recorded in the report. Usually it is no more than the recording of the fact plus, in some cases, specifying which members of the committee went on particular trips. Thus the Committee on Rural Bus Services (1959–61) set up a small subcommittee which made two-day visits to a number of areas to see what the problems were on the spot and to discuss them informally with local people; the Committee on the Fire Service (1967–70) made visits to eighteen fire brigades and other institutions in this country and also went to four other countries: and the Committee on Scottish Inshore Fisheries (1967–70) visited eleven fishing ports in the country.

The purpose of such visits is rarely explicitly stated. Sometimes it is fairly obvious. The committee charged with examining the conditions under which livestock are kept under systems of intensive husbandry (1964–5) naturally needed to see what the conditions were and it is not surprising that they visited fifty-four livestock establishments in various parts of the country. Nor is it surprising that the committee which was asked to examine the organisation and systems of control and accountability of large government industrial establishments (1968–71) spent a good deal of time visiting the Royal Ordnance factories and naval dockyards.

Even so, it is not always clear just how far committees are seeking information directly relevant to their work, or getting views more informally than is possible simply by taking evidence, or trying to reassure those who are being investigated that they are really anxious to give them all a fair chance to be heard. Probably in many cases there is a desire to achieve all three aims. One of the more explicit statements about the purpose of visits is made in the report of the Royal Commission on Local Government in Greater London.[1] In addition to the 114 meetings which the Commission held, they spent no less than 88 days in informal visits to local authorities. They stated the objects of these visits as being, first, to meet members and officers on their own ground; secondly, to gain familiarity with different areas and their problems; thirdly, to see administrative arrangements at first hand. They went on: 'the chance to see and to talk freely brought the written evidence to life for us; and we believe that this informality was also valuable in persuading the local authorities concerned that we were approaching their problems with open minds'.[2]

There could hardly be a better statement of the interaction between

[1] Cmnd 1164, 1960: the Commission was appointed in 1957 and thus falls outside the limits of the detailed study.
[2] Ibid., para. 24.

investigators and investigated designed both to inform and, more subtly and perhaps ultimately more important, to achieve a mutually tolerant atmosphere and 'oil the wheels' of the Commission's progress.

One further development has become of increasing importance in recent years – the visit to other countries. It has long been a tradition of committees of inquiry to seek information about the law and practice of other countries, mainly by the relatively simple method of asking for factual statements either via the representatives of those countries here or through our own representatives abroad. This method may be supplemented by examination of the relevant published literature and sometimes by questioning of experts on particular aspects. The result is usually a weighty appendix to the committee's report, packed with information,[1] although sometimes it may be merely a factual statement of certain limited aspects of the committee's field of inquiry.[2]

Increasingly, committees now also pay visits abroad, and again this may be done for a variety of purposes and in a variety of ways. The Maud Committee on the Management of Local Government, for example, appointed Dr A. H. Marshall of Birmingham University to carry out inquiries in six countries leading to a series of detailed reports on local government administration abroad which were published as a separate volume by the Committee. The primary object of these visits was to obtain more detailed information on the working of local government systems in these countries than could be gained from inviting purely factual statements.[3] On the other hand, the visits of members of the Committee of Inquiry into the Shipbuilding Industry to shipyards in six of the principal shipbuilding countries were presumably designed to find out at first hand how these countries were dealing with the management and other problems of modern shipyards, and generally to provide them with ideas which might prove applicable to the British situation. None of this is, however, explicitly set out in the Committee's report, which merely refers to the fact of the visits and makes fleeting references elsewhere.[4]

Again, the purpose of some visits abroad is much clearer than others. When, for example, the growing cost of the slaughter policy for dealing

---

[1] A good example is the report of the Committee on Privacy (Cmnd 5012, 1972), Appendix J.

[2] E.g. the Report of the Committee on Decimal Currency (Cmnd 2145, 1963) contains some limited information on the position in certain Commonwealth countries.

[3] See report of Committee, Volume 4, *Local Government Administration Abroad* (HMSO, 1967).

[4] Cmnd 2937, 1966, p. 7.

with fowl pest led to the appointment of a committee in 1960 to review this policy, it was clear that the main issue was whether to continue the policy, or to substitute, in whole or in part, a policy of vaccination. Since some other countries already operated a vaccination policy it was clearly desirable in the interests of making a fair assessment of the two policies to gain as much information as possible about the practical operation of vaccination policies in other countries. The Committee's special study of the Netherlands, USA and Canada, with extensive tours of these countries, may therefore be seen as an extension and counterpart of the visits they paid in this country to see the effects of current British policy.[1]

On the other hand, it is not so easy to see why the Committee on Allotments found it necessary to make a 'brief official visit' to Holland, Germany, Denmark and Sweden except in the context of their desire to induce a change of attitude on allotments policy on the basis of the rather different approach of these continental countries.[2] This Committee, however, highlights one of the important facts about visits to other countries. Whereas practically all committees of inquiry make visits to places within this country as part of the traditional and accepted means of making inquiries, only a relatively small proportion make foreign visits, and there is far from being any consistent policy or rule to act as a guide for determining which do and which do not. The Committee on the Patent System, for example, was very much concerned with the international implications of the growth in the use of patents and with the different systems operative in different countries. It could have, but apparently did not, argue that visits to other countries' patent offices might have been illuminating to observe procedures and discuss problems.[3] The committees on rural bus services [4] and foot-and-mouth disease [5] did, and the committees on the major ports [6] and the use of antibiotics in animal husbandry [7] did not make visits abroad. Perhaps one can sum up by saying that there are a large number of committees whose field of inquiry does not make foreign visits particularly relevant and who do not make such visits, and a small number of committees for whom they are relevant and who do make them; in between is a sizable minority of committees where the question of foreign visits is an open one to be decided by the committee's own view of the problem referred

[1] Cmnd 1664, 1962, pp. 2–3: also Appendixes I, II and IV.
[2] Cmnd 4166, 1969, esp. p. xviii and Chapter 14.
[3] Cmnd 4407, 1970.
[4] HMSO, 1961.
[5] Cmnd 3999, 1969.
[6] Cmnd 1824, 1962.
[7] Cmnd 4190, 1969.

to it (and no doubt by its ability to persuade the Treasury to accept that point of view).

Of the various formal means by which committees of inquiry seek to inform themselves about the problems to be resolved, invitations to submit written evidence form the basic and most characteristic means and foreign visits (at present at least) the rarest. Few committees use all the means which have been referred to in the preceding pages and among those which do there are wide variations in the extent to which they use particular means.

It was suggested at the beginning of this chapter that one of the reasons for interest in the methods of operation of committees of inquiry was that it might lead to suggestions for improving the way in which committees undertook their task. So far as the means employed by committees to get information and views are concerned, there seems to be no consistency of approach, each committee simply deciding as it goes along what, if any, means it will employ other than simply inviting evidence.

THE INFORMAL APPROACH

The committee's view of its task
But questions such as 'ought committees to commission more research or carry out more surveys of public opinion or collect more statistical information?' have wider implications. As was mentioned earlier,[1] it has been argued that the membership of committees should be chosen according to their ability to direct research and organise evidence, implying that these are overriding priorities in the work of a committee. Andrew Shonfield, a member of the Duncan Committee on Overseas Representation, has described how the Committee were the 'victims of a pragmatic fallacy', expected to plunge into the subject of investigation and find out what was significant as they went along; whereas they ought to have had guidance on the theory behind existing policy, for example, and ought to have had an 'investigating arm' so that they could have directed their inquiries into the most profitable channels and not relied exclusively on the conventional evidence-taking and visits. He implies, though without explicitly saying so, that the pressure on the Committee to produce a quick report coupled with the conventional necessity to obtain evidence and examine witnesses were major factors shaping the committee's report.[2]

[1] Above, p. 99.
[2] Andrew Shonfield, 'In the Course of Investigation', *New Society* (24 July 1969), pp. 123–5.

What is implicit in these criticisms is a view not only about the kind of information which committees ought to have but also about the way in which they should approach their task and use the information. It is necessary, therefore, to look at the influences on committees and the practical and informal ways in which they operate as well as the purely formal steps which they take to get information if we are to understand the process by which committees reach decisions and the limits within which practical guidance can operate.

A basic question here is the general view which a committee takes of its task since this affects its use of evidence and other means of investigation, and largely determines the kind of report which it produces. Sometimes a committee makes explicit reference in its report to its general view, though more often one is left to infer it.

The Committee on Carriers' Licensing, for example, went out of their way to stress that they had not taken a narrow view of their subject but had thought it necessary to consider the principles underlying the system and other possible objectives which it might serve. A consequent difficulty was that this involved them in a series of problems which 'proceed almost indefinitely onwards'. They met this difficulty by drawing attention to, but without pronouncing upon, these other problems on which licensing had a bearing. As they pointed out, much of the evidence was directed to detailed points concerning the operation of the existing system, and they could quite well have spent their whole time dealing with these. If they had, then it is hardly likely that they would have concluded, as they did, that the entire system of carriers' licensing should be abolished.[1]

The Geddes Committee on Carriers' Licensing had on the face of it a not dissimilar task to that of the Jenkins Committee on Company Law – of reviewing a piece of existing legislation in the light of changing conditions.[2] Yet the Jenkins Committee explicitly saw their task in narrower terms, of reviewing the suggestions made for change in the evidence, providing others of their own as a result of discussions of the evidence in committee and finally recommending 'those which it would in our view be both practicable and desirable to adopt'.[3] Hence it is not surprising to find the Jenkins report full of specific references to

---

[1] *Carriers' Licensing*, report of the Committee (HMSO, 1965), paras 0.8–0.10.

[2] Geddes's terms of reference were 'in the light of present day conditions, to examine the operation and effects of the system of carriers' licences . . .'; Jenkins's 'to review and report upon the provisions and working of the Companies Act 1948 . . . and generally to recommend what changes in the law are desirable'.

[3] Cmnd 1749, 1962, paras 8–10.

suggestions which came up in the evidence, nor to find that 'at our request the written evidence contributed was, to facilitate collation, for the most part arranged in accordance with headings listed in a standard form of questionnaire provided by us'.[1] The questionnaire was indeed a formidable document over three pages long with twenty-nine headings ranging from directors' duties to the arrangements for audit.[2]

Again, the Committee on the Marriage Law of Scotland made quite clear their general philosophy that 'proposed innovations have to be justified by something more than a conclusion that on balance they would do more good than harm . . . our proposals are intended to strengthen the estate of matrimony, while changing our law as little as possible'.[3]

It is perhaps not surprising that a committee with this general view was also very traditional in its approach to sources of information and views, relying mainly on written evidence and the 'skilled advice and help' of its secretary who as the Deputy Registrar-General 'was in a unique position to guide us in the technical law and practice of his department'.[4] In contrast, the Committee on Consumer Credit stated forthrightly their view that 'reform of the existing legal tangle is badly overdue' and emphasised the need for 'liberation of the consumer credit industry from the antiquated provisions, and from the official restrictions, that hobble it'.[5] In reaching their detailed conclusions the committee drew extensively on the special surveys which they commissioned.

Clearly, important questions to be discussed below arise in connection with the reasons for these differences in approach, but meanwhile it must be noted that it is comparatively rare to find in a report a general statement of approach in quite so explicit a manner as those quoted. In the more usual form of report there is a brief introductory statement of the number of meetings held, the amount of evidence received and of any visits or other sources of information used, and then the report goes straight into a discussion of the problem remitted to it and what the committee think should be done about it. There is often little or no reference explicitly in the report to the source of views which are discussed, although there is sometimes reference to more general statements such as 'most of the evidence was in favour of X' or 'some of those who gave evidence argued in favour of Y'.

Thus the Committee to Examine the Arrangements for the Protection

[1] Ibid., para. 3.
[2] Ibid., Appendix A.
[3] Cmnd 4011, 1969, para. 7.
[4] Ibid., para. 3.
[5] Cmnd 4596, 1971, introductory letter.

of Field Monuments referred to the range and volume of the evidence which it had received emphasising the complexity and urgency of the problem and said that it had considered closely the suggestions made, but the report gives no indication of what had influenced its views.[1] The Committee on Immigration Appeals devoted a short chapter of its report to dealing with some of the questions raised in evidence but this was largely to point out that the Committee's terms of reference did not permit them to consider whether controls on Commonwealth immigration should be relaxed or abolished but only whether there should be an appeals system from the decisions of immigration officers.[2] The Committee on Senior Nursing Staff Structure described at some length the various sources of information and opinion which it had used, but much the greater part of its report was concerned with an exposition of its views on a new structure with much reference to factual information but little to the evidence submitted.[3]

As these examples illustrate, difficulties of interpretation mainly arise over the reasons for a particular committee's general approach to its problem. Even without an explicit statement in its report one can of course, by reading the report itself, see whether it took a narrow or wide view of its task, but whether this was because of the circumstances of its origin, the nature of the subject, the particular membership of the committee or some other reason, is sometimes hard to judge. More importantly, it needs a certain degree of detailed knowledge about the particular committee. One difference, for example, between the Committee on the Marriage Law of Scotland and that on Consumer Credit may well have been that the pressure for changes in the former was less strong and on a narrower front than in the case of consumer credit. This in turn may mean that government had a much more positive attitude to the question of change in the case of consumer credit and this was reflected in the choice of members and the consequent different approaches of the two committees to their tasks and their different use of sources of information and views.

Again, the explicit statement in the report of the Geddes Committee on Carriers' Licensing of its relatively broad approach to its task was to some extent foreshadowed by the Minister (Mr Marples) in his announcement of the Committee during a debate on the Beeching Report on the Railways: 'We must get an informed view of what part our road transport will have to play in the transport pattern and how it

---

[1] Cmnd 3904, 1969, p. vii, paras 5–6.

[2] Cmnd 3387, 1967, paras 59–66.

[3] Report of the Committee on Senior Nursing Staff Structure (HMSO 1966), paras 5–8, chs 4–6.

can be made to do so efficiently.' [1] By contrast the President of the Board
of Trade (Mr Maudling) in announcing the appointment of the Jenkins
Committee on Company Law said merely: 'The time has now come for a
fresh review . . . because ideas and practices have changed since the
war and it is desirable to examine what modifications are needed in
the light of recent experience to take account of these changes.' [2]

The whole question of the influence of ministerial and departmental
pressures is crucial but difficult. Clearly, chairmen and members of committees are aware of what ministers and departments expect or hope that
a committee will achieve; sometimes this is fairly obvious from the way
the terms of reference are drawn up, or from informal discussions at the
start of a committee's work. Committees, however, do not necessarily
take their cue from ministers and their departmental advisers. At the
same time, to the extent that committees hope that what they eventually
recommend may have some practical influence, they are likely to pay a
good deal of attention to the attitudes of those who appointed them.

Use of evidence and other sources

The difficulties of determining the influences on committees and their
relative importance apply even more to their use of information and
views in arriving at the specific conclusions embodied in their reports.
There are, of course, some obvious general constraints within which all
or nearly all committees operate. Apart from the basic limitation provided by the terms of reference, time is the most prominent one since
even without any specific pressure on a committee [3] it is usually expected
to report within about two years. Quite apart from other reasons, there
is always the danger that if a committee goes on for too long the circumstances which originally gave rise to it may have changed so much that
its findings are outdated almost before its report is printed. [4]

Perhaps even more important are the psychological pressures
operating on a committee. It seems to be the unspoken aim of committees to achieve a unanimous report presumably on the grounds that a
unanimous report will carry more weight, and committees sometimes

[1] H. C. Deb. 676, 29 April 1963, 738–9: the Committee referred to this speech
in their report (para. 0.9).
[2] H. C. Deb. 614, 26 November 1959, 569–73.
[3] E.g. the Committee of Inquiry into the Shipbuilding Industry was asked to
(and did) report within a year (Cmnd 2937, 1966).
[4] As may well happen with the Commission on the Constitution which
although appointed early in 1969 did not report until the autumn of 1973;
among other reports which have taken a long time to produce, that by the Committee on Death Certification and Coroners (Cmnd 4810, 1971) is outstanding in
recent years, having taken six and a half years.

draw attention as a noteworthy fact to the unanimity of their reports.[1] In spite of some prominent examples in recent years of minority reports,[2] it is indeed true that the great majority of reports are broadly unanimous, although occasionally disagreements on certain points are noted in the text of the report,[3] or in notes of reservation or dissent.[4]

Again, one may draw attention in a general way to the influence of departmental officials, sometimes, though rarely, as members of committees, more often as assessors to Committees [5] and most frequently as providing the secretariat. Committees of inquiry almost invariably have government officials as secretaries [6] and they usually come from the department sponsoring the committee. In the very rare cases where they do not there is usually some special reason.[7] The secretary may influence the work of the committee in two main ways, through such direct means as his handling of the material coming to the committee or drafting of its report, and through the fact that to some extent he can act as a channel for his department's views on specific topics, and draw on material from past committees.

DIFFICULTIES OF INTERPRETATION AND PRACTICAL PROBLEMS

In relation to specific committees, however, one needs to probe a good deal further in order to elucidate how they came to write the report which they did in fact write. Once more, what the committee say in their report may provide some information, but it often needs to be interpreted. The Committee on Industrial Designs, for example, relied on

[1] E.g. the Crowther Committee on Consumer Credit.

[2] E.g. the Royal Commission on Local Government in England and the Committee on the Age of Majority.

[3] E.g. the Fulton Committee on the Civil Service (Cmnd 3638), paras 75–84.

[4] E.g. again the Fulton Committee, pp. 101–3: and the Royal Commission on Local Government in Scotland (Cmnd 4150, 1969).

[5] Eg. HMIs are frequently appointed to act as assessors to committees appointed by the Secretary of State for Education and Science.

[6] The original secretary of the Committee on the Enforcement of Judgement Debts came from the British Institute of International and Comparative Law, although he was later succeeded by a Home Office official (see Cmnd 3909, 1969).

[7] For example when a committee was set up in April 1959 to examine the financial structure of the Colonial Development Corporation, a secretary was appointed from a 'neutral' department, largely because of the suspicion which the CDC and especially its chairman, Lord Reith, had developed for the Colonial Office (on this see especially report of the Corporation for 1958, H. C. 214, 2 June 1959); this Committee is perhaps, however, a borderline case between a committee investigating a particular event and one investigating a general problem (for the Committee's report see Cmnd 786, 1959).

the evidence showing dissatisfaction with the operation of the Designs Act, 1949, and 'substantial support' for the application of the principles of the law of copyright to industrial designs, for its view that the main question remaining to be decided was whether the latter should be in addition to or substitution for the existing system.[1] It may well be that the committee arrived at this view after due consideration of the evidence, but it is at least as likely that they were aware that the main reason for their appointment was pressure to apply the law of copyright to industrial designs. Reliance on the evidence presented does not necessarily mean that members start work without views on the problem.

In other words, what tends to be missing from study of published information is any indication of the process by which the committee proceeded from its first meeting to the day when it signed its completed report. The report itself naturally tries to make the whole process appear to be orderly, logical and tidy, whereas anyone who has ever sat on a committee knows that things are frequently muddled and strong disagreements have to be papered over by compromise formulas.

When there are minority reports some small hints are provided of the ways in which committees operate and of the use they make of information. The majority of the Committee on the Age of Majority, for example, came out strongly in favour of reducing the age from 21 to 18. They relied in part on arguments based on 'What the Young Think', (the title of one section of the report); unfortunately, this included a sample survey of people aged 16 to 24 who favoured keeping the age as 21 by a majority of two to one. The majority dismissed this piece of information on the grounds that the results might have been very different if those interviewed had been 'interested and involved' in the problem. Two members who put in a minority report in favour of keeping the age as 21 maintained on the contrary that the survey was a reliable expression of opinion.[2] There is some indication here of the kind of arguments which must have gone on in the Committee, but not of how important those arguments were in relation to the ways in which the various members of the Committee arrived at their conclusions on the main problem before them. To do this one would need to go back to the circumstances in which a reforming Labour Lord Chancellor (Lord Gardiner) set up the Committee, and especially the extent to which members were chosen with the expectation, or at least the hope, that they would recommend fairly fundamental changes in the law, as well as to examine the actual discussions which went on in the committee, the nature of the evidence, the strength of personality of the different

[1] Cmnd 1808, 1962, para. 4.
[2] Cmnd 3342, 1967, paras 91, 523–7.

members of the Committee, and especially the chairman, and so on.

Underlying all this is indeed the question how far chance factors play a part in the kind of report which a committee produces. How significant, for example, for the Fulton Committee's findings was the fact that one of its members, Dr Norman Hunt (now Lord Crowther-Hunt), was able for a period to spend the whole of his time on the Committee's work and worked with the secretary on the drafting of the report? [1] Or that similarly Dr Roy Parker, a known supporter of a family service, happened to be on sabbatical leave during part of the time that he was a member of the Seebohm Committee, was then paid by the Ministry of Housing and Local Government to work for one day a week for the Committee and acted as editor of the Committee's report? [2]

It seems clear that ideally to answer these and similar questions about the working of committees one would need to be a silent observer of a committee's proceedings, noting the way in which discussions were carried on and the different influences contributing to its decisions. Even if the practical difficulties of bringing in an outsider in this way could be overcome, it would of course only illuminate the working of a particular committee. This indeed is the main disadvantage of the detailed case-study approach. Short of doing this, one has to rely on discussion with participants in a number of committees and on published information. The former suffers from the disadvantage that memory of events which may have taken place several years ago is not always very reliable. It also poses the problem of how many participants (and in how many committees) one needs to get a reliable picture. The chairman's view may be different from that of the average member, and the secretary may well see things in another light altogether.

The reports of committees, as has been seen, permit some limited inferences to be made about the way committees operate in practice. There is a dearth of published information, however, which describes at all specifically or in detail how particular committees arrived at their conclusions. This is not surprising. Such descriptions would have to be done by people who had participated in a committee and they might well feel unable, even if they had the time or the inclination, to reveal too much about what is still largely a private process. Professor Maurice Kogan, who was Secretary of the Plowden Committee on Primary Education,[3] has provided one of these rare descriptions in which he dis-

[1] Richard A. Chapman (ed.), *The Role of Commissions in Policy-Making* (Allen & Unwin, 1973), p. 17.

[2] Ibid., pp. 152–3.

[3] *Children and their Primary Schools*, a report of the Central Advisory Council for Education (England) (HMSO, 1967).

cusses the way in which working-parties considered specific aspects of the Committee's terms of reference and produced reports which were largely incorporated in the Committee's report, how the Chairman influenced the shape and content of the report, and how research findings led to particular recommendations of the Committee.[1] He points out that there were many issues coming within the Committee's terms of reference on which the Committee did not have adequate information and concludes that 'time, its own composition and the state of research in these areas, were all against it'.[2]

The very interest and rarity of this description raise questions which can hardly be answered in the present state of our knowledge about committees of inquiry. How typical, for example, is the Plowden Committee? There is one obvious sense in which it was not typical. It was a report of the Central Advisory Council for Education (England) specially constituted 'to consider primary education in all its aspects and the transition to secondary education'. Thus the Committee was a standing body (though of an unusual kind) given very broad terms of reference to consider a whole segment of education, rather than an *ad hoc* body asked to consider a specific problem. It was also, as Kogan points out,[3] a body whose function was to sum up 'practices in education' and the present state of progress as seen at the time that the Reports were written, rather than to offer specific proposals for action to meet current political and other pressures.

The question is whether, because of its origins, the Plowden Committee operated in practice in a significantly different manner from that of other committees of inquiry. One can only answer this by summing up the pros and cons. On the one hand, it was a very large committee and this was connected with its advisory status and in turn affected the way in which it operated through working parties. On the other hand, there seems to have been a variety of influences – evidence, research findings, personality and experiences of members – operating on the way in which conclusions were arrived at, with nothing to suggest that these were significantly different from those experienced by many committees of inquiry. Again, the fact that the Department perhaps felt the Committee to be something of a nuisance, for reasons connected with its status,[4] may have played a part in influencing its work particularly in

[1] Maurice Kogan, 'The Plowden Committee on Primary Education' in Chapman (ed.), op. cit., pp. 91–5).
[2] Ibid,, p. 95.
[3] Ibid., p. 84.
[4] Ibid., pp. 88–9.

the direction of a practical report acceptable to the Department, but doubtless other committees set up as the result of political pressure have also found themselves in a similar kind of dilemma.

CRITICISMS OF METHODS OF WORKING

There are, thus, difficult practical problems in trying to assess for one committee, let alone a whole series of committees, how and why they came to write their report in the particular way in which they did. It is in the light of this discussion that one should examine criticisms which are made of the working of committees of inquiry, and suggestions for improvement. Criticisms are most frequently made of a particular committee, as when the British Omnibuses Public Relations Committee accused the Committee on Rural Bus Services of failing to appreciate the problems involved and of producing incomprehensible and unworkable proposals; [1] or when a *Times* leader suggested that there were 'uncomfortable gaps' between the Hunt Committee's analysis of the problems of the intermediate areas and its recommendations.[2] Even more frequent are complaints that a committee has ignored or paid insufficient attention to evidence or information which would, so it is claimed, have made a vital difference to the committee's report. For example, a committee set up by the Lord Chancellor in 1965 to review the law relating to the recovery of debts and allied matters reported at length in 1969, one of its principal recommendations being for the abolition of imprisonment for civil debt and the introduction of attachment of earnings as a means of enforcing money judgements; [3] Miss Elizabeth Ackroyd (then Director of the Consumer Council) immediately drew attention to the fact that the Committee had not taken into account the Council's evidence, based on North American experience, of the dangers to which attachment could give rise.[4]

An academic critic, Jeffery Stanyer, has gone much further in examining the methods of operation of the Maud Committee on the Management of Local Government and the Redcliffe-Maud Royal Commission on Local Government in England.[5] Among other criticisms

---

[1] Cf. H. C. Deb. 637, 28 March 1961, 1302.
[2] *The Times*, 25 April 1969, leading article 'Pattern for Growth'.
[3] Cmnd 3909, 1969.
[4] In a letter to *The Times*, 19 February 1969.
[5] Jeffery Stanyer, 'The Maud Committee Report' in H. V. Wiseman (ed.) *Local Government in England 1958–69* (Routledge & Kegan Paul, 1970): Jeffery Stanyer, 'The Redcliffe-Maud Royal Commission on Local Government' in Chapman (ed.), op. cit.

of the Maud Committee he claims that they relied too much on the evidence of 'insiders', i.e. people in or connected with local government, that they seemed to be unaware of the literature on management and that their research into local government management in other countries was badly designed and had not produced useful comparative information.[1] Somewhat similar criticisms are made of the Redcliffe-Maud Royal Commission. Stanyer here pays particular attention to the quality of the analysis of the problems of local government structure provided by the Commission and criticises it mainly on intellectual grounds, finding in it both factual errors and illogicalities of argument; but he also criticises it for failing to investigate 'political-administrative considerations'.[2]

Most of such criticisms appear to have as their target either the composition of a committee's membership or, more seriously, its calibre. It is, of course, a matter of individual judgement to decide in a particular case whether criticisms of the kind levelled at the Jack Committee on Rural Bus Services or the Payne Committee on Judgement Debts are justified. Where, as in these two examples, the criticisms come from partisans who argued for different solutions, one is inevitably drawn into value-judgements about what is the right approach to the problem under investigation. To the outside observer it may often appear that such partisan criticism springs more from disappointment at the viewpoint adopted by the committee than from any failure in the way they have tackled the problems presented to them.

However, a more fundamental question is involved here, and is highlighted by the criticisms made by Stanyer. If such criticisms are judged to be true, do they relate only to particular features of the committee under examination, or do they have implications for the use of committees of inquiry in general? Stanyer deliberately limits his evaluation of the Redcliffe-Maud Commission, judging it in terms of its formal justification, that it 'holds out to the citizenry at large and to those specially affected by the subject under investigation the prospect of a greater degree of reasonableness in the ultimate decision, and a guarantee that their perceptions and interests will be properly considered'.[3] On this basis he sets out to demonstrate the failings of the Commission as he sees them, particularly in relation to the crucial argument (on the relation between size of local authority and performance), on which, wrongly in his view, they relied on 'insider' evidence from civil servants rather than on the special studies commissioned from out-

[1] Ibid., especially pp. 58–63.
[2] Ibid., especially pp. 134–40.
[3] Ibid., p. 110.

siders.[1] Stanyer does not specifically draw any conclusions as to why the Commission should have operated in this way but since he accuses them of arrogance and of wasting public money when 'it would have been so easy to have made a much better job of the task set' one can only conclude that his criticism is basically of the way the particular individuals of which the Commission was composed set about their task. Another presumably better-chosen group of individuals would, one supposes, have done a better job.

The point here is not to judge whether Stanyer is right or wrong in his particular criticisms of the Redcliffe-Maud Commission. But the implication is that, at any rate judged from the standpoint of 'the prospect of a greater degree of reasonableness', the crucial practical question is the calibre and ability of the members. Implicit in Stanyer's argument is acceptance of Beattie's view that members of committees ought to be chosen for their competence to direct research and organise evidence.[2]

Acceptance of this argument has, however, far-reaching consequences, since it implies that the only or at least the overriding need is for an intellectually convincing answer, the right answer in academic terms, and that everything else should be subordinated to this aim. If this were the position many committees would no doubt be in the situation in which Stanyer views the Redcliffe-Maud Commission of being set a task 'which was nothing more or less than applied social science'.[3]

Correspondingly, it would be comparatively easy to offer practical guidance on the ways in which committees should operate to achieve their ends and on the kind of people who should be appointed to them.

Undoubtedly, thorough analysis of evidence and other information and the elaboration of proposals based on that analysis form a major part of the function which committees of inquiry are intended to perform. The point at issue is how far other considerations ought to come into the reckoning, as they undoubtedly do in practice. In appointing committees, for example, how much attention, if any, should governments pay not only to getting people of the necessary intellectual calibre, but to achieving a balance of membership and a representation of interests with a view to obtaining not only an intellectually satisfying report but (what is not always the same thing) one which is also acceptable to those most likely to be affected by it? And how much attention ought members of committees to pay not only to trying to carry out a rigorous analysis of the problem presented to them, but to reconciling

[1] Ibid., pp. 137–40.
[2] Above, p. 99.
[3] Op. cit., p. 139.

divergent views among themselves and trying to find an acceptable solution even if it may not be the one to which analysis strictly points?

Clearly, different committees may face very different situations in practice in regard to these matters. In some cases, evidence, information and members' experience may all point to the same solution and argument will be chiefly about secondary though still important questions; in other cases, there may be no agreement or certainty about the significance of the evidence, the relevance of research findings or the merits of alternative solutions. But the fundamental issue raised by consideration of the ways in which committees operate is whether one should view them primarily as means for clarifying current problems and providing solutions to them which can be justified in rational terms or whether one should view them as serving more complex aims.

This issue will be further discussed in the concluding chapter, but it can be seen that there are practical difficulties in applying the rationalist view. One is the difficulty in accounting for the use of committees on such a large scale when it might be thought that many questions could more easily be examined by a single person, as is sometimes done now,[1] with a gain in clarity of analysis. What indeed are the advantages of having a committee at all in such circumstances? Again the proposition that other things being equal governments ought to choose members of committees for their intellectual capacity may seem reasonable enough, but one then has to ask when, if ever, other things are equal and whether in fact much of the difficulty about judging committees of inquiry arises because, whatever the theoretical merits of pursuing a single aim, in practice it proves necessary to pursue several aims which are not always easy to reconcile.

[1] Among recent examples are Lord Mountbatten's inquiry into prison escapes and security (Cmnd 3175, 1966) and Lady Sharp's inquiry into transport planning, *Transport Planning: the Men for the Job* (HMSO, 1970).

CHAPTER 6

COMMITTEE REPORTS
AND THEIR CONSEQUENCES

A major characteristic of committees of inquiry is that they provide written reports and that these reports are published. Any examination of the use and role of committees of inquiry must therefore be concerned with the consequences which committee reports have as public documents contributing to ideas about and debate on the problems discussed in them. Nor is this simply a matter of increasing our understanding of the part played by committees of inquiry. The question arises whether from examining the consequences of committee reports it is possible to develop criteria for judging how effective committees are with a view to suggesting ways of improving their effectiveness in future. This chapter is, therefore, concerned broadly with three questions:

1 What consequences can follow from committee reports?
2 How can those consequences be assessed?
3 What significance does the analysis of these two questions have for developing criteria of effectiveness?

The word 'consequences' has been deliberately chosen because it implies a chain of causation, and the first thing to be done is to examine in what ways committee reports may be said to have consequences at all. It is possible to distinguish two broad categories of consequences. The first category consists of consequences which can be related directly to the committee's analysis of a problem and, more particularly, its specific recommendations; the second consists of less specific and more indirect consequences, such as contributing to a change in the climate of public opinion.

ACCEPTANCE OF RECOMMENDATIONS – GENERAL PROBLEMS

A simple sequence view of committees of inquiry would see them as going through the following stages: first, appointment because a difficult problem has arisen on which there is no certainty whether and if so what action should be taken; secondly, examination of the problem and production of a report with suggestions for action to be taken; thirdly, action taken, or not taken as the case might be, on the suggestions made. The problem here is to examine this third stage and its relation to the preceding stages. What we want to know is, basically, how far the recommendations of committees of inquiry are carried out, and, following from that, whether this information can be used to develop at any rate one criterion for judging the effectiveness of committees. The critical point here is the connection between the making of a recommendation and its subsequent implementation. To the extent that the second is a consequence of the first it may be some measure of the influence of committees. To the extent that other factors may be involved it becomes much harder to determine what part committees play in influencing subsequent events and hence in using the degree to which committee recommendations are implemented as a measure of effectiveness.

Analysis of these questions involves both theoretical and practical difficulties. A basic difficulty is to determine what is meant by saying that a committee's recommendations have or have not been implemented. Most committee reports contain a summary of conclusions and recommendations, but even the most cursory glance at committee reports is enough to indicate a great range, not only in the number of such recommendations but even more in their relative importance, and in the different approaches of committees to the presentation of their views.

One would, of course, expect committees like those on footpaths [1] or the hospital pharmaceutical service,[2] with their relatively limited scope, to have briefer summaries than, say, those on the Scottish salmon and trout fisheries,[3] or the police [4] with broader problems to examine. But some committees like those on the patent system [5] or local government in Scotland [6] have lengthy summaries of twelve pages or more, and many more, like those on shipping [7] or the London taxicab trade [8] devote between six and nine pages to such summaries, without there being any very obvious connection between the length of these summaries and the complexity of the problems or analysis.

[1] 21 recommendations in 2 pages (Report of the Committee, HMSO, 1968, pp. 22–4).

[2] 15 recommendations in $1\frac{1}{2}$ pages (report of the Working-Party, HMSO, 1970, pp. 44–5).

[3] 127 conclusions and recommendations in 8 pages (Cmnd 2691, 1965, Ch. xi).

[4] 111 conclusions and recommendations in 10 pages (Cmnd 1728, 1962, Ch. x).

[5] Cmnd 4407, 1970, pp. 172–84.

[6] Cmnd 4150, 1969, Ch. 3.

[7] Cmnd 4337, 1970, Ch. 26.

[8] Cmnd 4483, 1970, Ch. 13.

The reason is very largely that committees employ different techniques in presenting their recommendations. Many, like that on the patent system, do simply present a dry catalogue of recommendations in summary form. Others, aware perhaps that few people are going to read their report right through, yet conscious that bare summaries may be misleading, attempt to induce the reader at least to follow up in the main body of the report those recommendations in which he is interested. Thus, the Fulton Committee's two and a half pages of main findings are barely intelligible without studying the detailed arguments elsewhere in the report; [1] and the Sainsbury Committee on the Relationship of the Pharmaceutical Industry with the National Health Service kept its summary of recommendations to just over three pages, no doubt in the hope that readers would turn to the 27-page chapter headed 'Our Proposals'.[2]

One consequence of this situation is that merely to look at the summary of conclusions and recommendations is not necessarily an adequate starting-point for assessing whether a committee's recommendations have been carried out. One committee may list 150 recommendations, of which a large number are carried out; another may only list 50, of which only 20 may be carried out. But the first committee may have listed all its recommendations however minor, whereas the second may have selected only what it regards as major recommendations. It is therefore necessary as a first step to decide which are the important recommendations of a committee, before looking at the extent of acceptance.

Often, it will be obvious that some recommendations are key ones, in the sense both that they relate to matters of principle or substance rather than detail and that they follow from the main strand of a committee's argument. But sometimes decision will be difficult and may necessitate examining rather more closely the problem presented to the committee and the arguments it has followed in its analysis. This is especially true where, as with the Committee on Consumer Credit, the problem is complex and may consist in fact of a series of related problems.

The difficulties of assessment are obvious when it is realised that government may either accept, modify or reject each individual recommendation. The fact that a government has accepted 50 per cent of a committee's recommendations is meaningless unless we know what the significance of those recommendations is to the committee's analysis.

[1] Cmnd 3638, 1968, pp. 104–6: there was also a list of 158 recommendations tucked away in 12½ pages of close print at the back of the report (pp. 194–206).
[2] Cmnd 3410, 1967, Parts I and V.

Moreover, it is common for governments to announce that they accept a committee's report 'in principle' but then to modify it considerably in practice. It is thus a matter for judgement, and often difficult judgement, rather than simple fact to determine the extent to which a committee's recommendations have been carried out, except for the rare cases where a committee's report is either accepted or rejected *in toto*.

Time presents a further difficulty. It frequently happens that a government's immediate reaction to a committee's report is to announce that consultations are to be held with interested parties before any decision is made about it. These consultations may take months or even years, and further months or even years may pass before the government announces its decision. The decision may be that certain recommendations are to be implemented and others involving legislation will be implemented in a modified form when a suitable opportunity occurs. Further months or years may pass, ministers or even governments may change, and if and when legislation is ultimately brought in it may seem to bear a somewhat tenuous relation to the committee's original recommendations. Basically the problem is that the time-factor adds a further dimension to the original difficulty. It is a question of assessing not only whether but also within what period a committee's recommendations have been carried out.

ACCEPTANCE OF RECOMMENDATIONS – EXAMPLES:

Committee on Court of Criminal Appeal

Some examples of different committees will illustrate the practical problems. In February 1964 the Lord Chancellor (Lord Dilhorne) and the Home Secretary (Mr Brooke) jointly appointed a committee which had the task of examining whether the Court of Criminal Appeal should be merged with the Court of Appeal and in any case whether any changes should be made in the constitution, powers and practice of the court.[1] The Committee concluded that there should be a single Court of Appeal with two divisions, one for civil and one for criminal appeals.[2] They also made a number of detailed recommendations, some substantive, for example, that the power of the court to increase sentence should be abolished, and some procedural, for example, that any notice by the full court saying that leave of appeal had been refused should give reasons for the decision.[3] Five months after the Committee had reported

[1] Cmnd 2755, 1965.
[2] Ibid., para. 84.
[3] Ibid., para. 260.

the Home Secretary announced acceptance of its recommendations, and legislation was passed the following year.[1]

This is almost as straightforward a story as it is possible to have: there was one central issue, together with a number of lesser but still important issues and, finally, some minor issues. The Government accepted the Committee's recommendations on the first, and broadly those on the second, and some of those on the third group of issues. Even though not every recommendation of the committee was put into effect, there would be no dispute that the Committee's report was implemented.

Committee on Major Ports

A rather more complex example is the Committee on the Major Ports of Great Britain appointed by the Minister of Transport in 1961 under the Chairmanship of Lord Rochdale to consider the adequacy of the major docks and harbours for national needs and whether methods of working could be improved.[2] The Committee's recommendations fell under several different heads, but one of the most important was that a National Ports Authority should be established with statutory power to control capital investment and prepare schemes for amalgamations; the committee wanted the publicly-owned docks to be grouped with private docks on an estuarial basis under new independent port authorities; they made a large number of detailed recommendations to port authorities over such matters as finance, access and labour relations; and they made a number of recommendations about specific ports, e.g. that Southampton should be developed as a principal cargo port.[3]

A few months after the Committee had reported the Government made a statement accepting the 'central thesis' of the report that future development should be in accordance with a national plan; they proposed that a National Ports Council should be set up to formulate and supervise the carrying out of such a plan; but government was to retain control of capital investment.

The central question to be considered about the Rochdale Committee is the extent to which its recommendations were accepted. It should be emphasised that the main concern is with recommendations addressed to the Government; as the Minister, Mr Marples, pointed out, two-thirds of the recommendations were for consideration by those con-

[1] See H. C. Deb. 721, 24 November 1965, WA 74: H. C. Deb. 731, 11 July 1966, 1107–46: and Criminal Appeal Act, 1966.
[2] Cmnd 1824, 1962.
[3] Ibid., paras 140–53, 660.

cerned in the industry.[1] One significant recommendation which was rejected by the Government related to the financing of new investment in the ports. The Committee took the view that government loans should only be available for this purpose in exceptional circumstances, whereas the Government's view was that such borrowing would be necessary if new investment was to be sustained. This in turn affected the decision on the nature of the proposed new authority which, in the Government's view, should not control capital investment in the way proposed by the Committee, and should be advisory rather than executive in character. In particular, the Committee's proposal that the authority should have power to direct ports to undertake improvement schemes was rejected by the Government.

However, despite the rejection of these and some other major recommendations (e.g. that relating to the grouping of ports under estuarial authorities), as well as some minor recommendations, the Government did in fact largely accept the Committee's recommendations which were implemented in the Harbours Act, 1964. The key to the situation is the view expressed very early in the Committee's report that 'some measure of national planning and co-ordination is essential if resources are to be used to the best advantage': hence arose the proposal for a non-operational National Ports Authority, on discussion of whose functions and powers they had spent a good deal of their time.[2]

Acceptance by the Conservative Government at that time of the need for a national body of this kind, even if not precisely in the form recommended by the Committee, was a significant change of policy.

Committee on Rural Bus Services

Problems of a rather different kind are raised by another Ministry of Transport committee which was set up in 1959 under the chairmanship of Professor Jack 'to review present trends in rural bus services . . . [and] to consider possible methods of ensuring adequate services in future. . . .' The Committee agreed that services were not adequate, and that some form of outside assistance was needed, but could not agree on whether this should be in the form of a remission of fuel tax, or a direct subsidy, or, as one member (Mr Harry Nicholas) wanted, through public ownership of the industry. The majority of the Committee were in favour of subsidies administered by county councils but partly financed by the Exchequer.[3]

Shortly after the Committee's report was published in 1961 a Con-

[1] H. C. Deb. 680, 10 July 1963, 1264.
[2] Cmnd 1824, 1962, para. 8.
[3] Rural Bus Services, report of the Committee (HMSO, 1961).

servative backbencher (Mr Rupert Speir) moved an adjournment debate to draw attention to it and in the subsequent months a certain amount of pressure was maintained by a group of Conservative backbenchers actively concerned with the rural transport issue to try to secure some action.[1] Government spokesmen pointed to the difficulties of either subsidies or remission of fuel tax until, in August 1962, Mr Marples announced that since no 'generally acceptable solution' had been found he proposed to put in hand detailed studies in a few selected areas.[2] However, eighteen months later, following these studies and further discussions he announced that there was still 'no unanimity about what is the right solution to this problem' and he proposed to carry out some practical experiments in selected rural areas.[3] Before these were completed a general election brought a Labour Government to power which introduced subsidies to bus operators as part of its general transport policy, and subsequently nationalised the industry.[4]

To answer the question 'were the Jack Committee's recommendations accepted?' by saying 'not immediately but ultimately' seems straightforward enough but begs a number of questions. It is true that the Conservative Government in the three and a half years between the publication of the Committee's report and the general election of October 1964 did not adopt any of the various suggestions put forward by the Committee; but at the same time they did not either say that they proposed to do nothing about the problem of providing rural bus services or put forward any alternative plan of action. Ostensibly the various studies and experiments put in hand by Mr Marples were designed to see whether an agreed and acceptable policy was attainable despite the failure of the Committee to find one.

The Conservative Government at that time, and Mr Marples in particular, found the idea of subsidies unacceptable,[5] but in view of the pressures for some action to be taken and, in particular, the quite strong feeling in certain sections of the Conservative Party that a policy was needed for dealing with the rural transport problem generally,[6] it was politically impracticable to reject Jack without putting something

[1] See H. C. Deb. 637, 28 March 1961, 1297–1304; 641, 7 June 1961, WA 90; 649, 22 November 1961, 1339–41; 651, 11 December 1961, 48–98.

[2] H. C. Deb. 651, 11 December 1961, 95–7; 664, 1 August 1962, WA 92–4; 668, 27 November 1962, WA 42–4.

[3] H. C. Deb. 691, 11 March 1964, WA 61.

[4] See White Paper, *Transport Policy* (Cmnd 3057, 1966), paras 78–9: Transport Act, 1968, S.34.

[5] As indeed was alleged by the Labour Minister of Transport (Mrs Castle), see H. C. Deb. 736, 23 November 1966, 1380–1.

[6] The Party's 1951 election manifesto had promised action on this topic.

in its place. Hence, the studies and experiments at least offered the promise that an alternative policy would ultimately be found, although it is of course a matter for speculation what the Conservatives would have done about rural bus services if they had been returned to power in 1964.

Thus, even a straightforward factual statement about acceptance or rejection needs a certain amount of background information to make it intelligible. It is theoretically possible, for example, that a post-1964 Conservative Government might have been driven to the conclusion that there was no alternative to some kind of action, such as remission of fuel tax, involving Exchequer help for bus operators. We do not know. We only know that they did not do so before the election and we can infer from their actions and the political situation that this amounted to a rejection of the Jack Committee's analysis.

This elaboration of the Conservative Government's failure to act on the Committee's report may not be strictly necessary for a simple factual answer to the original question. But to view the Labour Government's commitment to a policy of subsidisation as in some way a consequence of the report does require acceptance of a specific interpretation of how that policy was arrived at. The fact that a different government was involved from that which originally appointed the Committee itself makes it difficult to be sure how far one can talk in terms of cause and effect. Labour policy would almost certainly have been the same without the Jack Committee, although this is not to say that the committee's report was not useful in helping to focus some of the issues in that policy.

Committee on Industrial Designs

The Jack Committee illustrates the difficulty of answering the question whether a report has been accepted or not without being drawn into discussion of what constitutes acceptance or rejection. The problem recurs in a different form with the report of the Johnston Committee on Industrial Designs. The Committee was appointed in 1959 to consider whether any changes were needed in the law relating to the protection of industrial designs, and concluded in 1962 that in addition to the existing statutory provisions providing for protection of registered designs there should be a design copyright giving protection for up to fifteen years.[1] This recommendation was accepted in principle by the President of the Board of Trade (Mr Heath) two years after the Committee reported, but without any guarantee of when legislation would

[1] Cmnd 1808, 1962.

be introduced.[1] Two years later the Labour Minister of State (Mr Darling) said that although the Government was not reluctant to legislate on this question, there was the difficulty of finding parliamentary time.[2] The following year he hinted that less complex legislation than that proposed by the Johnston Committee might provide an interim answer,[3] although in the event it was left to a private member (Mrs Jill Knight) to introduce a bill dealing with the design copyright question in a somewhat different way; this bill was 'heartily supported' by the Government.[4]

Here the basic problem is one of judging intentions against performance. The Committee's recommendations were accepted not only by the Government which appointed it but in effect by its successor, but they were not carried out. But it is not enough simply to state these facts. The consequences of the Johnston Committee have been practically nil,[5] in spite of the fact that its recommendations were accepted. This seems to call for some elucidation.

Lack of parliamentary time was the main reason which prevented the introduction of legislation on the lines recommended by the Committee and this in turn was related to the fact that such legislation would have required a large and complicated bill on a relatively minor question of industrial property law. The danger in such a situation is that the longer implementation of a committee's proposals is delayed, the more likely are circumstances to change and to make it difficult to implement them without further inquiry. This is what has happened in the case of the Johnston Committee. Controversy surrounding the 1968 Act, which gave protection to some people, e.g. fashion jewellers, but created difficulties for certain engineering firms which reproduced but did not design standard parts, was a major factor in the appointment in 1973 of a further committee of inquiry into the whole question of the law of copyright.[6] It is therefore still a question for the future whether and, if so, to what extent, the original Johnston recommendations will eventually be incorporated in legislation.

[1] H. C. Deb. 691, 19 March 1964, 1566.
[2] H. C. Deb. 731, 14 July 1966, 1692.
[3] H. C. Deb. 740, 1 February 1967, 468–72.
[4] Design Copyright Act, 1968; see H. L. Deb. 296, 16 October 1968, 1373–7.
[5] In an article 'The Jewellers' Charter Becomes an Engineers' Nightmare' (*The Times*, Business News, 22 January 1973), David Jones and Adrian Hope remark that the Committee's report 'has become known as a useful cheap textbook for students of design law but otherwise has done little except collect dust on shelves'.
[6] See article quoted in previous note, also subsequent correspondence (*The Times*, 24, 26, 30 January, 5th February 1973); and *The Times*, 15 August 1973.

Committee on Company Law

Of all the practical difficulties arising from the attempt to make an assessment of whether a committee's recommendations have been accepted, probably the greatest arise in the case of those committees examining many-sided and complex questions and making large numbers of recommendations, particularly if implementation is carried out in piecemeal fashion. The Committee on Company Law, for example, made recommendations on numerous topics, often of a detailed and technical nature, ranging from the issue of shares of no-par value to a new system of control for unit trusts.[1] Legislation on some of these many questions was promised shortly before the 1964 election, but with the change of government the measure which eventually passed as the Companies Act, 1967, was more limited in scope. Not until 1973 was legislation promised to implement much of the remainder of the Committee's Report.[2]

If the Conservative Government had carried out their intentions announced in 1964, one could have said that the Committee's recommendations had largely been accepted and carried out. The actual course of events means that a simple assessment of the Jenkins Committee in terms of acceptance or rejection is even more difficult than in the case of the Jack or Johnston Committees.

In one sense it could be argued that the 1973 White Paper and subsequent legislation following it represents the carrying-out of the original decision to implement the Committee's recommendations. The circumstances, however, in which the 1973 White Paper was produced differed considerably from those of 1964 so that although it may be true to say that much of what the Jenkins Committee recommended was ultimately embodied in legislation, the question is whether this in itself provides an adequate basis for judging effectiveness, or whether in addition it is necessary to look at the reasons why recommendations are accepted or rejected, and implemented or not implemented.

The question is important in relation to the discussion at the beginning of this chapter. That a committee's recommendations were accepted and implemented, or accepted but not implemented, or partly implemented and partly rejected does not in itself adequately deal with the consequences of a committee's report. If, for example, a government does nothing about a report but later as a result of subsequent events decides to implement it in whole or in part, the fact of ultimate

[1] Cmnd 1749, 1962.
[2] See the White Paper, *Company Law Reform*, Cmnd 5391, 1973.

implementation is of less importance than the reasons which led to it. It seems necessary, therefore, to try to understand why reports are or are not accepted as well as whether they are accepted. This in turn involves a number of problems which are again best considered by looking at some examples.

REASONS FOR ACCEPTANCE OR REJECTION:

Committee on the Truck Acts
The Committee on the Truck Acts (1959–61) under the chairmanship of Mr David Karmel, QC, seems at first sight to provide a fairly simple and straightforward example. Here was a committee asked to consider a limited area of statutory provisions dating back to 1831 'in the light of present-day conditions' and to make recommendations. It concluded that although the time had not come to abolish the statutory provisions, they ought nevertheless to be repealed and replaced by a new Act better designed for twentieth-century conditions. No action was taken on this recommendation, and, therefore, the committee was in this sense unsuccessful.

In terms, however, of the reasons for this lack of success the story is much more complex. To begin with, there were two strands in the appointment of the committee. First, in the late 1950s there was considerable public interest in the question of the payment of wages through banks and whether the Truck Acts were an obstacle to this development; this question was resolved through the amendment of the Truck Acts by the Payment of Wages Act, 1960, which thus dealt with one important issue on which the Karmel Committee might have made acceptable recommendations. Secondly, and partly because of the attention thus thrown on the Truck Acts, the question arose whether the wider issue of the relevance of these Acts in modern conditions ought not to be examined. The question was put to the Minister of Labour's National Joint Advisory Council in 1958, and they concluded that the many uncertainties and anomalies in the application of the Acts justified review by a small independent committee, a conclusion which was accepted by the Minister.[1]

The situation thus facing the Karmel Committee when it was set up was a not uncommon one. A fairly general agreement among those directly concerned that existing arrangements were to some degree unsatisfactory was not matched by any agreement on whether anything and if so what needed to be done about the situation. The British

[1] Annual report of Ministry of Labour, 1959 (Cmnd 1059), pp. 71–2.

Employers' Confederation wanted the abolition of the Truck Acts on the grounds chiefly that they inhibited employers from making arrangements involving deductions from wages, even though these might benefit workers (e.g. contributions for recreational facilities); the TUC, on the other hand, merely wanted the Acts to be consolidated and extended to cover more workers, with modifications designed to eliminate the main ambiguities.[1]

The Committee steered a middle course between these two positions; it wanted a new Act which would remove legal obstacles to the provision of benefits and allowances in kind, universal in its application (with a few exceptions), but with the provision of new administrative machinery in the form of local tribunals to deal with appeals and grievances.[2] The question is why nothing was done either to implement these recommendations or to introduce any alternative plan. The question requires consideration of the main factors involved:

1   The attitude of the Department. From the origin of the Committee it is clear that the Ministry of Labour had a fairly neutral attitude; reform or abolition of the Truck Acts was not something on which it had strong views, but if it could be shown that changes were both practicable and acceptable to those mainly involved it would probably have been prepared to act;

2   The Committee's view of its task. In view of (1) and the composition of the Committee, it is likely that a compromise solution was inevitable; but it was difficult to find a compromise which was workable, especially in view of

3   The attitudes of interested parties. What is important here is not so much the views of e.g. the BEC and the TUC, but how strongly they were prepared to push them, and how tenaciously they were prepared to maintain them.

It seems doubtful whether a committee set up in the circumstances of the time could have produced a practical scheme acceptable both to employers and workers, and one which the Ministry of Labour could have endorsed. The dice, one could say, were loaded against this Committee. The official language of a later committee set up to review the subject of payment of wages conveys the rather unenthusiastic tone in which the Karmel Committee's report was received. Referring to the consultations held on the report it said 'these consultations have shown that there are considerable reservations concerning legislation along

[1] Report of the Committee on the Truck Acts (HMSO, 1961), paras 18–21.
[2] Ibid., para. 23.

these lines and no further action has been taken to implement the report'.[1]

Committee on Statutory Smallholdings

The Committee on the Truck Acts, although relatively straightforward in a factual sense since no action was taken on its recommendations, turns out to be more complex when the factors involved in its lack of success are examined. By comparison, one may examine the Committee on Statutory Smallholdings which was, on the face of it, much more successful. The Committee was appointed in July 1963 by the Minister of Agriculture, Fisheries and Food (Mr Soames) with Professor M. J. Wise as Chairman, mainly to report on the working of existing smallholdings legislation and the economic position with a view to recommending what future provision and administrative and financial arrangements should be made.[2] Much of what the Wise Committee recommended was enacted in the Agriculture Act, 1970.

Although in announcing the Committee the Minister simply said that it was time that an independent body should look at the working of a policy dating back to the Agriculture Act of 1947,[3] there was no doubt that both the Treasury and the MAFF felt that a review of policy was needed. The former had in effect imposed a ban on the provision of new smallholdings in 1956 largely on the grounds that continuation of existing policy was likely to be very expensive and difficult to justify on financial grounds. A key question was indeed whether the policy of trying to turn selected agricultural workers into farmers at public expense could still be justified. The Committee made two reports, the first concerned with local authority smallholdings; here they argued that the 1947 Act was no longer relevant in view of changes in the agricultural situation; they wanted the obligation on local authorities to provide smallholdings in accordance with demand to be abolished; the amalgamation of existing holdings where necessary so that each could provide a reasonable living; tenants to be selected according to qualifications and experience; and the diminution of Exchequer financial assistance. Most of these recommendations were accepted (some in a modified form) by the Government.[4] The second report dealt with smallholdings owned by the Minister, some of which are managed by the Land Settlement Association. So far as the latter were concerned the

[1] *Methods of Payment of Wages*, a report of a committee of the National Joint Advisory Council (HMSO, 1972), p. 4.
[2] Cmnd 2936, 1966; Cmnd 3303, 1967.
[3] H. C. Deb. 678, 29 May 1963, WA 128–9.
[4] H. C. Deb. 760, 7 March 1968, WA 156–8.

Committee thought that the existing system was no longer relevant to the needs of agriculture, and suggested two possible ways in which existing tenants might become members of voluntary horticultural co-operatives. The Government, however, took the view that the LSA system should continue, although somewhat modified to allow tenants more freedom in the use of centralised services.[1]

In considering the various factors which contributed to the relative success of the Wise Committee, the attitude of the department principally concerned is again a key factor. The MAFF were moved to reconsider the provisions of the 1947 Agriculture Act relating to smallholdings largely through the Treasury's initial financial concern, but once having been drawn to its consideration the Ministry were bound to find a strong case for revision. For example, the statutory requirement on local authorities to meet the demand for smallholdings ran increasingly against the trend of policy for efficient agriculture towards large units. On the other hand, for historical reasons there were strong sentiments in favour of smallholdings. This is turn provided the political motive for retaining the system. So far as local authority smallholdings were concerned, therefore, the conflict or potential conflict between financial and agricultural efficiency considerations on the one hand, and political considerations on the other provided the main reason for setting up the Committee. It was thus essential that the Committee should be independent and not representative of the interests concerned.[2]

It follows that the sponsoring department was already disposed to certain changes in the system of provision by local authorities. What it hoped that a committee would provide were the facts and arguments derived from its own inquiries to confirm that these were indeed the kind of changes needed, and to elaborate on them where necessary. As the Minister (Mr Peart) said in relation to the Committee's first report, the Committee's views on reorganisation and amalgamation were very much in line with the Government's farm structure policy.[3] It is hardly surprising, therefore, that on these and most other major proposals relating to local authority smallholdings, the Committee's proposals were accepted and put into effect, although, as is almost invariably the case, there were modifications in detail.[4] There is also no doubt that the

[1] H. C. Deb. 764, 10 May 1968, WA 145-7.

[2] Cf. Mr Soames's reply to Mr Peart on trade union representation on the Committee (H. C. Deb. 679, 19 June 1963, 435).

[3] H. C. Deb. 760, 7 March 1968, WA 156-8.

[4] For example, the Government put more emphasis on practical experience than technical knowledge as qualifications for tenants (ibid., also S.I. 1970, No. 1049).

Government were anxious to have the financial arrangements revised, and again the Committee's report pointed the way to abandonment of the system of a central contribution to annual losses and its replacement by a more limited system of grants to assist in the amalgamation of holdings of less than commercial size.[1]

The situation was rather different with regard to the Committee's proposals on the Land Settlement Association holdings. Here there was clearly a conflict between the advantages of the existing strongly centralised system, particularly over grading and marketing of produce, and the desire of the smallholders for a less rigid system. Here the Wise Committee put the emphasis on moving towards a system of voluntary co-operatives; in other words, their approach ran counter to the whole philosophy on which the LSA scheme was founded, with its basis in a contractual obligation on the part of the tenants to make use of the Association's central services. The Government in effect rejected this approach, but adopted a compromise position which maintained the contractual obligation but with some modifications in favour of tenants.

Several points may be made about this account of the Wise Committee. In the first place, it was not a committee to examine smallholdings policy in general. Its terms of references were directed specifically towards a review of the existing system and to its improvement, and not, for example, to the question whether, in the changed conditions of the 1960s, there ought to be a system of government-sponsored smallholdings at all. The latter raised politically controversial questions which the MAFF did not want or feel it necessary to tackle by means of a committee. It followed, secondly, from this that the Committee's main purpose was to smooth the way for changes in the system. In general, no doubt many of those changes could have been foreseen, but the precise form of them was open to argument, and the advantage of a committee was that these arguments could be set out in a public document and related to the facts and opinions presented to the Committee. Thirdly, the only major point on which the Committee's recommendations were not accepted, those concerned with the LSA, shows the complexity of factors involved in the acceptance or rejection of recommendations.

Both practical reasons (e.g. the view that the Committee had attached too much importance to the idea of voluntary co-operation) and political reasons, especially unwillingness to face the political odium of attacking or seeming to attack the established LSA scheme,[2] played a

[1] H. C. Deb. 760, 7 March 1968, WA 156–8.
[2] The LSA was established during the Depression as a means of providing work on the land for the unemployed.

part in the Ministry's view that the Committee's LSA proposals went too far.

Committee on Higher Education

Neither the Committee on the Truck Acts nor the Committee on Statutory Smallholdings touched very large issues of public policy. It is doubtful whether many people either knew of their existence or were much affected by what happened to their proposals. The report of the Robbins Committee on Higher Education,[1] on the other hand, generated a good deal of interest and comment. Moreover, as might be expected from a committee covering such a wide and important field, it produced a large number of recommendations. Immediately after it reported the Government issued a White Paper in which it accepted much of the Committee's basic thinking and its calculations on which it had based proposals for the expansion of higher education, as well as a number of its detailed recommendations.[2] 'Few official reports', one study claimed, 'have led to such immediate changes in government policy.'[3] What, then, were the reasons for this success?

The first point to notice is that, as the study already quoted makes clear,[4] the most successful proposals were those concerned with the assumptions on which the numbers of places to be provided in higher education were to be calculated. In particular, the Government accepted the assumption that higher education should be available for all qualified school leavers, and it was this which represented a distinct change of policy. On the other hand, the Committee made recommendations on matters ranging from the machinery of government, where they wanted a separate Ministry for Arts and Science responsible for the universities, to university administration (e.g. they wanted a review of the structure of university staffing); many of these recommendations were rejected (like that for a separate Ministry) or modified or deferred.

The first question, then, is the familiar one of determining whether the Robbins recommendations which were accepted represented the main or essential part of the Committee's analysis. Once more this question can only be answered by reference to the circumstances in which the Committee was appointed. One important strand here was the increasing demand for higher, and particularly university, education. To the extent that the need to find a means of dealing with this demand was

---

[1] Cmnd 2154, 1963.

[2] *Higher Education*, Cmnd 2165, 1963.

[3] Richard Lazard, John King, Claus Moser, *The Impact of Robbins* (Penguin, 1969), p. 22.

[4] Ibid., p. 22, cf. p. 61.

a primary reason for the appointment of the Committee, the Committee's recommendations designed to provide for an expansion of places were a key part of its Report.

Even accepting this as a simplified view of what the Robbins Committee was about, and regarding the Government's reaction as indicating a broad acceptance of the Committee's analysis and recommendations, examination of the reasons for that acceptance reveal a complex situation. A variety of reasons has in fact been advanced, from the imminence of the 'bulge' of children born in the immediate post-war years [1] to the desire of the Conservative Government to 'make up' for their disagreement the previous year with the University Grants Committee over university salaries and other matters.[2] More subtly, the Minister of Education at the time (Sir Edward Boyle) has pointed to the fact that the two major education reports appearing in 1963 (Newsom [3] and Robbins) drove home the view that the pool of potential ability was larger than many had suspected.[4] The implication is that one factor in the ready acceptance of the Robbins report was the receptiveness of one of the ministers mainly concerned to the argument and evidence in the report that a large-scale expansion of higher education was both necessary and desirable. On the other hand, one might also argue that the setting-up of the Committee in the first place indicated a disposition to expansion. A combination of this disposition together with the force of the arguments advanced by the Committee can thus be seen as the main factors leading to the acceptance of the Robbins report and to the great expansion of higher education in the following years.

Even if this very broadly represents the situation, so brief an account cannot do justice to the report of a committee dealing with such an inportant and complex subject. Any full account of Robbins would need, for example, to examine the relationship of recommendations which were rejected to the central argument of the Committee as well as the reasons for rejection. It would also need to look at what was happening to the longer-term recommendations, as, for example, that a higher percentage of students in universities should have broader courses for their first degree.[5] However, the object here is not to offer yet another inter-

---

[1] Ibid., p. 22.

[2] Sir Edward (now Lord) Boyle in Maurice Kogan (ed.), *The Politics of Education* (Penguin, 1971), p. 93.

[3] *Half Our Future*, a report of the Central Advisory Council for Education (England).

[4] In Kogan, op. cit., p. 91.

[5] Although this is primarily a matter for the universities rather than the Government, the latter may be involved indirectly e.g. through any consequences for university expenditure.

pretation of Robbins, but rather to illustrate the difficulties and the need for skilled judgement in assessing both the extent to which the Committee's recommendations were accepted and the reasons for acceptance.

FACTORS IN ACCEPTANCE OR REJECTION

Quality of reports

The examples of committee reports and their recommendations in the preceding discussion have concentrated on the principal arguments used and the political and other circumstances contributing to the reception which those recommendations received. For the most part, the discussion has not dealt with the intrinsic merit of particular arguments and recommendations as a factor contributing to their acceptance nor with the fact that recommendations may differ widely, e.g. in their specificity or degree of novelty. This is not because these aspects are unimportant, but because they need to be treated in a rather different way.

It was remarked earlier that committees sometimes draw attention to the fact that their recommendations are unanimous, and it is often said or implied that lack of unanimity may affect the success of recommendations.[1] One object of appointing committees is to try to achieve collective agreement, and in fact most committees are unanimous on most of their recommendations, but it is certainly open to doubt how far a unanimous recommendation contributes to its acceptance or, conversely, how far openly expressed disagreement by members of a committee contributes to the rejection of a recommendation. So much depends on the individual circumstances of a particular committee, and, especially, on the motives behind its appointment; and also on the importance of particular recommendations to the total analysis and report of a committee. The fact that the Committee on the Age of Majority, for example, split 9–2 on the principal question of whether the age should be lowered from 21 to 18 and that the Committee on Decimal Currency split 4–2 on one of their principal questions did not prevent the majority views from being implemented in both cases. Nor did the massive memorandum of dissent by Mr Derek Senior in which he rejected the whole basis of the scheme of reform propounded by his colleagues on the Royal Commission on Local Government in England prevent the Labour Government's acceptance of the essentials of the scheme put forward by the majority, although the scheme was not in the

[1] E.g. Peta Sheriff, 'Factors Affecting the Impact of the Fulton Report', *International Review of Administrative Sciences*, 3 (1970), pp. 215–16.

end implemented because of the change of government in June 1970. A committee which cannot agree provides a government which has in any case no great desire to act with the excuse for continuing inaction.[1] But where a problem requires some action to be taken it does not automatically follow that reservations, memoranda of dissent or minority reports necessarily prevent action although they may hold it up since they provide opponents of a particular set of proposals with ammunition to hand.

There is perhaps also a distinction to be drawn here between memoranda of dissent implying a fundamental disagreement on a major point of principle, and reservations or notes of dissent affecting a particular recommendation or group of recommendations which may not vitally affect the committee's central arguments. Failure to agree on a central issue, as in the case of the Committee on Rural Bus Services,[2] is a more serious matter, both because it tends to delay a decision where a problem has to be resolved and because it provides a convenient excuse for doing nothing where the problem is not regarded as urgent. Particular recommendations, however, may be and frequently are rejected by governments without affecting acceptance of a major line of argument, and it would be rash to suppose that this happens more frequently with recommendations which are not unanimous without at any rate studying much more closely a large number of rejected recommendations and the reasons for their rejection.

The fact that a recommendation is unanimous tells us nothing about its quality. Indeed it could be argued that since unanimity may conceal an uneasy compromise between conflicting views it may sometimes result in poor recommendations which satisfy nobody but are the best that can be done in the circumstances.[3] But this raises the whole question of what influence, if any, the quality of a recommendation has on the likelihood of its acceptance, and, again, there is not a simple relationship, but rather a complex series of relationships.

Quality itself covers a number of distinct aspects. It may refer to the logic of the argument; or the ingenuity of the solution proposed; or the practical appeal of a proposal. Recommendations may have quality in

---

[1] A most notable example occurred in the 1920s with the Royal Commission on London Government which split into three groups on the fundamental question of whether and, if so, how London government should be reorganised.

[2] Above, p. 133.

[3] This is presumably why Sir Kenneth Wheare (*Government by Committee*, Oxford University Press, 1955, p. 80) argues that it may be better to have conflicting views clearly stated; although again one might suppose that this would chiefly apply only to certain kinds of committees.

all or none or some of these senses. A proposal may, for example, be an ingenious solution to a problem without necessarily following from a well-argued analysis; conversely, a committee may present a reasoned and well-argued analysis of the problem without being able to suggest any very new solution or one which is acceptable to the Government and to the interests concerned.

Again, it is necessary to examine the effect of quality in relation to specific examples. Jeffrey Stanyer's account of the Redcliffe-Maud Commission [1] claims that the report was accepted by the Labour Government in spite of the illogicalities and poor quality of its arguments; he attributes this largely to the fact that the Commission gave great weight to the evidence of the government departments which therefore welcomed the report and that the Labour Government relied a good deal on civil service views in coming to a decision.[2] Another commentator has argued that some of the Fulton Committee's recommendations on the civil service were accepted either because they were in such general terms that acceptance would have little practical effect or because acceptance gave the appearance of a great willingness to reform even though the consequences of acceptance would not in practice prove to be so far-reaching.[3]

It is of course open to argument whether these particular analyses of particular committee recommendations are correct. What they do draw attention to is the fact that a committee's report and even more its specific recommendations have to meet a variety of challenges in order to gain acceptance. Neither a well-argued case nor a new and ingenious solution to a problem are in themselves guarantees of success for a committee, because in the last resort a government subject to conflicting pressures and not least the pressure of priorities frequently adopts a pragmatic view and accepts a solution which is workable in both a practical and political sense, even if it is not based on the most impeccable logic; conversely, it may reject a well-argued report because the conclusions to which it points conflict with other aims, such as the need to gain the support of certain interests. A certain amount of window dressing, of accepting recommendations with little practical effect, is probably as inevitable as is the rejection of recommendations with troublesome implications.

There is nothing necessarily wrong in this. Governments appoint

[1] Above, p. 124.
[2] Jeffery Stanyer, 'The Redcliffe-Maud Royal Commission on Local Government', in Richard A. Chapman (ed.), *The Role of Commissions in Policy-Making* (Allen & Unwin, 1973), p. 128.
[3] Sheriff, op. cit. pp. 216–17, 218–19.

committees to help them in deciding what to do. That help may be in the information provided in a committee's report, or in its analysis of a problem or in its proposals for action – or of course in all three. But what the Government decides to do in the end will be affected by a great many other factors as well, not excluding the effect of a committee's report on public opinion, a topic which is discussed further below.

Again, the whole subject needs to be kept in perspective. Reactions to a report, taking the whole range of committees of inquiry covered in this study, most frequently take the form of modified acceptance. Admittedly modification can take a great many forms, usually involves a watering-down of the less acceptable proposals and can sometimes result in a very emaciated version of the committee's proposals being carried into effect. Nevertheless, it is the committees on social studies, or footpaths, or higher education, or senior nursing staff structure, or immigration appeals which are more typical in terms of acceptance than the often more-publicised committees whose reports are either positively rejected more or less in their entirety or are simply not carried out, apart perhaps from one or two recommendations, without any indication being given of the Government's attitude.

There are, as always, no sharp dividing-lines between, say, a committee whose report is accepted but in such a modified form that it becomes unrecognisable and one whose report, although rejected, provides at least part of the basis for subsequent action. Nevertheless, government reaction to a report like that of the Hunt Committee on the intermediate areas [1] amounts to a more positive rejection of the Committee's thinking than, say, its reaction to the first report of the Wilson Committee on noise.[2] It is indeed rare for a government to state categorically that it rejects a committee's main finding as the Secretary of State for Scotland did with the report of the Committee on the Generation and Distribution of Electricity in Scotland,[3] or as the (Conservative) Secretary of State for Education and Science did with the reports of the Labour-

[1] Cmnd 3998, 1969: the Secretary of State for Economic Affairs (Mr Shore) made a statement on the day the report was published in effect rejecting a major part of the Committee's approach (H. C. Deb. 782, 24 April 1969, 668–83).

[2] Cmnd 1780, 1962: the Government accepted that there should be numerical noise limits for new vehicles, but considerably modified the timing and to some extent the actual limits proposed by the Committee. See Alistair Aird, *The Automotive Nightmare* (Hutchinson, 1972), pp. 105–7.

[3] Cmnd 1859, 1962: the Committee proposed a single electricity board for the whole of Scotland, but the Government claimed that it had not established that the existing two boards could not provide electricity economically (see H. C. Deb. 680, 10 July 1963, 1244).

appointed Public Schools Commission.[1] Nor is it all that common for governments simply to do nothing about committee reports, as has so far happened with the committees on experiments on animals [2] and on industrial designs.[3] Some positive reaction and subsequent action usually arises from a committee's report, even if only after an interval of time. Indeed this is bound to be so unless one adopts the extreme and unrealistic position that the only object of committees of inquiry is to enable governments to avoid taking any action at all.

WIDER CONSEQUENCES OF COMMITTEE REPORTS

This discussion does, however, lead on to a wider topic. Given that Committees do generally have some success judged by the degree to which their recommendations are accepted and acted upon, but that this success depends not only on the merits of their arguments but also on the political and other circumstances in which particular committees operate, are there other consequences which committee reports have and should their success or otherwise be judged by these other consequences? A particular question which arises here is the extent to which (by, for example, influencing public opinion) committee reports may indirectly contribute to acceptance or rejection of their recommendations in the longer term.

The reports of committees are public documents. They often contain a wealth of information in addition to discussion and specific recommendations for action. They are commented on by newspapers, by professional and technical journals, sometimes by academic commentators. The question is, therefore, what the significance of such reports is, not simply in terms of the reactions of civil servants and ministers poring over them in their offices, but in this wider public context.

Sir Geoffrey Vickers has indeed argued that what committees recommend by way of action may be less important than their ability to provide 'the authority which appointed them and also all who read their report with a common basis for forming their own appreciations', that is, of judging the nature of the problem and ways in which it may be

---

[1] The Commission published two reports in 1968 and 1970: despite the brave words of the Secretary of State (Mr Short) (H. C. Deb. 787, 17 July 1969, 865–6) the first report was not well received at the Labour Party conference in 1968 and was something of an embarrassment to the Government; what action if any they would have taken on that and the second report (on the direct grant schools) is impossible to say, but the Conservative Secretary of State (Mrs Thatcher) following the election decisively rejected both reports (H. C. Deb. 806, 19 November 1970, 1403–4).

[2] Cmnd 2641, 1965.　　　　　　　　　　[3] Cmnd 1808, 1962: see above, p. 135.

resolved.[1] From a slightly different angle, others have argued that royal commissions are sometimes used for their educative value, that is, they are deliberately appointed in order to prepare the way for change by giving respectability and authority to ideas which may be acceptable to government but are ahead of public opinion.[2] Somewhat similarly, it has been argued that the function of the reports of the Central Advisory Councils for Education has been to sum up current thinking on education with the effect of legitimising new thinking about the relation between education and society.[3]

That committee reports can have an effect on public opinion which goes far wider than their specific recommendations is well illustrated from one of Sir Geoffrey Vickers's examples, the Buchanan report on *Traffic in Towns*. One could indeed argue that simply by focusing attention in a systematic way on an issue which previously most people had been aware of but had not considered in all its implications, the Committee made a major contribution to increasing awareness of the extent of the problems involved and the advantages and disadvantages of possible solutions, quite apart from whether its specific proposals were or indeed could be brought into operation.[4]

The Buchanan Committee was, however, a rather unusual committee both in its methods of operation [5] and in the nature of its subject. Many committees, perhaps the majority, are concerned with subjects which do not have the direct interest of or impact on the general public as does traffic in towns. Practically everybody is affected by traffic and has views on the policies followed by public authorities to deal with it, whether in the form of the Greater London Council's 1960s proposal for a motorway box round central London or Nottingham's 1970s plan virtually to ban the private car from the city centre. By contrast, relatively few people have much direct interest or concern in the teaching of Russian or the patent system or the importation of Charollais cattle.

However one defines public opinion, and whether one qualifies it by the adjective 'informed' or not, one is thus dealing in most cases not so much with public opinion, as with opinion among those who are likely

[1] *The Art of Judgement* (Chapman & Hall, 1965), p. 50.

[2] Cf. H. M. Clokie and J. W. Robinson, *Royal Commissions of Inquiry* (Stanford University Press, 1937), p. 139.

[3] Maurice Kogan, 'The Plowden Committee on Primary Education' in Richard A. Chapman (ed.), *The Role of Commissions in Policy-Making* (Allen & Unwin, 1973), pp. 84–5.

[4] See Peter Self, *Administrative Theories and Politics* (Allen & Unwin, 1972, pp. 115–17), for some of the administrative problems involved in the Buchanan proposals.

[5] See above, p. 81.

to be directly affected by any action on a committee's report. The report may have an educative effect on them, or may change their appreciation of the problem in Sir Geoffrey Vickers's sense, or alternatively they may merely look to see whether it accepts or rejects the views which they or their representatives put to the committee.

What is being emphasised here is that the effect of a committee's report may depend not only on the strength and cogency of its arguments but on the degree of receptiveness to persuasion among those who read it or, in most cases, read about it. If a subject is of broad general and political interest there is perhaps more chance of informed public debate about it than if it is one which interests only those who are already partisans. The real difficulty is to decide in either case what consequences follow either in the shorter term for the acceptance or rejection of a committee's recommendations or in longer-term changes in attitudes.

WIDER CONSEQUENCES – SOME EXAMPLES

Committee on Cannabis

Some committees, by the nature of the subjects which they investigate as well as the recommendations which they make, seem much more likely to make their impact on longer-term attitudes than on short-term decisions. When the Advisory Committee on Drug Dependence, for example, in 1969 published a report of one of its subcommittees advocating, among other things, a reduction in the maximum penalty for possessing cannabis,[1] it can hardly have been surprised at the Home Secretary's immediate and forthright rejection of its advice.[2] The subject of drug-taking and its consequences was controversial, not least among members of the medical profession,[3] and one liable to rouse strong emotional reactions, as was evident from comment on the report in the Press and on radio and television, to say nothing of parliamentary reaction.[4]

[1] Cannabis, report by the Advisory Committee on Drug Dependence (HMSO, 1969).

[2] H. C. Deb. 776, 23 January 1969, 661–5.

[3] The British Medical Journal, for example, thought the Committee's recommendations more likely to increase than diminish the use of a drug 'that causes mental disorientation' (BMJ, 18 January. 1969, p. 133), whereas The Lancet quoting the Committee's view that cannabis was less dangerous 'than either drugs like the barbiturates or alcohol' thought the proposals right (The Lancet, 18 January 1969, p. 139).

[4] The Home Secretary (Mr Callaghan) in a debate on the report referred to the need to call a halt to the advancing tide of permissiveness, which led The Lancet to deplore the use of such 'colourful' language (H. C. Deb. 776, 27 January 1969, 959; The Lancet, 1 February 1969, p. 246).

For the Government in 1969 to have adopted a more liberal attitude to the question of penalties for possessing cannabis would have meant going ahead of much public opinion. This is a subject, however, on which argument is likely to recur and on which attitudes may change; certainly the advocates of change are still to be heard.[1] But if attitudes do change it will be for future historians to decide what part, if any, the report on cannabis played in that change. Certainly the report was unusual in the extent of public interest which it aroused, and this in part was related to its origins.[2]

Committee on Experimental Importation of Charollais Cattle

By contrast, the suggestion made in the late 1950s that some Charollais bulls should be imported from France for experiments in cross-breeding with British breeds was not one which was likely to excite any great interest in the general public, although it aroused intense controversy among cattle breeders. The decision to set up a committee to look into the whole question in 1959 was taken, according to the Minister principally concerned, because of 'the wide divergence of views in the industry'.[3] The Committee consisted of a legally-qualified Chairman (Lord Terrington), a veterinary surgeon, and two former civil servants in the agriculture departments. The Committee concluded that imports should be allowed to enable the Ministry to conduct trials, and this was eventually done.[4]

At first sight, this seems to be a simple case of a committee influencing the 'appreciation' of a problem by those directly concerned with it. The main opposition to the proposal to import Charollais cattle came, however, from the National Cattle Breeders' Association before the Committee was appointed; it did not change its opposition once the committee had reported in favour of the proposal. What really changed was the attitude of the MAFF, from a fairly neutral attitude of being mildly in favour of conducting experiments but unwilling to go against the opposition of a powerful sector of the industry and also inhibited by the statutory restrictions on imports under the Diseases of Animals Act,

[1] E.g. Dr Henry Miller in *Medicine and Society* (Oxford University Press, 1973) has claimed that the prohibition of cannabis does more harm than good.

[2] Mr Callaghan made much of the fact that the Government had not specifically asked for this subject to be investigated, presumably referring to the fact that the Advisory Committee was able to initiate its own inquiries; however, it seems likely that the Government began to have doubts only when it saw the direction in which the inquiry was going.

[3] The Minister of Agriculture, Fisheries and Food (Mr Hare) in replying to a parliamentary question (H. C. Deb. 605, 14 May 1959, WA 174–5).

[4] Cmnd 1140, 1960; H. C. Deb. 638, 20 April, 1961, WA 121–2.

1950, to one in which it used the backing given by the Committee's report to try to overcome the opposition.[1]

But the consequences can also be viewed more widely. The experiments which the Ministry carried out showed that some of the opposition had been based on a mistaken view,[2] and eventually led to the importation of Charollais cattle more widely. Indeed, it could be argued that one consequence of the Charollais argument was that it contributed to a general liberalisation of the Ministry's policy with regard to the import of foreign breeds, leading to an amendment of the 1950 Act in 1972. Before that date, largely because of the fear of encouraging disease, the policy was to ban imports with few exceptions; whereas now, imports of livestock are running at some 1,200 animals a year.

Committee on Noise

The cannabis and Charollais committees were deliberately chosen as examples of committees considering single and relatively well-defined problems. Some committees, however, range over a whole area of problems; correspondingly, their analysis and recommendations, as was seen earlier, may be very much more complex than those of these two committees. What are the implications for the assessment of the consequences of committee reports?

The Committee on Noise has been referred to several times before, largely because it is an example of a committee considering a large, ill-defined and many-faceted subject. It had to deal with technical questions (e.g. how do you measure noise?), questions of physical and mental health and questions of law. Its recommendations were numerous and wide-ranging, from very specific proposals for statutory restrictions on the noise levels to be permitted for new motor vehicles, to more general proposals (e.g. that industry should pay much more attention in design and installation to the problems of noise).

The consequences of the Committee's reports can also be viewed from several different angles:

1   How far were specific proposals acted upon either by government or by private industry, professional bodies and the general public?
2   What effect have their more general proposals had?
3   What consequences have there been for general attitudes to the question of noise?

[1] Cf. the tone of the Minister's (by now Mr Soames) statement (H. C. Deb. 631, 8 December 1960, 1430–2).
[2] For example, it was found that Charollais matured more quickly than the NCBA believed.

These questions become progressively more difficult to answer as they increase in generality. It is comparatively easy to determine whether the Committee's proposal that new cars should not emit noise exceeding 85 DBA has been carried out; more difficult to judge how far the Committee's view that office machine noise could be reduced has been acted on; and still more difficult to determine whether and if so to what extent people's attitudes to noise have changed as a result of the Committee's reports, or what contribution the reports have made to the effective control of noise.

Ultimately, answers to these questions depend on what view one takes of the noise problem. When the Committee's first report, on motor vehicle noise, was published in 1962 the *Economist* welcomed it on the grounds that it showed that noise from this source was not an inevitable price of progress, but something which could be checked by the specific measures recommended by the Committee.[1] Similarly, Lord Hailsham welcomed the Committee's second and more general report as a 'major contribution to public understanding of the problem and of ways to mitigate it'.[2] One may perhaps read into both these statements the implication that the educative effect of the Committee's report in persuading people that something can be done about noise is of equal importance with actually carrying out specific proposals.

Yet equally if noise is an important problem then it is clear from the Committee's reports that quite large changes in attitude are needed if effective steps are to be taken to limit the growth in noise, let alone reduce it. Most people would accept that during the 1960s more public concern was expressed about the problem of noise, as indeed about environmental problems generally; it was part of the movement of protest against supersonic airliners and large container lorries, just as it formed part of the protest movement against the Roskill Commission's choice of Cublington for the third London airport, and in numerous much more local protests against sites for go-kart or speedway racing, or proposals to extract gravel in hitherto quiet country areas. What is much more difficult to estimate is the contribution which the Wilson Committee made to this greater awareness as compared with, say, people's evidence of their own senses about the extent of the noise problem.

Again, many of the Committee's proposals were essentially of a long-term nature; the encouragement of research into cheaper sound insulation for buildings, for example, or the improved training of architects and builders might not have measurable consequences on the problem of noise for many years; and others if implemented would have pre-

[1] *The Economist*, 21 July 1962, p. 270.
[2] H. L. Deb. 251, 2 July, 1963, 648.

vented further noise rather than affected existing noise, like their proposal that adequate criteria needed to be developed before any increase in the use of helicopters should be permitted in city centres. Thus, on those who were indifferent or apathetic to the noise problem, the Committee's proposals probably made little or no impact. Whereas those who viewed noise as one of the more intolerable evils of modern living were liable to see them as inadequate, particularly as some of the more specific of them (e.g. that grants should be payable towards the cost of sound-proofing houses near Heathrow Airport) were initially rejected by the Government.

One could therefore say that on a narrow front the Wilson Committee on Noise was moderately successful in making some impact with its specific proposals. It has probably also made some, though hard to assess, contribution to increased awareness of the need for more effort in the direction of controlling noise. The difficulty is to be more precise about this latter influence, which, perhaps, inevitably, must remain a matter for debate.

CONCLUSIONS – CRITERIA FOR JUDGING THE EFFECTIVENESS OF COMMITTEES

Much of the preceding discussion has pointed to the practical difficulties of discovering what consequences actually followed from the reports of particular committees. A more fundamental problem is to relate such information, if it can be discovered, to possible criteria for judging the effectiveness of committees of inquiry. The accounts of the Wilson and Robbins committees, in particular, indicate how formidable this problem is.

The basic difficulty here is that the effectiveness of committees needs to be related to a view of the purpose which committees serve, and this, as was seen earlier, is neither a simple matter nor one on which there is any general agreement. Different committees may in practice serve different purposes, and particular committees may have more than one purpose. And these purposes may look rather different according to whether the viewpoint is that of a civil servant concerned with setting up the committee in the first place, a member of the committee, an outside interest group directly affected, an academic observer or a member of the public with an intelligent interest in the problem under investigation. Because of these conflicting viewpoints and practical variations it becomes exceedingly difficult to assert with confidence a single purpose which committees ought to serve and hence to relate this to criteria for judging how effectively they carry out this purpose.

One may consider, for example, the contrast between two possible ways of viewing how committees ought to be used. The first, which one might call a naïve rationalist view, would see the appointment of a committee as a means of finding a rational answer to a particular problem which has arisen; the second, which might be called the appreciative view (from Sir Geoffrey Vickers's use of the term), would see committees as a means of opening up a problem to public exposure and discussion, of giving it a different perspective. It should of course be made clear at the outset of this discussion that these are not intended to be mutually exclusive points of view. The aim is rather to show the different consequences for judging the effectiveness of committees which follow from emphasising one or the other viewpoint.

The naïve rationalist view naturally puts most emphasis on the intellectual quality of a committee and its report. The important thing is to ensure that the problem is thoroughly analysed and a logical and coherent solution propounded for it, and committees will be judged accordingly. One difficulty about such a view is what part, if any, it assigns to the practical consequences of a committee's report. Rational analysis and solutions may or may not be accepted and put into practice. This may be held not to matter provided that the job has been done and is on record in the published report. More likely the assumption will be made that rational analysis will, and indeed must, make a difference. This could be in several ways: it might, for example, be held that a good report in this sense is for that very reason more likely to be put into practice than a bad one. In which case, there should be a correlation between the quality of reports and their effectiveness in practical terms. Or it could be held that even though a good report was not implemented, it would, because of its quality, influence attitudes over a longer term.

This latter view comes closer to the contrasting appreciative view which would presumably be less concerned with whether a committee's report was implemented than with its effect on the ways in which a problem is viewed.[1] The difficulty, however, is to see how one can derive from this viewpoint practical criteria for judging the effectiveness of committees. The point of changing our appreciation of a problem is presumably to enable us to deal with it more effectively because we see in a new light what was previously difficult or insoluble. If the committee enables us to do this through its analysis of the problem then one would also expect its proposals, based on that analysis, to be ones which for the same reason are easier to adopt. But if the extent to which proposals are

[1] Cf. Sir Geoffrey Vickers's view of the Robbins Committee's Report on higher education as 'not merely a plan for a reorganisation of our institutions. It is also a plea for the reorganisation of our thought' (op. cit., pp. 59–60).

adopted is not to form the basis of criteria for judging effectiveness, we are left with a far harder task. For whether or not a committee has changed our appreciation of a problem is a matter requiring considerable knowledge of the circumstances of the origin of individual committees and a considerable degree of judgement first of the essential factors in a committee's analysis and, secondly, of how and in what ways that analysis has influenced attitudes.

What makes the task of establishing criteria all the harder is the fact that, as was suggested above, it is rarely, if ever, possible simply to adopt a single viewpoint. Practically the only common feature shared by all committees of inquiry is that they are asked to look at some problem which has arisen, to analyse it and, usually, to make recommendations on it. It is undeniably implicit in this situation that the committee should make the best analysis of which they are capable, and this would hardly be in dispute between those setting up the committee, those serving on it, and those observing it from outside. What is in dispute is what 'best' means in this situation, and, more particularly, best for whom? To answer 'best for the public interest generally' may be simply to beg the question since the question then becomes 'how (and by whom) is the public interest to be determined?' Is the best answer one which is the most intellectually satisfying, or one which is acceptable to the interests most directly concerned, or one which accords with the political outlook of the minister responsible, or one which most appeals to (informed) public opinion? Or one which attempts to achieve all of these things? And if the latter, should all be regarded as of equal importance or is it better where aims conflict to concentrate on one particular aim?

We are hardly in a position to answer these questions yet, mainly because they seem to require much more work – and much more detailed work – on individual committees to see how far it is is possible to classify them according to different criteria and what information about their consequences can be reliably obtained. If, for example, it were generally true that committees were mainly used as a means of getting support for policies already decided upon, and their members and terms of reference deliberately chosen to this end,[1] there would be little point in judging committee reports according to whether they were intellectually satisfying or not. The question would be whether they had done well or badly the task for which they were appointed. This is not to deny that one might want to raise a deeper and more significant question in such circumstances of whether it was right to employ com-

[1] Cf. R. V. Vernon and N. Mansergh, *Advisory Bodies* (George Allen & Unwin, 1940), p. 25.

mittees in this way. And of course one would need to take into account the fact that even if this was the real reason for many committees it was not the ostensible reason for their appointment.

Again, there is a general expectation that committees will base their analysis to some degree on the evidence which they receive. Since this evidence often comes for the most part from interested parties this means in effect that committee reports tend to meet some at least of the expectations of interested bodies. So much so that it is a matter for comment when a committee in effect rejects the views of all interested parties.[1] But the expectation is itself based on a view of the purpose – or at least one purpose – of committees, namely that they should not only find an answer to a problem but find one which, if not welcomed by all interested parties, at least seems, and is seen, to treat seriously the arguments put forward by them. Some committees seem to concentrate on this aspect of their work, conceiving it to be their job largely to weigh up the evidence they receive, much as courts of inquiry in industrial disputes have tended to hear both sides and then propose a compromise formula as a means of ending a dispute. Others, on the other hand, although they may acknowledge the usefulness of the evidence, have clearly relied on other means for arriving at their conclusions and proposals.

Whether a committee operates more in one of these ways or in the other may be partly a function of the nature of its inquiry, or of the nature of its membership, or some extraneous factor, such as changing attitudes over time to the purpose of committees, or the ways in which they should operate.[2] The question of whether and how far a committee should seek to relate its analysis to the evidence presented to it, and how far to its own inquiries, thus involves judging the appropriateness of such methods in the particular circumstances of individual committees rather than attempting to define criteria valid for all committees.

Perhaps in the end the best way of looking at the problem of effectiveness is from the point of view of committee members. Their aim must surely be to have some effect on future events. A committee whose report has no discernible consequences on the handling of the problem which it was set up to examine is, so far as its members are concerned, a failure. But of any particular committee we are anxious to know what

[1] Cf. the comment by *The Times* (3 May 1972) on the report of the committee set up in 1969 to examine the registration of builders: 'a special brand of ingenuity is required to produce a Government-commissioned report on a topic of national interest which succeeds by the conclusions it draws, in alienating all interested parties, even those with diametrically opposed views'.

[2] It may be, for example, that committees are much more likely now than, say, fifty years ago to seek their own information and go beyond a judicial-type function.

kind of consequences it had and why, and whether its task was relatively easy because what needed to be done was obvious or relatively hard because there was no agreement either on what the problem was or how it should be dealt with, if at all.

Thus the committee's ultimate aim as seen by its members centres largely on persuasion, but whom it has to persuade – government, interest groups, the public, or even some of its own members – is not something to be determined in the abstract, but by the circumstances of each particular committee. Thus the search for general criteria of effectiveness becomes meaningless (except at so high a level of generality that nothing can be deduced from it) precisely because general comparisons run up against the familiar difficulty of the inability to compare like with like. Can one really apply the same criteria to the Karmel Committee on the Truck Acts and the Robbins Committee on Higher Education, the Terrington Committee on the Experimental Importation of Charollais Cattle and the Jack Committee on Rural Bus Services?

It is no denigration of the work of the Robbins Committee to say that political and professional circumstances provided them with much greater opportunities for effectively influencing the course of events than the Jack Committee. One may still significantly argue how well each committee made use of its opportunities, but this is a judgement which needs to be based on detailed knowledge and assessment of each committee's background and the context in which it operated.

What the argument comes to is this. Looked at in terms of the distinctions made at the beginning of this chapter, it is certainly possible, and indeed indispensable for an understanding of committees of inquiry, to examine the consequences which follow from committee reports, both in terms of the degree to which recommendations are put into effect and in terms of wider effects. Such examination leads inevitably to consideration of the factors which are important in determining these consequences and hence to a concentration on the circumstances in which individual committees operate.

But it is a big leap from this pragmatic approach to consequences in the light of the individual circumstances of committees to the formulation of general criteria of effectiveness. It is a leap which cannot be made without at least much more detailed analysis of many more committees. Is there no alternative then to the case-study approach? And if so how many cases would have to be studied to make at any rate the possibility of generalisation feasible? This dilemma has haunted discussion in much of this study. Before trying to sum up what can be said about committees of inquiry and what more needs to be done, it is time to look at alternative approaches to see what they may yield.

CHAPTER 7

COMMITTEES OF INQUIRY
AND THE POLICY-MAKING PROCESS

THE POLICY-CENTRED APPROACH

Two important points which have emerged from the discussion in preceding chapters are:

1 Committees of inquiry are only one of a number of means by which governments seek information and advice from outside sources, and there are no firm dividing-lines between these various means.

2 Appointments of committees of inquiry, their proceedings and publication of their reports are not simply a series of individual, though related, events, but part of a continuing process which does not begin with the appointment of a committee nor end with acceptance or rejection of its report.

One can of course, as was argued earlier, deal with the first point by definition, but then the question arises whether to draw the definition broadly or narrowly; in either case, it seems necessary to discuss the relationship of committees of inquiry coming within the definition to other means of investigation and advice which come outside if the definition is not to seem merely arbitrary.

The second point is even more fundamental since it affects the standpoint from which committees of inquiry are viewed. All analysis implies abstraction, and to that extent distortion of the thing analysed, but there is perhaps a peculiar difficulty in isolating committees of inquiry for study. The basic approach of this study is to try to analyse what part committees of inquiry play in the formulation of policy both as an aid to understanding better the processes at work in policy-formation and as a basis for offering practical guidance on their use and operation in future. The emphasis is, as it surely must be, on the idea of process. We may concentrate our attention on a specific period of time, namely that between the appointment of a committee and the publication of its report, but we have to be constantly aware of the action and interaction of events.

The appointment of a committee, for example, is certainly a specific event in time, but its understanding requires knowledge of the often complex circumstances which gave rise to it, not simply for the sake of idle curiosity but because the circumstances of its origin powerfully affect the limits within which a committee can operate, and hence have a bearing on the influence which it can exert on future policy. Again, the appointment of a committee does not simply lead to a suspension of the various activities and pressures which were already being brought to bear on the problem it is asked to examine; rather it affects the situation in ways which are not easy to assess because of the interaction between the committee's activities and these other activities. Or again the fact that a certain period of time elapses between the appointment of a committee and its report, and perhaps even more between its report and any action taken on it, again emphasises that committees are operating within a context which may change and may sometimes change quite rapidly.

The danger is that by concentrating on individual committees in isolation we may give a misleading view of how they operate and the part they play, as though entrusting a problem to a committee somehow removed it on to a different plane, detached from the pressures which gave rise to it in the first place when what we want to know is precisely what difference the appointment of a committee makes, and what contribution it makes within a process of policy-making which may extend over a considerable period of time.

However, there are obvious practical difficulties in trying to go beyond a fairly simple analysis of individual committees. In particular, to try to examine a heterogeneous collection of committees of inquiry which happened to be appointed within a specific period of time (in this case ten years) becomes an impossible undertaking if for each one there has to be a kind of detailed case-history extending in some cases over many years.

The question to be considered in this chapter is whether it is possible to examine committees of inquiry rather differently. Instead of looking at the fact that a committee was appointed to examine, say, the organisation of civil science, one might instead consider how civil scientific policy had developed and what part the committee on the organisation of civil science had played in the development of that policy. In other words, instead of looking first at a particular committee and working outwards from that, one would look at a specific policy or possibly, as is discussed below, an area of policy with a view to assessing the contribution which committees of inquiry had made to the development of policy. Discussion will be concentrated on whether, and if so how, such an approach would be possible, leaving to the next and final chapter discussion of whether, if it were feasible, such an approach should be in addition to, or a substitution for, other approaches.

It is not claimed that the policy-centred approach will always be necessary or appropriate. Where a committee is appointed in unusual or exceptional circumstances, its use and function may be examined without the need to elaborate on wider policy issues. An example is the Committee appointed in 1959 under the Chairmanship of Lord Sinclair of Cleeve to examine the financial structure of the Colonial Development Corporation, as it then was.[1] The problem was of a very limited nature and only occupied the Committee of three for three months. The Committee is chiefly interesting for the light which it throws on the tensions which had arisen between the CDC and the Colonial Office, rather than for the illumination of policy issues.[2] Clearly it would be possible to discuss in relation to the development of British government policy on assistance for the emerging Commonwealth countries the part played by this particular Committee, or, perhaps more significantly, why only this one issue had over a long period of time been thought to require a committee of inquiry to resolve. But such a discussion would hardly in the circumstances carry much further our understanding of committees of inquiry.

It does not follow from this that we can ignore all policy areas where committees of inquiry are rarely if ever used. It may be, as was discussed in an earlier chapter,[3] that at least in broad terms comparison between areas in which committees are used and those in which they are not may be useful for illustrating the role of committees. More specifically, examination of a particular policy area may help to define more clearly the circumstances in which they are used.

There were, for example, considerable developments during the 1960s in government policy towards the admission of Commonwealth immigrants, notably the decision to restrict such immigration embodied in the Commonwealth Immigration Act, 1962, and the Labour Government's further restrictions foreshadowed in the 1965 White Paper, *Immigration from the Commonwealth* (Cmnd 2739) and carried out in the 1968 Act. This policy was not evolved as a result of the recommendations of committees of inquiry, although the 1965 White Paper was preceded by a high-level mission under Lord Mountbatten to Commonwealth countries; and the only question referred to such a committee was whether Commonwealth immigrants (and also aliens) should have

[1] Cmnd 786, 1959.
[2] See above p. 120, n. 7.
[3] Above, p. 43.

a right of appeal against a decision to refuse them admission or to require them to leave.[1]

Study of the evolution of policy in this area might, by showing the reasons for the contrast between what was and what was not referred to a committee of inquiry, help in the examination of certain hypotheses, e.g.:

1 That committees are not appointed where a problem is urgent and/or politically important or sensitive, or perhaps simply where a government is quite sure what it wants to do;

2 That committees are appointed where a government is not sure what to do and/or reluctant to take action without outside backing.

This kind of approach is, however, essentially rather negative. It is concerned not so much with what influence committees have on policy and how that influence is exercised as with the reasons why a great many policy questions are settled in other ways. We need also a more positive approach, through consideration of policy questions which seem to owe something to the influence of committees. This might be approached first by looking at an example of an individual and fairly self-contained policy issue, Scottish land tenure reform.

SCOTTISH LAND TENURE REFORM

In July 1969 the Labour Government issued a White Paper proposing the abolition of the feudal system of land tenure in Scotland and its replacement by a new system with two forms: (a) absolute ownership and (b) occupation for a limited tenure. This reform would require major legislation which could not be ready before 1971.[2] In the event, the Labour Party was defeated at the 1970 election, but two years later the Conservative Government issued a Green Paper substantially on the same lines at least to the extent of proposing the abolition of feudal tenure; it was proposed that land should be held on a system of absolute ownership, but major decisions on how this was to be achieved were to depend on comments and discussions following the Green Paper.[3]

[1] Cmnd 3387, 1967. Questions affecting immigrants already in this country were, however, considered by a standing body, the Commonwealth Immigrants Advisory Council.

[2] *Land Tenure in Scotland*, Cmnd 4099, 1969, esp. paras 23–5, 50–1.

[3] *Land Tenure Reform in Scotland* (HMSO, 1972), esp. paras 17, 81, 95 (cf. also para. 6 for the Conservative commitment to reform in their 1970 election manifesto). The Land Tenure Reform (Scotland) Act, 1974, is the first stage of the legislation intended to give effect to these proposals.

The Labour Government's decision was not taken as the result of the recommendation of a committee of inquiry investigating Scotland's system of land tenure, since no such committee had been appointed. But in 1964, shortly before the election in that year, a committee had been appointed under the Chairmanship of Professor J. M. Halliday 'to examine and report on existing conveyancing legislation and practice . . . .' The Committee found among other things that the multi-tier structure of land ownership was one of the factors which complicated conveyancing, and therefore recommended a scheme for considerably modifying the existing system.[1] It was, according to the Secretary of State (Mr Ross), as a result of this report that it was decided to examine 'the possibility of major reform of the Scottish system of land tenure itself'.[2] This examination took the form of preparation of a memorandum of proposals by officials, its circulation to interested parties and subsequent discussions leading to the preparation of modified (and fuller) proposals in the White Paper.[3]

The Halliday Committee itself was appointed as a result of the recommendations of an earlier committee appointed in 1959 under the Chairmanship of Lord Reid 'to consider the case for introducing registration of title to land in Scotland. . . .' The Reid Committee concluded that the existing system of registration of deeds should be amended but could not agree whether there should be a full system of registration of title, as the majority of seven members wanted, or, as two members preferred, a modified scheme of certification. The Committee agreed that, whether or not it was decided to introduce registration of title, there ought to be a small expert committee to examine the question of amendment of the conveyancing statutes, and they also thought that, if it was decided to introduce registration, there should be another small expert committee to work out the details.[4]

Thus, there is a sequence of events beginning with the appointment of the Reid Committee in 1959 to examine a seemingly restricted and indeed rather technical subject chiefly of concern to lawyers and ending with legislation in the 1970s on a much wider front.[5] Sequence does not, however, necessarily mean cause and effect. Nor was 1959 necessarily

[1] Cmnd 3118, 1966.
[2] H. C. Deb. 751, 26 July 1967, WA 146.
[3] Cmnd 4099, paras 9–11.
[4] Cmnd 2032, 1963 (cf. p. 29 above).
[5] The programme outlined by Mr Ross was, first, to deal with the 'most objectionable' features of existing legislation which was done in the Conveyancing and Feudal Reform (Scotland) Act, 1970, then, to abolish the feudal system and, finally, to introduce registration of title to land. (See Proceedings of Scottish Grand Committee, 17 February 1970, col. 5.)

the beginning of the story,[1] just as 1974 may well not be the end of it.

The White Paper of 1969 claimed that the Halliday Committee's report had had a widespread welcome from the legal profession and others concerned with land transactions, and that this was 'one of the factors' which had confirmed the Government in its conclusion that there should be an examination of the whole system, its advantages and disadvantages, to see whether a better system could be devised.[2] The Committee's Report was thus important in the sequence of events in focusing attention more clearly and distinctly on the problem than had been done before; as well as in making clear through the evidence which it received and the recommendations which it made that there was support for some change in the system. Clearly this was not the only reason for reviewing the system of land tenure but it was an important reason for looking at that particular time at something which otherwise might have been left to some indefinite future date. However, equally clearly, to elucidate how precisely the decision to change the system of land tenure was arrived at would require a much more detailed case-study taking into account the various political and administrative pressures involved, and the interaction of a number of factors.

TRENDS IN AGRICULTURAL METHODS

If a number of difficult questions are raised by a relatively self-contained policy issue like that of Scottish land reform, elucidation is likely to be a more complex matter where the issue itself is hard to define. An example would be policy towards trends in modern methods of farming. This indeed is not so much an issue as an area of policy and would require for its full elucidation a discussion of many aspects of the work of the Ministry of Agriculture, Fisheries and Food. Within this general area there have been a number of problems examined by committees of inquiry, especially those of 'factory farming',[3] the use of antibiotics [4] and, more recently, soil structure and fertility.[5]

[1] The question of registration of title to land in Scotland itself had a lengthy history going back at least to a royal commission of 1906, as the Reid Committee briefly reported (Cmnd 2032, paras 9–10).

[2] Cmnd 4099, para. 7.

[3] Report of the Technical Committee to Inquire into the Welfare of Animals Kept under Intensive Livestock Husbandry Systems (Cmnd 2836, 1965).

[4] Report of the Joint Committee on the Use of Antibiotics in Animal Husbandry and Veterinary Medicine (Cmnd. 4190, 1969).

[5] *Modern Farming and the Soil*, report of the Agricultural Advisory Council on Soil Structure and Soil Fertility (HMSO, 1970).

There is a two-fold problem here, that of relating the report of each committee to the development of policy on the individual problem issue, and that of determining whether one can connect these individual studies within a general policy area. One characteristic of all three problems investigated by committees of inquiry was that the latter followed a period of considerable agitation and controversy. The Swann Committee, for example, on the use of antibiotics followed an earlier joint committee of the medical and agricultural research councils which had reported in 1962, and the accumulation of evidence which seemed to show considerable danger that if the use of antibiotics were not restricted in animal husbandry, human resistance to certain infections could be weakened.[1]

It may be, therefore, that it is enough to examine these committees simply against the background of the individual problems which had arisen, to see them perhaps as a response to pressures. Certainly, there is evidence in all three cases that the Government was unwilling to act, and, in the case of both the Brambell Committee on Factory Farming and the Swann Committee on Antibiotics, only acted following the recommendations in those reports. Yet, as before, it would be necessary to establish just what the connection was between the committee reports and the development of government policy.

It is difficult to leave the matter there, because of the possible wider implications of these individual issues. Can they be seen, for example, as part of wider changes in policy? Since the war agricultural policy, as has been pointed out,[2] has been largely characterised by what has amounted almost to a partnership between the agricultural departments and the National Farmers' Union. Does the significance of more recent developments lie in the fact that the departments may now be evolving (or may need to evolve) a more positive policy towards the methods of modern agriculture, and, if so, what part have committees of inquiry played in this?

These questions arise partly because of the different nature of the policy changes involved as compared with, say, Scottish land reform. In the case of antibiotics, for example, what was involved was the introduction of controls where there had been none before and in the case of factory farming there was the question whether codes of conduct should be made voluntary or mandatory. But in neither case was the emphasis

[1] See on the Swann Committee, Bernard Dixon, 'Antibiotics on the Farm – Major Threat to Human Health', *New Scientist* (5 October, 1967), pp. 33–5; also the same author's *What is Science for?* (Collins, 1973), pp. 137–9.

[2] Peter Self and Herbert J. Storing, *The State and the Farmer* (Allen & Unwin, 1962), p. 230.

on reviewing a long-established system; rather, it was the need to take action to deal with innovations which had grown up in practice which chiefly characterised the agricultural changes.

Perhaps even more important for a policy-centred approach is the differing nature of governmental responsibilities in relation to different areas of government. Government responsibility for agricultural policy, for example, is largely a question of influencing, by financial and other means, the nature and quantity of the crops and livestock produced by the farmers and farm-workers who work in the industry. Such influence may be very extensive, ranging as it does from the price which the farmer receives for many of his products to the structure of the industry, but it falls short of control and direction of what individual farmers do. Correspondingly, the policy issues which may arise are many and varied but probably lack any definite unifying connection, outside the central question of the nature of central government support for the industry.

NATIONAL HEALTH SERVICE

General medical questions

The situation is very different if one considers an area of government policy in which there is much more direct government responsibility, like the national health service. Here, not only is central government directly responsible for determining general policy but it also has responsibilities for administering the service mainly through appointed agents but also in part (until 1974) through local authorities. Correspondingly, the policy issues which arise tend to be very clearly linked to the basic issue of 'what is the best and most effective way of providing this group of services?' At the same time, issues may vary very considerably in importance and generality, from the right structure of the NHS itself to the role of special hospitals: or from concern about the cost of the NHS as a whole to concern about the work, training and qualifications of hospital engineers. And although there is this central core of issues which centres on the organisation and administration of the NHS itself there are also a great many other issues of a medical nature which arise and which have direct or indirect consequences for the NHS. They may be issues of considerable public concern and controversy like drug addiction or the fluoridation of water supplies or the relationship between smoking and cancer of the lung; or they may be comparatively much more straightforward like the question of vaccination against measles; or involve international diplomacy like the question of relations with the World Health Organisation.

It is comparatively easy to separate those issues which concern the organisation and administration of the NHS from the more general issues. A number of questions then arise: for example, are there significant differences between the ways in which these two kinds of issue are handled? What part do committees of inquiry play in the resolution of the two kinds of issue, and what is their relationship to other means of dealing with them?

As a start, one might examine some at least of the important medical issues which have arisen in recent years and compare those where committees of inquiry have been employed with those where they have not. Such an undertaking is fraught with difficulties. There is to begin with the ambiguity of the world 'important'. If it is defined as meaning politically important, then an issue which is important in this sense may well not be so important from a purely medical point of view. Indeed, this is perhaps inevitable, because what gives many issues their political importance is the fact that they have broader social consequences and are not simply medical issues.

This is strikingly illustrated by the way in which the issue of drug addiction became prominent. An inter-departmental committee under the Chairmanship of Sir Russell (later Lord) Brain and consisting of seven doctors and a pharmacist was appointed in 1958 by the Ministry of Health and Department of Health for Scotland to examine the question of drug addiction from the medical point of view, and was especially concerned with precautions against over-prescribing, and with arrangements for treating addicts. In its report, the committee took the view that addiction was a small problem and was not on the increase, and they generally relied on the 'prevailing healthy attitude of the public to this problem and the efficacy of the measures in Great Britain'.[1]

Three years later, however, the departments took the unusual step of reconvening the Committee to examine the problem again in the light of evidence and public concern that addiction was in fact on the increase. The Committee's second report did recommend new measures (a system of notification for addicts, provision of treatment centres, etc.). But equally important was the different tone of the report; for the Committee now acknowledged the 'complex variety of social, medical and psychological factors' involved in habituation to drugs and recommended a broadly-based standing advisory committee to keep the whole problem under review.[2]

[1] *Report of the Inter-Departmental Committee on Drug Addiction* (HMSO, 1961), paras 24, 34.

[2] *Drug addiction*, the second report of the interdepartmental committee (HMSO, 1965), paras 41, 42.

Since then the Advisory Committee on Drug Dependence has been established,[1] and the whole question of what should be done about drug-taking has becone a controversial issue of public policy. The evolution of policy was therefore in several distinct stages: growing public alarm about what was happening led the government to appoint the second Brain Committee. The committee both contributed to a change of policy and was also instrumental in focusing public attention on the issues involved.[2]

Drug-taking is an example of an issue which became prominent and required government to take an attitude, if not to adopt a positive policy. To that extent it has similarities with cigarette-smoking in relation to health and particularly its connection with the incidence of cancer of the lung; there is also a similarity in that it is not simply the medical consequences of smoking which need to be taken into account but its social and economic aspects. But the main origin of concern about the implications of cigarette-smoking was in the patient work of a small band of research workers in the 1950s who started to demonstrate that there was a statistical connection between smoking and the incidence of cancer of the lung. No committee of inquiry was appointed to look into the question. On the other hand the Royal College of Physicians issued a report on 'Smoking and Health' in 1962 which may have served in some ways to focus public attention more seriously on this question. Certainly it seems to mark a point at which most responsible medical opinion, both inside and outside the Ministry of Health,[3] took a firm stand about the dangers of cigarette-smoking.

Organisation and administration
Whether or not comparisons of policy-issues in this way could help to elucidate the part played by committees of inquiry, it remains true that few such committees have been appointed to examine this type of general medical problem. On the other hand, in looking at the issues which have arisen in connection with the organisation and administration of the NHS, there are a great many committee reports which are

[1] Significantly, it advises the Home Office, not the health departments.
[2] The publication of the Committee's report was, for example, followed by a good deal of correspondence in *The Times* and articles with titles like 'The Spread of Drug-Taking, A Growing Evil Among Teenagers' and 'Pushers Who Lead to a Slow Suicide' (*The Times*, 2, 4, 20, 21, 28 December 1965).
[3] It is noticeable that when Sir George Godber became Chief Medical Officer at the Ministry in 1961, much stronger emphasis was put on the dangers of cigarette-smoking (see, for example, *On the State of the Public Health* for 1960 (Cmnd 1550, 1961), p. 8; for 1961 (Cmnd 1856, 1962), p. 10; for 1962 (HMSO, 1963), p. 103.

relevant although not all of them are reports of committees of inquiry. Indeed at first sight it appears that hardly any question going beyond purely day-to-day management is resolved without first being the subject of a committee report.

It is, of course, well known that in the running of the national health service the departments are assisted by an elaborate system of statutory advisory committees consisting of the Central Health Services Council and its standing committees and corresponding bodies in Scotland. In addition simply to giving advice, the councils and the committees frequently set up committees to examine specific problems; they may be committees of the CHSC (or joint committee with the Scottish HSC) or subcommittees of the standing advisory committees. These committee reports are frequently published. Some of them are wholly or mainly advisory in character, whereas others function as committees of inquiry. In addition, and quite separately from this advisory machinery, *ad hoc* committees are appointed to examine different problems, of which some again are committees of inquiry, whereas others are more in the nature of advisory committees.

Two problems arise here. One is the relationship between committees of inquiry and purely advisory committees. The other is whether all the questions considered by committees whose reports are published are questions of policy. The common element in these two problems is that the focus of this study is on committees of inquiry concerned with policy questions and yet one cannot ignore the connections with other kinds of committees considering other questions.

The difficulties over defining the elusive word policy were discussed in the introductory chapter. There are, however, some questions considered by committees concerned with the national health service which are mainly of a procedural or operational nature and which it is tempting to omit from consideration here on those grounds. An example is the subcommittee appointed to consider the organisation of work in operating theatres and the pattern of staffing required.[1] Another is the working-party which was asked to suggest revisions to the guidance given on the equipment and training of staff in the ambulance services.[2] Clearly such examinations of procedural or organisational problems could have implications for policy, but they are not themselves policy questions.

[1] *The Organisation and Staffing of Operating Departments*, a report of a joint subcommittee of the Standing Medical Advisory Committee and the standing Nursing Advisory Committee (HMSO 1970).

[2] Report by the Working-Party on Ambulance Training and Equipment (Pt. I, HMSO 1966).

Even after the elimination of committees considering problems of this kind, there remain a fair number which are concerned with policy questions, and although some of these are clearly more important policy questions than others, they should not be disregarded for that reason alone. Nevertheless, in considering and contrasting the use of committees of inquiry and advisory committees it may be useful to see how far the former are and the latter are not asked to consider questions which are of political (or even potentially political) importance.

During the late 1960s the question of the future structure of the national health service became a major political issue with the publication of two Green Papers by the Labour Government (in 1968 and 1970); [1] this was subsequently followed by a White Paper by the Conservative Government [2] and by the National Health Service Reorganisation Act, 1973, under which the administrative structure of the NHS underwent its first major overhaul since its establishment in 1948. This change was not the result of the recommendations of a committee of inquiry, although, as has been pointed out, [3] the idea of the *ad hoc* area health authority now brought to fruition had its roots in the war-time discussions preceding the introduction of the NHS and was helped on its way by the medical profession's own unofficial committee of inquiry which reported in 1962 (the Porritt Committee); and that Committee itself was to some extent a reaction to the government committee of inquiry (Guillebaud) which had examined the cost of the NHS in the 1950s. Other committees of inquiry which had a possible influence, if only negatively, on the decision to recast the structure of the NHS were the royal commissions on local government of 1966-9 and the Seebohm Committee on Local Authority and Allied Personal Social Services of 1965-8. More positively, the Royal Commission on Medical Education of 1965-8 recommended that teaching hospitals should no longer be separately administered by boards of governors in England and Wales but should be brought within a single unified system, as to a large extent already happened in Scotland. [4]

On the face of it, therefore, the decision to abolish the 1948 structure

---

[1] *National Health Service. The Administrative Structure of the Medical and Related Services in England and Wales* (1968); *National Health Service. The Future Structure of the NHS* (1970). There are separate Green Papers for Scotland and, in 1970, Wales.

[2] *National Health Service Reorganisation: England* (Cmnd 5055, 1972). A consultative document was issued in 1970.

[3] J. R. Butler and R. J. C. Pearson, 'Face-lift for the NHS – a Major or Minor Operation?' in W. A. Robson and B. Crick (eds), *The Future of the Social Services* (Penguin, 1970).

[4] Cmnd 3569, para 16.

of the NHS and substitute one based on area health authorities responsible for all health services in their area owed little directly to committees of inquiry. However, in examining this question one would need to look at two distinct aspects, the idea of a unified structure, and the alternatives of a unified structure under local government control or one separately administered on an *ad hoc* basis. The extent to which the findings of committees of inquiry, although not directly related to these questions, yet had some influence on the decisions taken, would need to be separately considered for each of these questions.

But if government did not seek the views of committees of inquiry directly on the major issue of administrative structure it certainly made use of both committees of inquiry and advisory committees, *ad hoc* and standing, to examine details of the structure, particularly of the hospital service. The following are examples of reports of committees in recent years which have examined aspects of the structure or staffing of the hospital service:

1 Joint Working-Party on Medical Staffing Structure in the Hospital Service (1958–61).
2 Working-Party on Special Hospitals (1959–61).
3 Committee of Inquiry into the Recruitment, Training and Promotion of Administrative and Clerical Staff in the Hospital Service (1962–3).
4 Committee on Senior Nursing Staff Structure (1963–5).
5 Subcommittee on the Selection, Function, Training and Deployment of State Enrolled Nurses (1966–71).
6 Joint Working-Party on the Organisation of Medical Work in Hospitals (1966–7).
7 Committee on the Functions of the District General Hospital (1966–9).
8 Committee on Hospital Scientific and Technical Services (1967–8).
9 Working-Party on the Hospital Pharmaceutical Service (1968–1970).
10 Working-Party on the Responsibilities of the Consultant Grade (1968–9).

Only one of these committees was called a committee of inquiry and only two (on state enrolled nurses and the district general hospital) formed part of the standing advisory machinery. Nevertheless, it might seem at first sight that all these committees could be regarded as wholly or mainly advisory in character, their function being to advise the minister (or ministers) how best to run the hospital service within policy objectives already laid down. But by the criteria adopted here (following Sir Kenneth Wheare) of regarding an advisory body as one which is expected to offer advice on the basis of its members' experience and knowledge, four committees (state enrolled nurses, special hospitals, consultant grade and organisation of medical work)[1] are perhaps better treated as advisory, although even these four were also concerned to some degree with inquiry. The Committee on State Enrolled Nurses, for example, a subcommittee of the Standing Nursing Advisory Committee, consisting almost entirely of nurses, did take some evidence and seek information by questionnaire.

Moreover all these committees were concerned to some degree with questions of policy rather than simply procedural or operational questions. This is perhaps most evident in the case of the committees concerned with staffing structure (medical, administrative and clerical, senior nursing, scientific and technical, pharmaceutical). These committees differ in the extent of the inquiries which they were asked to carry out; the Committee on Hospital Scientific and Technical Services, for example, was asked to look at both 'the future organisation and development' of these services as well as the 'broad pattern of staffing required',[2] whereas the Working-Party on Medical Staffing Structure was merely asked 'to study . . . the principles on which the medical staffing structure in the Hospital Service should be organised'.[3] Nevertheless, particularly if they are considered together, they represent a considerable body of information, analysis and advice on the organisation and staffing of the hospitals. The important point, surely, is that since the state assumed responsibility for the provision of a national health service, questions about the organisation and structure of hospitals have become questions of public policy, and therefore ministers need and seek advice, and often investigation based on inquiry, into these relatively detailed questions in a way which is neither necessary nor appropriate to, say, the development of government policy in relation to private industry.

General analysis

By the same token, many of these detailed inquiries are likely to have a relatively low political content. However important the functions of the

[1] The last-named was not in any case strictly a government committee but a joint committee of the Ministry of Health and the Joint Consultants Committee, each nominating six members.

[2] *Hospital Scientific and Technical Services*, a report of the Committee 1967–8 (HMSO, 1968).

[3] *Medical Staffing Structure in the Hospital Service*, a report of the joint Working-Party (HMSO, 1961).

district general hospital or the organisation of the hospital pharmaceutical service are to ensuring the smooth and effective running of the hospital service, they are not likely in themselves to provoke much public controversy or public debate. This can be seen by comparing the ten committees mentioned above with two committees of inquiry also appointed during this period which did arouse (and arise from) more general public interest.

The Royal Commission on Medical Education, whatever its precise origins,[1] did derive part of its *raison d'être* from public concern over possible shortages of doctors; and the Committee on the Relationship of the Pharmaceutical Industry with the National Health Service was much concerned with a continuing public controversy over whether the drug firms were making excessive profits from their contracts with the NHS. Not only were these issues wider in scope than those considered by the ten committees but they were politically more highly charged.

In considering the use and relationship of these various means of advice and inquiry, one important factor is the nature of the advisory machinery set up under the National Health Service Act, 1946, and the National Health Service (Scotland) Act, 1947. The membership of the bodies constituted under those Acts is mainly drawn from the professions most closely concerned in providing health services and, in particular, the medical profession. The advisory machinery therefore provides a means, as a recent study has put it, for ministers to receive essential technical advice and, particularly, advice 'agreed by the different branches of the medical profession and by other interested parties'.[2] It follows, therefore, that where issues arise which are not simply or predominantly the concern of the medical and other professions, use of the advisory machinery may not be the best way of making progress. At the same time it must be noted that there may be significant differences of view how far an issue is a medical issue, and in any case there may be practical reasons why a minister may wish to sound out the views of the professions even over matters with wider implications. Nevertheless, one would expect to find a broad difference between matters on which advice is sought simply through the standing advisory machinery, and matters where something more than advice is sought going beyond the advisory machinery. The question is whether one can go further than this in identifying the kinds of issues which arise and the kinds of bodies which are involved in investigating them.

[1] See above, p. 61.
[2] PEP Study Group, *Advisory Committee in British Government* (Allen & Unwin, 1960), p. 170.

Such an analysis might, following the earlier discussion, distinguish three categories:

1   Operational questions on which advice is needed: these form the great bulk of questions handled by the statutory advisory machinery; examples include the care of younger chronic sick patients, the classification of proprietary preparations, the revision of nurses' uniforms; [1] the results of advice in many cases appear as circulars or memoranda to the authorities concerned with day-to-day administration (hospital boards, executive councils etc.).

2   Minor policy questions requiring both information and advice: these are the questions for which there is most overlap between the use of the standing advisory machinery and *ad hoc* committees; examples drawn from hospital structure and staffing have been discussed above, but the field is wider than this.[2]

3   Major policy questions: here one could distinguish questions which are referred to *ad hoc* committees of inquiry (like relations with the pharmaceutical industry) from those which are not (like the future administrative structure of the NHS): although advice may be sought through the standing advisory machinery on certain aspects of these questions, the influence of the advisory machinery is more likely to be felt indirectly.

The first of these categories is outside the scope of this study. The third can be treated in principle no differently from those questions discussed at the beginning of this chapter, that is, consideration of the specific policy issues in which committees of inquiry have been used, the influence which committees have had on the policy outcome and comparison with issues in which committees have not been used.

It is the second category which requires closest examination from the point of view of the distinctive and specific policy area of the national health service. Such an examination would attempt to assess the contribution made by committees of inquiry to the evolution of policy in the administration of the NHS through considering the kind of questions referred to such committees, the reasons for their appointment and the consequences of their reports.

---

[1] These examples are all taken from the 1968 report of the Central Health Services Council (H. C. 315, 1969).
[2] For example, there were reports on *The Field of Work of the Family Doctor* (HMSO, 1963) by a subcommittee of the CHSC's Standing Medical Advisory Committee: and on *Hospital Building Maintenance* (HMSO, 1970) by an *ad hoc* committee.

Clearly one of the most difficult aspects of such an undertaking would be to try to find any common thread or pattern linking these disparate inquiries, not least because of the uncertainty of definition of committees of inquiry. The Working-Party on Special Hospitals, for example, which was asked to consider their future role, was chaired by a senior official of the Ministry of Health and contained a number of officials among its members.[1] The Committee on the District General Hospital, on the other hand, although it too was basically concerned with redefining the role of a certain type of hospital, was, as a committee of the Central Health Services Council, chaired by a member of the Council (Sir Desmond Bonham-Carter, a former director of Unilever), and its membership consisted largely of doctors.[2] The reasons why the former has been treated as an advisory committee and the latter as a committee of inquiry depend largely on the nature of the tasks which each was given and the ways in which they carried out those tasks. But it is at least arguable that they were equally important in terms of their significance for policy-making.

A considerable amount of work would be involved, therefore, in assessing the use and role of committees of inquiry in the development of policy for the NHS. Yet ideally their use there should be compared with their use in other policy areas to test various hypotheses which might be put forward. It was suggested above, for example, that the comparatively frequent use of committees of inquiry for NHS questions might be related to the nature of government responsibilities for the administration of the service. Another factor which might need to be taken into account is that the Government needs the goodwill and advice of the strong and well-organised medical profession, as is evident from the elaborate statutory machinery for consultation and advice, and that this in turn creates an atmosphere favourable to the use of committees even for matters which are not directly medical in content. For such matters, like the organisation of hospital scientific and technical services, will nearly always be of considerable interest and concern to the medical profession.

SOCIAL SECURITY

A contrast might be drawn, for example, with the other half of the Department of Health and Social Security. The administration of the social security system is a direct responsibility of central government,

---

[1] *Special Hospitals*, report of the Working-Party (HMSO, 1961).
[2] *The Functions of the District General Hospital*, report of the Committee (HMSO, 1969).

yet it makes scarcely any use of committees of inquiry. Clearly there are obvious contrasts in the nature of the administration of the NHS and the social security system respectively. The latter, being essentially a system of payments of benefits, does not have the complex administrative and financial problems which derive from the provision, staffing, equipment and maintenance of institutions like hospitals. Nor correspondingly is it so directly involved with organised professional interests as the NHS is with the doctors.

At the same time, given the lively political interest in social security, there is no lack of policy questions in some of which at least committees of inquiry might have been involved. Even if major policy questions, such as the reconstruction of the pensions scheme or the even more recent proposals for a system of tax credits linking the tax system with social security, have owed nothing to committees of inquiry, might one not have expected them to have played some part in lesser but nevertheless important issues such as the extension of an existing benefit or the creation of a new benefit? Yet in the ten-year period covered by this study only one *ad hoc* committee of inquiry was appointed and that was concerned with what was essentially a technical medical question, so that it is very much on the borderline with an advisory committee.[1]

Part of the answer may well be sought in the statutory arrangements for standing advisory committees under the National Insurance Act, 1946, and particularly the National Insurance Advisory Committee. The NIAC, containing both independent and representative members, is mostly occupied with commenting on draft regulations prepared by the minister, but from time to time more general questions are referred to it. For the most part these general questions are of a restricted kind. For example, in 1966 the committee was asked 'to review the present level of the earnings limit for retirement pensions. . . .',[2] but it was not asked to consider the more fundamental and politically controversial question of whether there ought to be an earnings limit at all; nor indeed has this question been the subject of an independent committee of inquiry since the national insurance scheme was started in 1948. Occasionally the Committee may be asked to look at somewhat broader questions; for example in 1952 it looked at the whole question of time limits for claiming benefits.[3] However, even taking all these general questions together, they do not constitute a very large area of investigation. In the five years

[1] Report of the Committee on the Assessment of Disablement (Cmnd 2847, 1965).
[2] Question of the Earnings Limit for Retirement Pensions (Cmnd 3197, 1967).
[3] Cmnd 8483, 1952.

1964–8, for example, only four such questions were considered by the NIAC.

Examination of questions of this kind by the NIAC is in some ways akin to examination by a committee of inquiry. For example, the NIAC does not simply pronounce on these questions on the basis of its members' own knowledge and experience, but receives written representations and may examine witnesses orally. On the other hand, the nature of the questions examined is usually so restricted that there is correspondingly little scope for general analysis of the problem, as is evident, for example, from the report on the earnings limit.

A more significant question would be to assess the extent to which cumulatively the various reports of the NIAC including those on draft regulations have contributed to the development of the system in a way which perhaps parallels the contribution of committees of inquiry in the NHS. The PEP Report published in 1960 claimed a high success for the implementation of NIAC Reports, but this may be partly due to the Committee's unusual statutory position in relation to reports on draft regulations.[1] To put this success into perspective one would have also to assess the contribution of the few *ad hoc* committees of inquiry which have been appointed,[2] and also to evaluate at least in a broad way the way in which other sources of information and ideas have influenced discussion of major policy questions.

LAW REFORM

The basic problem
If the need to consult with well-organized professional interests is one factor contributing to differences in the way in which policy questions are resolved, and hence may have a bearing on the use and role of committees of inquiry, we should consider government relations not only with the medical profession but also with the legal profession. Here the relationship is not only of very long standing, but also involves constitutional as well as administrative considerations in view of the independence of the judiciary.

There is a basic difficulty about considering this question. Many

---

[1] The Minister is required either to accept the Committee's recommendations or to give his reasons for rejecting them (National Insurance Act, 1965, s. 88).

[2] It is of interest to note that *ad hoc* committees of inquiry were appointed in 1969 to examine the problems of one-parent families and in 1971 to review the measures for detecting and preventing abuse through wrongful claims to social security benefits.

questions of public policy, and certainly most major questions, are likely to involve questions of law and hence to be of direct concern to the legal profession. Whether the question is one of amending existing laws, such as those relating to companies or Sunday observance, or of legislating for something not previously governed by statute, such as the right of an individual to privacy, the legal profession will be closely and directly concerned. Yet these are not simply legal matters. It is the social and economic implications of legislation which are the main concern of public policy. There are, on the other hand, many matters where the technical legal aspects seem to be the main concern and where the wider implications are less relevant to public policy. For example, the elimination of ancient statutes which have fallen into disuse, or the redefinition of old but still active statutes in line with modern conditions might be examples of what is often termed 'law reform'.

The problem is where to draw the line between social and economic problems involving legislation, and law reform. Some indeed would deny that it can be done. The first Chairman of the English Law Commission has claimed: 'In my four years at the Law Commission, I have never yet found a problem of law reform that was worth doing anything about which did not have an important social element. . . . And it is because of the existence of that social element that law reform should never be entrusted to lawyers alone.' [1] Nevertheless, the extent of the 'social element' varies considerably and law reform is generally taken to be concerned with those issues and areas of policy where the element is comparatively small.

The point is important because law reform involves a number of specific standing advisory bodies composed entirely of lawyers, as well as in some cases *ad hoc* committees of inquiry which may or may not be composed entirely of lawyers, in addition to other possible influences on policy. In contrast, what one might call substantive issues of social and economic policy may, as has been evident throughout this study, be the subject of examination by advisory bodies or committees of inquiry but not by committees of lawyers.

Any examination of the use and influence of committees of inquiry on law reform would thus be concerned both with the boundaries of the subject and with the relationship between *ad hoc* and standing advisory committees. Before the Law Commissions were established in 1965, there were two main bodies of the latter kind, the Law Reform Committee set up in 1952 (and the successor of the Law Revision Committee of 1934) in the field of civil law, and the Criminal Law Revision Com-

---

[1] Mr Justice Scarman in *What's Wrong With the Law* (BBC Publications, 1970), p. 87.

mittee set up in 1959. There was also a separate Law Reform Committee for Scotland.

On the whole these committees functioned as advisory committees rather than committees of inquiry, that is to say, on the whole they did not take formal evidence from other people and organisations, but mainly operated on the basis of the experience and knowledge of their members; they were also largely concerned with questions which did not raise wide issues of social policy. This was particularly true of the Law Reform Committee which dealt mostly with subjects like innocent mis-representation (10th report, Cmnd 1782, 1962) and acquisition of ease-ments and profits by prescription (14th report, Cmnd 3100, 1966). Rarely did this committee take evidence from other people.[1]

The qualification 'on the whole' becomes more important in con-sidering the Criminal Law Revision Committee. Most of the reports of the Committee have been on relatively narrow topics on which members have offered their expert advice without taking evidence or making formal inquiries. Examples are the 4th report on the order of closing speeches (Cmnd 2148, 1963) and the 5th report which considered whether the law should be amended to allow a trial to continue when a member of the jury dies or is discharged (Cmnd 2349, 1964). Two of their reports are, however, of more significance both in policy terms and for the consultations (though falling short of formal taking of evidence) which the Committee carried out. These are the 8th report on theft and related offences (Cmnd 2977, 1966) which they themselves described as 'much the largest and most difficult subject' they had investigated, and which led to substantial changes in the law; and the 11th report on evidence which is discussed further below.

The Law Commissions
These advisory committees have remained in existence,[2] but they have now been overshadowed by the creation in 1965 of the Law Commis-sions, charged with keeping the law as a whole under review and making recommendations for systematic reform. These novel and in many ways unique bodies raise, through their methods of operation in particular, the whole question of the part played by inquiry and advice in law reform. The White Paper which preceded the creation of the Commis-sions made a distinction between matters which might be handled by the Commissions or by existing reform committees, and those where it

---

[1] E.g. sixteenth report on privilege in civil proceedings (Cmnd 3472, 1967).

[2] Recent reports of the Law Reform Committee include the seventeenth on evidence of opinion and expert opinion (Cmnd 4489, 1970) and the eighteenth on conversion and detinue (Cmnd 4774, 1971).

might be appropriate 'particularly where important social questions may arise, for a topic to be referred to a Departmental Committee or a Royal Commission'.[1] This was explained more fully by the Solicitor-General (Sir Eric Fletcher) in reference to the Commissions' programme of work: 'Where the programme covers a branch of the law which seems likely to be controversial in a political sense, or to have a broad social trend, it is highly unlikely that the detailed revision would be entrusted to the Commissioners themselves. In a case like this, it would be more appropriate that the matter should be referred, as is the practice today, either to a Royal Commission or to a departmental committee.' [2]

The difficulty, as always, is that the distinction between the two types of inquiry is not a very precise one. It is easy enough to distinguish at one end of the scale subjects which are relatively non-political and largely expert in nature, like those examined by the Law Reform Committee, and, at the other, subjects of broad social and political interest which have been examined by departmental committees, like the age of majority. But there is a large area in between of subjects with *some* social and political interest as well as an expert, legal content. This area also is important for the development of public policy, and hence for an assessment of the role of committees of inquiry.

In April 1964, for example, the Home Secretary appointed a committee to look at a limited part of the Licensing Acts, namely, whether machinery for regulating the number, nature and distribution of licensed premises was still needed in the war-damaged areas, or ought to be introduced in other areas e.g. areas of major redevelopment.[3] Again, in July 1963 the Lord Chancellor appointed a committee to consider the law on positive covenants affecting land.[4] These were both departmental committees of inquiry dealing with limited subjects, and, before the Law Commissions were instituted, it was highly characteristic of the departments most closely involved in law reform (the Home Office and the Lord Chancellor's Department) to appoint *ad hoc* committees of this nature. Even where committees touched on matters of considerable public concern, they were generally limited to a very specific aspect. Thus there was no committee on the jury system but one on jury service; [5] the law of illegitimacy was not examined but only the

---

[1] *Proposals for English and Scottish Law Commissions* (Cmnd 2573, 1965), p. 2.
[2] On second reading of the Law Commissions Bill (H. C. Deb. 706, 8 February 1965, 54–5).
[3] Report of the Departmental Committee on Licensing Planning (Cmnd 2709, 1965).
[4] Report of the Committee on Positive Covenants Affecting Land (Cmnd 2719, 1965).
[5] Cmnd 2627, 1965.

law of succession in relation to illegitimacy;[1] the law dealing with personal injury was not subjected to scrutiny but only the question of limitation of actions.[2]

The appointment of the two Law Commissions has affected the situation in two ways. First, they are expected to deal in a systematic way with areas of law in place of the piecemeal approach adopted in the past; secondly, the relationship between the operations of the Commissions and those of *ad hoc* committees of inquiry is important, not least because of the distinctive methods employed by the Commissions.

Part of the activity of the Commissions is of the relatively uncontroversial and limited kind associated with traditional law reform such as the elimination of obsolete statutes and consolidation with minor amendments of existing statutes. But another, and from the present point of view much more interesting, part of their activities does have wider policy implications, and has been matched by a distinctive method of working evolved by the Commissions. They have, for example, examined many aspects of family law and have issued reports on topics such as breach of promise for marriage (Law Commission No. 26), financial provision in matrimonial proceedings (Law Commission No. 25) and family property (Law Commission No. 52). As many of their proposals are incorporated in statutes so there is a continuing modification and adaptation of important social provisions which cumulatively, at least, is more analogous to examination by a committee of inquiry leading to change than it is to the more limited examination by advisory committees.

From the beginning the Commissions devoted much attention to their methods of working. They early decided that what was needed was periods of intensive research followed by extensive consultations with government departments, professional and other organisations and individual experts; accordingly, they began, not in the way of a traditional committee of inquiry, by inviting evidence, but by preparing for circulation and discussion papers setting out the existing state of the law and their own preliminary proposals, although sometimes they reversed the procedure by having preliminary consultations before going into the subject in detail.[3] As time has gone on, they have extended their researches, calling in the aid of the social survey division of the Office of Population Censuses and Surveys so that they 'hope to evolve a standard procedure for harnessing the social sciences to law

[1] Cmnd 3051, 1966.
[2] Cmnd 1829, 1962.
[3] The Law Commission, First Annual Report, 1965–6 (HMSO, 1966), paras 12–16.

reform which will become as much a part of our method as the working paper procedure itself'.[1]

In all this, the Commissions have attempted scrupulously to meet the obligation not to deal themselves with politically-charged questions or ones which raise large social issues. Thus in considering personal injury litigation the Law Commission proposed themselves to examine the methods and basis of assessment of damages but suggested an *ad hoc* committee to look at the jurisdiction and procedure of the courts and this was duly appointed.[2] And they thought that an interdepartmental committee should examine the financial limits on magistrates' orders, in domestic and affiliation proceedings, including the question of whether it was necessary to have limits at all; and again an *ad hoc* committee was appointed although its terms of reference were limited to considering what the limits should be and the machinery for determining them.[3] Again when the Lord Chancellor referred to the Law Commission the report on divorce, *Putting Asunder*, by a Church of England study group, the Commission stressed that their function was not to make recommendations on the controversial question of whether the grounds of divorce should be extended but to point out the implications of various courses of action.[4] It is clear, therefore, that in the more significant part of their activities the Law Commissions are operating neither simply as advisory committees nor precisely as committees of inquiry. They have a much wider sphere of activity than the former and are not limited to giving advice based on their own experience. On the other hand, they are not limited to specific topics with defined terms of reference as committees of inquiry are, nor are they required to invite the formal submission of views from anyone prepared to put them forward.

The basis of analysis
Theoretically, therefore, one could divide reports of committees concerned with law reform into three groups:

1   Those concerned with major questions of public policy; these are *ad hoc* committees of inquiry;

[1] The Law Commission, Seventh Annual Report, 1971–2 (H. C. 35, 1972), para. 2.

[2] Report of the Committee on Personal Injuries Litigation (Cmnd 3691, 1968).

[3] Report of Committee on Statutory Maintenance Limits (Cmnd 3587, 1968): in spite of the limitation the Committee concluded that financial limits should be abolished and this was accepted by the Government (H. C. Deb. 763, 2 May 1968, WA 228).

[4] *Reform of the Grounds of Divorce: The Field of Choice* (Cmnd 3123, 1966, paras 2–3).

2 Those concerned with less important questions of public policy; these would include *ad hoc* committees like that on personal injuries litigation, and some of the reports of the Law Commission and the Criminal Law Revision Committee;

3 Those concerned with minor, often procedural, matters; these are mainly standing advisory committees like the Law Reform Committee and the Criminal Law Revision Committee, but also including some of the work of the Law Commissions.

It is comparatively easy to see how to approach the question of assessing the contribution of the first group of committees to policy-making, although the actual assessment may not be so easy in practice. The approach is, however, the one sketched in the earlier part of this chapter. Again, the third group of committees does not present much difficulty since it is largely concerned with the provision of expert advice and does not have a profound bearing on policy-making.

It is the second group which presents most difficulties, both in terms of assessing its general contribution to policy-making, and in determining the relative importance of different kinds of committee. Perhaps the most outstanding point is the sheer quantity of activity represented by committee investigations in the sphere of law reform and the fact that the greater part of this activity is being carried out by lawyers. The Law Commission has constantly stressed 'the grass roots of law reform are to be sought elsewhere than in the field of law'; [1] nevertheless, it is only in inquiries into very broad policy questions that non-lawyers are much involved. Four members out of nine on the Royal Commission on Assizes and Quarter Sessions, for example, were not lawyers, including the Chairman, Lord Beeching. [2]

It is understandable that lawyers should be so closely involved in the work of these committees. Even on matters where considerations of social policy are particularly important, expert legal knowledge is essential to a full understanding of the existing position and the possible consequences of changes. And where it is a question of examining some of the more technical fields, such as the law of contract, the contribution of lawyers is obvious. There are parallels with the committees, consisting largely or entirely of doctors, enquiring into matters concerned with the national health service. In both cases, governments need the advice which the experts can provide to be able to evolve coherent and effective policies.

The differences are, however, of more significance than the parallels.

[1] First Annual Report, 1965–6, para. 137.
[2] Cmnd 4153, 1969.

The Government's relations with the doctors are primarily guided by the need to maintain their co-operation in the provision of a service. But the nature of the laws, their interpretation and revision, are issues of an altogether more fundamental importance in a complex, civilised society. Hence law reform can rarely be a simple matter of tidying up technicalities, nor is it just a matter of the relations between governments and the legal profession.

It is against this background that one should view the spate of committees examining often minute or even seemingly trivial questions. Although it would be necessary to look in detail at these various committees to answer with any certainty precisely how they have influenced the development of policy, it can hardly be doubted that law reform and indeed the legal system itself are fields where few major changes and scarcely any minor changes are made without there first being an examination by a committee, often composed entirely of lawyers. It is this which so strikingly differentiates this field of government policy from other fields.

It is much harder to distinguish the specific contribution of committees of inquiry. When it can be said of the Law Commission that it 'attempted a fundamental reconstruction of marital rights and property and, by the ensuing Act [Matrimonial Proceedings and Property, 1970], plus working papers which will lead to more Acts, has done rather more for women's rights than Germaine Greer and the liberationists can point to',[1] we are left in no doubt that the writer is stressing the contribution of the Law Commission to the development of policy; but for reasons which have already been discussed this contribution is made in a somewhat different way from that of a committee of inquiry. Again, there is no denying the importance of the report of the Criminal Law Revision Committee on evidence.[2] Its recommendations, particularly its proposal to restrict greatly the 'right of silence' of suspects interrogated by the police, aroused intense controversy and opposition not only from civil rights bodies but from among others, the Bar Council and the Law Society. Whatever outcome the Committee's recommendations finally have on policy, this is an area of major public concern. Yet the Committee is essentially an advisory body of lawyers, although in this case it did take soundings of opinions both before it began work and after it had reached preliminary conclusions.[3] It is a moot point, however,

[1] Hugo Young, 'Future of the English Judge' (an interview with Lord Justice Scarman), *The Sunday Times* (17 December 1972).

[2] Criminal Law Revision Committee, Eleventh Report: Evidence (General) (Cmnd 4991, 1972).

[3] Ibid., paras 3, 9.

whether this could be said to amount to 'taking evidence'. On the other hand, the *ad hoc* Committee under the Chairmanship of Lord Justice Winn which examined personal injuries litigation functioned in many ways like an advisory body, but deliberately modelled its methods of operation on those of the Law Commission, circulating working papers and, as the Committee put it, exposing their proposals 'to the spotlight of public comment during their formative period'.[1] Furthermore, it is difficult to regard the subject of the Winn Committee's deliberations as differing all that much from those regarded as appropriate for standing advisory bodies; assignment to an *ad hoc* committee involves a nice judgement of the degree to which a subject is more or less technical.

What is needed, therefore, is a careful analysis of the subjects examined by different committees, whether *ad hoc* or standing, and the contribution which their reports have made to the development of law reform. Then it should be possible to examine the extent to which inquiry rather than simply advice played a part in this development. In other words, rather than trying to classify individual committees or reports as being those of committees of inquiry or advisory committees, one would be looking at the extent to which the whole question of law reform had depended simply on seeking the advice of eminent lawyers and how far it had been based on inquiry, whether in the traditional sense of inviting and analysing evidence, or more broadly in seeking to obtain statistical or other information not readily or immediately available. Moreover, it would be important to trace the situation over a period of time. There have not been lacking critics who have found the pace and scale of progress inadequate. As one of them has put it, in reference to the deliberations of the Winn Committee: 'If these changes are the best that can be managed under the present system, we should look elsewhere for our answers.' [2] It is against this background that one would have to judge the claims made for the Law Commission and its expressed intention to harness the social sciences to law reform.[3]

CONCLUSION

One lesson which emerges from the discussion in this chapter, and particularly from the discussion in the last section, is that if the focus of attention is on particular policies or areas of policy the interest may be not simply in the contribution of committees of inquiry but in the extent to which changes in policy are preceded by investigation and analysis,

[1] Cmnd 3691, 1968, paras 4–9.
[2] Harry Street in *What's Wrong with the Law?* (BBC Publications, 1970), p. 55.
[3] See above, p. 182.

however carried out. Law reform is a classic, traditional area of policy in which government seeks advice, and to some extent inquiry, from outside the normal government machinery, by bodies composed very largely of lawyers, and rarely initiates changes without first seeking that advice. But in other areas, particularly perhaps those where the scale of government involvement has grown greatly during this century, such as social security, it is much more an open question how far information and advice will be sought from outside bodies and, in particular, committees of inquiry.

Moreover, the means by which governments choose to seek such advice may vary in different areas and may change over time as new approaches are tried to meet new situations. The Law Commissions illustrate one such new approach; in its practical operation it differs both from the traditional standing advisory committee on law reform and from the *ad hoc* committee of inquiry. Again, the use of various forms of consultative documents and of Green Papers which has developed since 1967 has enabled government to seek comment on proposals before final decisions are taken. In theory this could represent an alternative to the use of committees of inquiry or advisory committees at least in certain circumstances, although it is not yet clear how far consultation by such methods effectively influences policy.[1]

The significance of the situation for the present study is that it emphasises the difficulty of generalising about committees of inquiry. Not only does the extent of their use vary in different policy areas, but so too does the kind of question they are asked to examine, from major policy questions to relatively much more limited questions of administration and procedure. The consequences are important not only for an understanding of the part played by committees of inquiry in the policy-making process, but for considering whether, and if so how, they might be used more effectively in future. Questions like 'do judges make the best committee chairmen?' or 'should committees make more use of research?' hardly permit of any general answers unless it can be shown or assumed that there are sufficient common elements in the use of committees of inquiry to make general answers meaningful. But it is precisely this which cannot be assumed and so far at least has not been shown to be the case. On the contrary, a great deal of the analysis in this study has tended to the view that there are very wide-ranging differences in the nature of the investigations carried out by bodies falling within the definition of committees of inquiry. And certainly this is borne out by

---

[1] On this see Arthur Silkin, 'Green Papers and Changing Methods of Consultation in British Government', *Public Administration* (Winter 1973), pp. 427–448.

the discussion in the present chapter. The question then to be examined in the final chapter is 'what can be said of committees of inquiry?' And this question will need to be examined from a number of angles in relation both to the use of committees of inquiry and to the practical guidance which might be offered in future.

CHAPTER 8

THE ROLE OF COMMITTEES OF INQUIRY IN BRITISH GOVERNMENT

'A notable example of the wise combination of fact-finding and policy-forming in the modern state.' (Clokie and Robinson, *Royal Commissions of Enquiry*, Preface.)

'No-one would have expected the Royal Commission to come to definitive or authoritative conclusions. These are not possible given the nature of the problem. What could reasonably have been expected was that these issues and the alternative courses of action could have been discussed and made explicit.' (Robert Kilroy-Silk on the Donovan Royal Commission in Richard A. Chapman (ed.) *The Role of Commissions in Policy-Making*, p. 26.)

'The practice of instituting special enquiries or commissions into matters affecting the Highlands and Islands has become a Scottish tradition of great antiquity and occasional utility.' (Report of the Committee on General Medical Services in the Highlands and Islands, Cmnd 3257, 1967, para. 7.)

SCOPE OF THE CHAPTER

Much that has been written about committees of inquiry is at first sight puzzling. Favourable, and often highly favourable, references to their value in general are accompanied by strongly critical accounts of individual committees. Much of the praise has come from American scholars, the latest study of the royal commission viewing it as 'the best of its kind ever developed. . . . Its findings of fact are accepted by the knowledgeable as definitive; its policy directives almost invariably guide societal evolution. . . .'[1]

Although few British scholars have been quite so outspokenly favourable, there is nevertheless a general acceptance of the value of committees of inquiry and of their advantages among which have been

[1] Charles J. Hanser, *Guide to Decision: The Royal Commission* (Totowa, New Jersey, Bedminster Press, 1969).

listed flexibility, adaptability, impartiality and relative cheapness.[1] Even the Chapman study, which is highly critical of the Redcliffe-Maud and Donovan royal commissions and regards the Fulton Committee 'as a political expedient for a government seeking to create a reformist image', nevertheless approves the democratic (or potentially democratic) role of committees.[2]

Criticisms of individual committees are frequently made. They take, broadly speaking, two forms. They either criticise governments for giving the committee the wrong job, or drawing the terms of reference too narrowly or choosing the wrong kind or the wrong number of members; or they criticise the committee for failing to grasp the essentials of the problem, or for not getting or making proper use of relevant information or for providing unworkable or unacceptable solutions. On occasions both types of criticism may be made when it may be argued that the Government set up the wrong kind of inquiry, and that the committee even so failed to deal adequately with the question referred to it.[3]

There is, of course, no intrinsic reason why belief in the value of committees of inquiry should not be combined with belief that specific committees had failed to demonstrate that value. But widespread criticism of individual committees, if it is valid, implies either that there is something seriously wrong with the way they are being used in practice despite the theoretical advantages attached to their use or that those theoretical advantages require re-examination if not revision. A major clue to understanding the situation is that committees of inquiry can be viewed from two quite different angles, either: (a) narrowly and specifically as a device used by government to serve certain fairly immediate purposes of government; or (b) more broadly, as having a general purpose and value in a democratic society.

This is not the place to embark on a discussion of democracy, nor on whether these two approaches are always or necessarily in conflict. It is sufficient to be able to show that it makes sense to ask both how and why governments find committees of inquiry useful, and also whether there is any way in which such committees can serve a purpose additional to this specifically instrumental purpose. This chapter will con-

---

[1] T. J. Cartwright, *Royal Commissions and Departmental Committees in Britain* (University of London Press, 1974).

[2] Richard A. Chapman, *The Role of Commissions in Policy-Making* (Allen & Unwin, 1973), pp. 39, 185.

[3] As indeed Robert Kilroy-Silk argues both that the Donovan Commission ought to have been a different kind of inquiry and that even so it failed to deal adequately with the task which it set itself ('The Donovan Royal Commission on Trade Unions' in Chapman (ed.), op. cit., pp. 46, 69).

centrate on these two questions and the relationship between them in an effort to see whether they enable any general conclusions to be drawn about the use and role of committees of inquiry.

FOUR USES OF COMMITTEES

Much of the analysis in the earlier part of this volume has viewed committees primarily from the point of view of the governments which appoint them. This is because, in order to understand the use of committees, it seemed essential first to try to elucidate how and why governments thought it necessary or desirable to appoint them in specific cases. The basic assumption here is that since the decision whether to appoint a committee, and what sort of committee (through the choice of terms of reference and membership) is in the hands of government, then committees must be useful in some way to government, whether or not they have other uses or consequences. The implication is that they enable government somehow to make progress in ways which are better (or are thought to be better) than other possible courses which are open to them.

However, once we try to give specific content to this use of committees of inquiry, difficulties begin, and these difficulties arise because the circumstances in which committees of inquiry are judged to be useful do not by any means conform to a single pattern but cover a broad range. It is true that, as was indicated in Chapter 3, certain general characteristics are to be found – some definite event preceding the appointment of a committee, some record over a period of pressure for action or a change in policy – but these are hardly enough to give a clear and accurate picture of the situation. Why, for example, do governments sometimes announce a change of policy without first appointing a committee and sometimes insist in apparently similar circumstances that it is first necessary or desirable to appoint a committee?

The situation is even more difficult in considering the intentions of government in appointing committees. Are they trying to kill off an awkward issue, or postpone a decision, or resolve a controversial issue through compromise, or get endorsement for a favoured policy or find some other solution? Or are they perhaps just waiting hopefully to see what turns up? Or trying to do more than one thing? Or perhaps not quite sure what they do want? Examples can be plausibly given of committees which seem to fit these various categories, but if so we are dealing not with a single use but a whole range of uses. If indeed the device is as flexible as this, is there any hope of being able to say anything meaningful and accurate about committees of inquiry, except in the most general and superficial terms, and if there is not what implications does this have for any discussion of their effectiveness and how that might be improved?

The most obvious first approach is to attempt a classification of committees. This could be simply in terms of the reasons for their appointment as outlined in the previous paragraph. The question we would then be trying to answer would be: given that governments find committees of inquiry useful for a variety of reasons, are there nevertheless some reasons which are more prominent than others? If, for example, it was found that many or even a majority of committees were appointed because there was a positive desire by government to get problems resolved in the best way possible, rather than simply to put off or kill off awkward issues, this would help to give a clearer view of how to offer practical guidance, as well as giving a more explicit meaning to the problem of assessing the role and value of committees of inquiry. For it is one of the drawbacks of previous studies of such committees (whether confined to royal commissions or not) that, although they give examples of committees used in different ways, they offer no means of judging whether these are common and typical, or rare and exceptional uses.

However, since our concern is with the consequences as well as the origins of committees of inquiry, any classification should attempt to link the reasons for their use with the probable consequences, at least in terms of the ways in which governments react to their reports. With this in mind, it is possible to suggest a four-fold classification on these lines:

1   Committees set up reluctantly by a government under pressure with the object of staving off that pressure; committee may well fail to agree, but in any case reports likely to be accepted to the extent that they recommend no action or only minor action.
2   Committees set up to postpone an awkward issue; reports likely to be accepted to the extent that they indicate a solution not likely to be too troublesome.
3   Committees set up because the government is in doubt how an issue should be resolved; reports likely to be accepted to the extent that they indicate that an acceptable solution is possible.
4   Committees set up where government is fairly clear what course to adopt but needs independent backing before doing so; reports likely to be accepted to the extent that committee provides this backing.

Such a classification is not free from vagueness and ambiguity, nor is it the only possible classification which could be made. Nevertheless it indicates the relationship between the degrees of enthusiasm for a solution inspiring the setting up of a committee and the likelihood of a report either being acted upon or pigeon-holed. It is not difficult to make such a classification. It is a matter of common sense and could almost be done *a priori* without studying in detail a single committee report. Much more to the point is the question of how to use it.

There is first the practical question of how to assign a particular committee to a particular category. This question has been discussed at length in the course of this study. The basic difficulty is that it requires, in the case of most committees, a good deal of knowledge and judgement of the circumstances of each to be reasonably sure of assigning it to the right category. Nevertheless, in principle it can be done.

But secondly, even if the laborious work of classifying perhaps 200 committees during a certain period of time had been successfully carried through, how meaningful would it be? Do we not want to know whether such a classification is also related to the type of problem examined by committees? It might be, for example, that the committees in category 1 were few in number but on the whole of great importance in relation to social and economic problems. And this would in turn affect our view of the role and value of committees.

For reasons explained in the introductory chapter to this volume the material does not exist for conclusive answers to these questions. Nevertheless, the approach which has been made in terms of a broad examination of committees appointed during a period of ten years does suggest answers to some of the questions and also throws light on the reasons for them in a way which is very relevant to the central preoccupation of this chapter.

What the approach suggests is that more committees are likely to be found in categories 3 and 4 than in categories 1 and 2; in other words, there are more committees to be found in situations where government positively seeks an answer to a problem, whether it is an answer which it has already found or not, than in situations where its object is to avoid taking action. In spite of commonly-held views to the contrary, this is hardly surprising since it might prove difficult in practical terms (e.g. in getting people to serve on committees) to continue using a device which was largely negative in purpose. Nevertheless, it is necessary to examine more closely the reasons for this situation.

REASONS FOR POSITIVE USE

One clue is provided by the way in which committees of inquiry are defined. Previous writers have tended to confine their attention to the traditional kind of committee examining an issue which concerns, or ought to concern, informed public opinion; the kind of committee report which rates a leader in *The Times* and deals with issues like marriage and divorce, the organisation of the civil service or the future of the aircraft industry. It has been contended in this study, however, that it cannot be automatically assumed that such obviously important committees are necessarily representative of committees of inquiry as a whole. In particular, the great growth in government activity means not only that more questions have become issues in which government is involved but that that involvement is often of a direct and detailed kind. Correspondingly, committees of inquiry are appointed to look at a great many matters which in the past were not matters of public policy, like the organisation of hospital scientific and technical services or the remuneration of milk producers. Such questions are less likely to be the subject of general public debate, but they may nonetheless be highly controversial within their own context and have important implications for public policy.

The consequence is that the majority of committees of inquiry which are now appointed are likely to be concerned with issues which have to be resolved if the business of government is to be carried on, but they are issues which are of little concern to the general public and centre mainly on relations between the Government and professional or other organised groups. Correspondingly, the emphasis in drawing up terms of reference and choosing members is likely to be on seeking an analysis of the problem and its solution which can gain acceptance from the various parties concerned.

One can look at this in another way. The extension of government activity into spheres remote from the traditional concerns with such issues as law, order and defence has led to a great increase in the amount and range of consultation and discussion, both formal and informal, with outside organisations and interests, whose object is simultaneously to keep the government in touch with outside opinion, to provide it with advice and information and equally to serve as a channel by which government ideas and policies may be disseminated and put into operation as a result of mutual discussion and compromise. From time to time, however, issues arise which cannot be so easily disposed of through these 'usual channels'. This may happen for a variety of reasons: the issue may affect bodies or interests which are not in and cannot easily be accommodated in the normal procedure; the department or departments concerned may be divided in their approach; or the department may fail to agree with the organisations concerned on the right course to be adopted.

In this kind of situation governments are very likely to appoint committees of inquiry. Such committees have a rather broader approach to the problem than the normal advisory machinery through their membership, methods of working and the need to produce and publish a report setting out their view of the problem and how it should be tackled. They are therefore able – or this at least is the hope and expectation – to resolve the issue more satisfactorily; they may persuade one of the parties involved, for example, to accept modification of its point of view, or at least to acquiesce in some compromise.

It follows that the great majority of these committees are not concerned with large issues of policy or matters involving legislation. They are likely to have a high success rate in terms of acceptance by government of their basic analysis and, often, of many of their actual proposals since they are working in a limited but definite area with a well-understood job to do. These are the committees like those on the hospital scientific and technical services, or pressure vessels, or psychologists in the education services which rarely hit the headlines and of whose existence most of us are completely unaware unless we happen to be professionally involved in the subject.

It also follows from what has been said that this kind of committee is most likely to be found in those areas of government in which government has a close and direct involvement with both general policy and its practical operation. Hence education and the national health service are areas where one would expect to find them and where they are in fact commonly found. Similarly, central government administration is itself an area where committees of inquiry are often found, as with the committee set up in 1964 to examine the organisation of the scientific civil service, or that set up in 1968 to look at the organisation and control of government industrial establishments. And, as the examples of the committees on pressure vessels and on means of authenticating the quality of engineering products and materials show, they are also to be found where government extends or develops its interests, as with the Labour Government's Ministry of Technology.[1]

In contrast to these committees, which fall within a broad category of subjects in which government is actively seeking to resolve issues and problems as they arise as part of its ongoing responsibility, are those concerned with issues of policy on which the Government does not necessarily need to act, and indeed in which one of the main questions which arises is whether and to what extent government should act. These are the broad social and economic questions represented by, for

[1] On this, see *The Ministry of Technology, 1964–1969* (HMSO, 1969), especially paras 1–4 and 8–10.

example the Committee on the Law on Sunday Observance and the Royal Commission on the Press in the period covered by this study or by the committee on privacy which falls just outside it. Whether the Government can be persuaded to take action on these issues – and what kind of action – will depend on the individual circumstances in which each committee is appointed. But these are the kind of committees which are likely to be found in categories 1 and 2, as defined above, that is, committees appointed because the Government is either reluctant to act or at least wants to be assured that action is both desirable and practicable before coming to a decision.

These suggestions certainly do not pretend to give a complete and exhaustive explanation of why communities on the whole fall into the more positive categories. Moreover, there are, as always, practical difficulties even in identifying the type of problem assigned to particular committees. Committees like the Royal Commission on Medical Education or the Committee on Civil Air Transport or that on experiments on animals, for example, are certainly concerned with issues which directly affect government administration. But whether they are simply concerned with this or with wider issues of public policy, and to what extent, cannot be determined just by looking at the terms of reference or reading the committee's report, but requires study and knowledge of their individual backgrounds. At most we are dealing here with tendencies and likelihoods rather than hard-and-fast distinctions.

COMMITTEES AS A PRELIMINARY TO LEGISLATION

There is a further question of major importance in this connection to be considered in relation to the role of committees of inquiry. Writing in 1939, Sir Arthur Salter asserted that 'on all the more complicated social and economic problems, exploration by a Royal Commission is the usual preliminary to legislative action'.[1] Others have gone further. Herman Finer, for example, claimed: 'It is probably true to say that since the early part of the nineteenth century hardly a social, economic, or political statute of any importance has been drafted and introduced into Parliament otherwise than as a result of recommendations of a Royal Commission,'[2] and this view has tended to be echoed by later writers on British government and politics.[3]

---

[1] In R. V. Vernon and N. Mansergh, *Advisory Bodies* (Allen & Unwin, 1940), p. 8.
[2] 'The British System', *University of Chicago Law Review* (Spring 1951), p. 554 (quoted in Hanser, op. cit., p. 45).
[3] For example, A. H. Birch, *Representative and Responsible Government* (Allen & Unwin, 1964), p. 203.

These are bold claims, and they imply a much bigger role for at least some committees of inquiry than anything considered so far. It is therefore necessary to consider how far these claims are true or, perhaps one should say, still true. For they might well be largely true for the nineteenth century or even the first part of the twentieth century without necessarily still being true today. From the point of view of the present study the claim needs to be examined for two reasons: first, if it is true, what implications does it have for the earlier discussion of the circumstances in which committees are appointed and the reasons for appointment? Secondly, if it is true, what proportion do these highly important committees form of the total number of committees of inquiry?

One preliminary point should be made here. The quotations both refer to royal commissions, but for reasons discussed in Chapter 1 it would be misleading to restrict the discussion simply to one class of committees of inquiry, however important. The question will therefore be examined in terms of committees of inquiry in general.

It is easy enough to give examples of the kind of situation which Salter and Finer had in mind. The revision of the law relating to consumer credit, for example, proposed in a White Paper in Autumn 1973, was foreshadowed by and is indeed largely based on the recommendations of the Crowther Committee on Consumer Credit which reported in 1971. This is certainly a 'complicated social and economic problem'. Other examples in recent years where legislation was preceded by examination by a committee of inquiry include the control and administration of the police, the structure of local government in England and Scotland, and the age of majority. As some of these examples indicate, legislation does not necessarily follow at all closely the recommendations of a committee, yet it can be said in broad terms that before legislating the Government has chosen to have the subject investigated by a committee of inquiry. One can also add to these examples other complex questions investigated by committees of inquiry with a view to major legislation, although in fact for various reasons legislation has not been carried out; the problem of noise might perhaps be assigned to this category.

Once we move away from these fairly straightforward examples, however, where governments in effect say 'before deciding whether to legislate or in what form we will have this question examined by a committee of inquiry', there is a whole range of possible situations. Measures like the Iron and Steel Act, 1967, for example, which transferred a large part of the industry to public ownership, or the Post Office Act, 1969, which made the Post Office into a public corporation were certainly major pieces of legislation but they were not preceded by committees of inquiry. Nor were the various Prices and Incomes Acts of the Labour Government of 1964–70 or the Counter-Inflation Act, 1973, of its successor; or the series of measures designed to deal with the problems of immigration and race relations, like the Commonwealth Immigration Acts of 1962 and 1968 and the Race Relations Act of 1965; or many of the Acts concerned with housing problems, like the Rent Act of 1957 or the Housing Acts of 1961 and 1964.

These measures – and they are by no means an exhaustive list [1] – all dealt with complex social and economic problems. The difficulty is that, although none of them was preceded by a committee of inquiry in the way that the Family Law Reform Act of 1969 was preceded by the Latey Committee on the Age of Majority and the Russell Committee on the Law of Succession in Relation to Illegitimate Persons, it does not follow that these measures owed nothing to reports of committees of inquiry. In fact two important questions arise in this situation: first, what was the origin of these measures and, secondly, to the extent that committees of inquiry played little or no part in their origin, does this give any clue to the kinds of situations in which such committees are and are not used?

The answer to the first question would have to be sought primarily through empirical studies. Some elements are fairly obvious. The origins of the Iron and Steel Act of 1967, for example, would need to be traced back through the various post-war vicissitudes of the industry and the Labour Party's commitment to nationalisation dating back to the time of the Attlee Government; the controls on immigration introduced in 1962 would need to be seen in the context of increasing concern about the whole question of the impact of immigration and how that concern manifested itself through the party political machinery.[2] All this and much more would be needed in order to assess how specific policies were arrived at and given legislative form in Acts such as these; but on the face of it these particular policies owed little to committees of inquiry.

It is highly unlikely, however, that analysis of these and other policies would show any consistent pattern, either in the extent to which committees of inquiry played some part in the origins of particular policies, or in demarcating the circumstances in which committees of inquiry did

[1] Opinions may of course differ on what constitutes a major social or economic question, but apart from the examples given which for simplicity refer to fairly specific issues there are some wide-ranging Acts which owe little or nothing to committees of inquiry, e.g. the Transport Act, 1968.

[2] Cf. Sheila Patterson, *Immigration and Race Relations in Britain, 1960–1967* (Institute of Race Relations, Oxford University Press, 1969), p. 18.

and those in which they did not form a significant element in such origins. Many of the examples given, for example, are clearly not simply controversial issues but controversial in terms of party politics. The nationalisation of iron and steel and measures to deal with inflation clearly fall in this category. Different political parties have a commitment to different policies on these issues; they feel an urgent political necessity to declare where they stand on them; they are issues which figure prominently in election manifestos; and they are therefore issues on which policy is much more likely to be evolved through the party political machinery than through the use of committees of inquiry.[1]

Explanations of this kind will not, however, fit all of the examples given. Immigration was an issue which was controversial not so much between the parties as within them; it is certainly not inconceivable that a committee of inquiry, perhaps a royal commission, should have been appointed, say, in 1960. For the present analysis it does not matter whether such a step was ever considered or whether, for example, the constantly expressed belief of the Government at that time that immigration presented no special problems precluded any serious attempt at examination of alternative policies. What is important is that there was nothing of a specifically party political nature which would have been an obstacle to examination by a committee of inquiry at that time. Clearly, the situation changed about 1961 to the extent that the problem came to be not only recognised but recognised as urgent, and it has since remained as a controversial political issue,[2] so that later development of policy, and especially the fact that only one issue, that of an appeals system for immigrants, was remitted to a committee of inquiry,[3] has to be viewed in that context.

Housing policy perhaps illustrates even more clearly how difficult it is to relate the origins of legislation to any clearly-defined distinction between what is and what is not appropriate for consideration by a committee of inquiry. Since 1918 numerous Acts have been passed dealing either with general housing policy or more specifically with the question of rents. Housing is certainly a subject of considerable social and economic importance and one which arouses a great deal of public interest. Here, then, if anywhere, one would expect to find examination

[1] Even so, it does not follow that committees of inquiry are never appointed in such circumstances: cf. the Donovan Royal Commission on Trade Unions and Employers' Associations.

[2] For example, the Labour Party committed itself in its 1964 election manifesto to legislating against racial discrimination.

[3] On the origins of this committee, see Patterson, op. cit., pp. 48–57.

by a committee of inquiry as a preliminary to legislation if the Salter/ Finer view is correct.

In fact, the position is highly confused. Some aspects of policy have been so examined, but some have not; moreover the same aspect may sometimes be examined and sometimes not. In the inter-war years, for example, there was a tradition of appointing committees of inquiry before legislating on the question of rent restriction; there was the Onslow Committee of 1923 and the Rent Act, 1923, the Marley Committee of 1931 and the Rent Act, 1933, and the Ridley Committee of 1937 and the Rent Act, 1938.[1] Since the war, there have been two important Rent Acts, those of 1957 and 1965. The first was not preceded by a committee of inquiry, and has indeed been criticised on those grounds.[2] The second has a more interesting and complex origin since it was a measure passed by the Labour Government, following the report of a committee of inquiry set up by the previous Government. That committee was, however, nominally not a committee to investigate the Rent Acts but a purely fact-finding inquiry into the housing situation in Greater London.[3] It was not until 1969 that a committee was appointed specifically to review the operation of the Rent Acts.[4]

On more general questions of housing policy there has been a whole series of White Papers and Acts since 1945 dealing with such questions as subsidies, house improvement and slum clearance, but hardly any of these have been preceded by specific examination by a committee of inquiry. The aim in the case of this broad area of housing policy is thus not to try to find a specific connection between committees of inquiry and legislation but rather to identify the various factors which have contributed to successive changes of policy as these have been expressed in legislation, and to see whether and to what extent committees of inquiry form one of those factors. But whatever the explanation of the origins of the legislation it is clearly not possible to explain the presence

[1] See J. B. Cullingworth, *Housing and Local Government in England and Wales* (Allen & Unwin, 1966), pp. 18–25.

[2] Ibid., p. 47.

[3] The Milner Holland Committee (Cmnd 2605, 1965): it has been described by one of its members as 'the first comprehensive study of housing problems to be carried out by an independent committee since the Royal Commission on the Housing of the Working Classes reported in 1885' (D. V. Donnison, *The Government of Housing*, Penguin, 1967, p. 352). However, it also has to be borne in mind that the Labour Party was committed to repealing the 1957 Act even before the publication of the Milner Holland report (see 1964 election manifesto).

[4] The Francis Committee (Cmnd 4609, 1971).

or absence of committees of inquiry in terms simply of political commitment or the urgency of the problems.

RECURRING SUBJECTS FOR COMMITTEES

Not only, therefore, is it not true to say that major social and economic legislation is generally preceded by independent investigation by a committee of inquiry, but it is not easy to state comprehensively the circumstances in which governments do decide on investigation as a preliminary to legislation. As a general proposition it may be said that governments choose to use committees of inquiry when they judge it politically safe to do so, or perhaps better, when they judge it politically less risky than acting in any other way. This means that they tend not to use committees of inquiry when they have a commitment to a particular policy or they have to find an urgent answer or for some other reason they believe that they do not need a committee.

Such generalisations may be true but are not very revealing. We need to know what circumstances, or set of circumstances or conditions need to be fulfilled to be favourable or unfavourable to the appointment of committees, and this means falling back on examination of individual committees. An illustration can be provided by what one may regard as 'old favourites', subjects which tend to recur at intervals for examination by committees of inquiry, like the licensing laws, or coroners, or patent law. These certainly involve complicated social and economic questions in which a kind of tradition have been established of investigation by committee of inquiry before legislative changes are introduced. They are all questions, however, which are not vital in terms of party policy; they are all in that sense safe questions to remit to a committee of inquiry.

Can one say the same, however, of the police and broadcasting, both of which are also recurring subjects for investigation by committees of inquiry? Police powers, and the control and administration of the police, are matters which are fundamental to the nature and organisation of society. Indeed, it could be argued that for that very reason successive governments have been very wary of introducing major changes without first having a royal commission to set out and analyse the arguments. If so, the explanation is in very different terms from that in the preceding paragraph. The argument suggests in fact that a major reason why governments find it necessary or desirable to investigate police matters in this way is that such matters are important in constitutional as well as purely political terms, and that the former in effect overrides the latter.

Such an explanation will not fit the case of broadcasting, however. Here the tradition of general, wide-ranging inquiries at intervals might plausibly be attributed to the special nature of broadcasting services with their immediate and simultaneous impact on millions of people being reflected in the special arrangements for securing control over their use. Such a tradition has not prevented the introduction of major legislation not related to investigation by a committee of inquiry, most notably the introduction of commercial television in 1954.[1] And the tradition itself received at least a partial blow in the decision of the Conservative Government elected in 1970 not to proceed with the general inquiry under Lord Annan initiated by the preceding Government. Nevertheless, to the extent that there have been several inquiries into broadcasting preceding legislation, the explanation is not to be found simply in the political importance of the way in which broadcasting develops. Rather, explanations have to be sought, as in the case of the police, in terms of some more specific characteristic of the subject of broadcasting.

To sum up the argument at this stage: even to examine the use of committees by government simply from the point of view of the kinds of problems examined by committees, and the reasons why governments should find it necessary to appoint them is an undertaking of some magnitude. There is scarcely any generalisation which can be made without numerous qualifications and exceptions. Theoretically, detailed case-studies of a large number of committees could provide the necessary information for stricter classification and more fruitful generalisation. But apart from the practical difficulties of carrying out such case-studies, the question is whether it really makes sense to attempt the kind of generalisations which would be useful for theoretical or practical purposes about a device developed by government over the years to serve such a variety of purposes. For at one end of the scale it is little more than a somewhat more elaborate means of seeking advice and conducting consultations with those most directly affected by particular policies than the regular consultative devices such as standing advisory committees; and at the other end of the scale it can be a means of concentrating discussion on controversial public issues into a form in which government is able to draw conclusions for public policy.

[1] See H. H. Wilson, *Pressure Group* (Secker & Warburg, 1961), for a detailed account of the way in which the change of policy was brought about. Once again, the situation is not clear-cut: the Beveridge Report on Broadcasting had, *inter alia*, examined this question and rejected it except for one member (Mr Selwyn Lloyd). The question therefore is what part, if any, the Beveridge report played in the events leading to the Television Act, 1954.

THE VALUE OF COMMITTEES

These problems become more acute if one looks not simply from a narrow point of view at the circumstances in which governments make use of committees of inquiry but more broadly at the contribution which committees make to the development of policies and at their value generally. The distinction made earlier between committees as a device of government and committees as part of the democratic process here becomes particularly important.

Consider, for example, Wheare's summing up of the value of committees to inquire, a category which corresponds roughly to committees of inquiry as defined here. If, he says, a department 'means business, if it is really anxious to determine some issue of policy or to undertake some reform of administration, then the setting up of a committee to inquire may well have some value'.[1] This instrumental use of committees is straightforward enough and corresponds to categories 3 and 4 in the classification suggested earlier in this chapter, that is, it refers to situations where government has a positive attitude to the appointment of committees. Value here is to be assessed in pragmatic terms, the value to government in enabling it to get things done. Here then, in principle, is one way for testing the effectiveness of committees and the contribution which they make in enabling government to evolve policies.

This is not, however, all that Wheare says on the value of committees to inquire. He goes on to point to the value of a committee report as a contribution to the study of the subject, so that it may not necessarily be wasted even if the department does not intend to take action: 'It may perform an educative function, which in the end, perhaps, may lead to some action.'[2]

Here, the position is not quite so clear. For a committee may be intended to have an educative effect. It may be appointed by government partly to demonstrate that a certain course of action which has been advocated is impracticable or unlikely to succeed because of the irreconcilability of the interests involved – what may be termed a negative educative effect. Or it may be appointed partly because the Government believes that analysis and discussion of a problem by an independent committee will help to secure support for the kind of changes it has in mind, or will help in other ways to prepare the way for an acceptable policy—a positive educative effect. In either case, there

[1] K. C. Wheare, *Government by Committee* (Oxford University Press, 1955), pp. 88–9.
[2] Ibid.

there can be an intended educative effect which is part of the use made by governments of committees. To the extent that the committee does in fact achieve the intended effect, then it could be said to have value for government, even though its value may have been the negative one of enabling the Government to resist the pressure for change.

However, what Wheare appears to be suggesting is a rather different situation, one where a committee set up by government to avoid or at least postpone taking action produces a report which is unwelcome to the Government in that its analysis in fact stimulates public debate to the extent that action may in the end have to be taken. Value here is therefore to some degree independent of the intentions of government. This requires further analysis.

The starting point is an essential characteristic of committees of inquiry, namely, that once appointed they continue in being [1] until they have presented a report which is published and contains not simply their recommendations but some indication at least of how they arrived at them. This characteristic marks off committees of inquiry from the informal discussion and advice which form part of normal day-to-day administration, and from much of the advice received in more formal ways such as through standing advisory committees. In appointing a committee of inquiry government is deliberately choosing to invite advice in a particular form, that is, a public document. It can influence in many ways, and notably through its choice of terms of reference and members, the kind of committee which it wants, and it can attempt to influence the kind of reception which a committee's advice gets; for example, it can issue a statement or even a White Paper on the same day that a committee's report is published rejecting the whole or part of the report. But the fact remains that the advice is public and not private and provides an opportunity for the public if it is so inclined to make up its own mind about the issues involved.

It is this public nature of committees of inquiry which provides the possibility of their performing an educative function. The main question which then arises is whether and in what sense this educative function is to be regarded as a value, irrespective of whether it is a function intended by government in appointing committees or not.

The question has wide implications for political philosophy. Those, for example, who deplore the fact that much government activity is too secret may see in committees of inquiry a value simply in the fact that they imply a public discussion of issues as against the private discus-

---

[1] Rarely, committees may be dissolved before they have reported: the most notable recent example was the Royal Commission on the Penal System, appointed in 1964 and dissolved in 1966.

sions which form a major part of the normal advisory machinery of government.[1]

More specifically, the argument, as formulated usually in criticisms of particular committees, seems to imply a unique role for committees of inquiry in influencing public opinion. Because they are, or should be, impartial and are in a position to get relevant information and views, they can set out in a dispassionate manner the various arguments and the pros and cons of different solutions to a problem.[2] Thus, the report of a committee of inquiry, whatever the merits of its precise recommendations, should provide those who wish to make up their own minds with the material for making an intelligent assessment of the issues involved.

There is of course a further implication here, as is clear from Wheare's analysis. It is not just that general awareness of the arguments and possible solutions to a problem is a good thing in itself. The implication is that the educative effect on public opinion can in some way lead to better policy-decisions than would otherwise be the case, can in fact produce more rational policy-making. Just as governments, it is claimed, need accurate information and dispassionate analysis if they are to evolve rational policies, so, in so far as they can or should take account of public opinion in formulating policy, it is desirable that public opinion should be well-informed, and to this committees of inquiry can make a contribution.

COMMITTEES AND THEIR ALTERNATIVES

It is not possible, within the limits of this study, adequately to deal with the theoretical implications of these arguments. Two things can, however, be said about them here which are relevant to the general approach of this study. First, it is doubtful whether the claims made for the uniqueness of committees of inquiry in this respect can be sustained. Secondly, it is important to consider under what circumstances committees of inquiry can perform this broader educative function.

Consideration of the first of these two points involves looking at what happens if a committee of inquiry is not appointed to examine a particular problem. In that case there is a wide variety of possibilities, from a position in which government policy is simply made known with scarcely any supporting argument to situations where government

---

[1] Cf. Ian Gilmour, *The Body Politic* (Hutchinson, 1969), p. 189: his main thesis is that governments adopt too negative an attitude, fail to use the powers which they possess, and seek to cut down public conflict and impose secrecy.

[2] Cf. Robert Kilroy-Silk on the Donovan Commission quoted at the head of this chapter.

commitment to a particular policy or change of policy comes after a lengthy period in which there may have been protests and debates about the hardships or injustices caused by existing policies, discussions and analyses in the press or on radio or television, and academic studies of the issues involved. More recently, too, there has been the additional device of the Green Paper by which government seeks to generate discussion of issues before policies have been settled. Correspondingly, the opportunities for public opinion to be intelligently informed will range from practically nil to almost a surfeit of information and opinion on which to judge. Certainly, it cannot be argued that committees of inquiry are the only means for informing and educating opinion, nor that without them the opportunities for achieving a rational and soundly-based approach to policy questions are necessarily diminished. What can be said is that given the right circumstances committees of inquiry may make a distinctive contribution to the study of a problem, largely because they act as a focus for information and views in a way which other channels do not provide.

However, in considering what are the right circumstances we are brought back to the practical context, and particularly the political context, in which committees of inquiry operate, since these provide both the opportunities and limitations for their work. If, for example, we consider briefly how an academic study of a problem compares with that made by a committee of inquiry, we can say that the former has the advantage of being able to probe the subject as widely or as narrowly as the inquirer judges necessary for his purpose, that he need only concern himself with the truth of his analysis, and that his conclusions may be designed as much to stimulate informed debate as to provide practical answers to current problems. Committees of inquiry mostly work within much tighter constraints in all these ways, but correspondingly are better able to exert practical influence, not least through the way in which they receive and handle evidence, that is, through their knowledge of and responsiveness to the views of those most closely involved with the subject under discussion.

As a study of interest and other organised groups has put it: 'If informed opinion has crystallized, the report of a committee is likely to reflect it fairly well, whatever the state of mass opinion.'[1] This exactly indicates the advantages and limitations of committees of inquiry as compared with less formal channels of communication. They are expected to analyse the problem given to them as fully as their terms of reference permit but they are also expected to relate this analysis to the

[1] Allen Potter, *Organised Groups in British National Politics* (Faber & Faber, 1961), p. 200.

evidence which they receive. If they do this task well then their report will be a contribution to the subject in the sense of providing information about the kind of views held about the subject and their relative validity as seen by the committee.

What is important is that the limitations and constraints under which committees operate are not just unfortunate accidents which in an ideal world would be removed but essential ingredients in the way in which they function. Committees are not there, like academic inquiries, primarily to find the truth, but rather to find a reasonable way of dealing with a problem on the facts as they see them. To a large extent it is incidental to this purpose that in order to do this they need to set down facts and analyses which may not be available, or so easily available, elsewhere. This situation arises because government is rarely, if ever, completely neutral in its attitude to the questions which it entrusts to committees of inquiry. There may, it is true, be occasions when it is inclined to stand back and say 'let us see what a committee makes of it', but even there it has a direct interest in the outcome simply because some kind of reaction will then be required, if only in the form of resisting taking action on the committee's recommendation.

In a similar way, there is almost inevitably bound to be a considerable difference in the methods employed in the two kinds of inquiry. A large and comprehensive research programme may well be the most appropriate starting-point for an academic inquiry whose main concern is with the discovery of the truth. Committees of inquiry may, and in many cases ought to, seek information additional to that provided by traditional sources such as evidence if they are to make a proper assessment of the problem under examination. But such additional seeking of information, even if it amounts to research in the accepted sense, cannot play the same central role as in an academic inquiry and must be severely restricted in time and scope by the need to find practical answers within a reasonable period of time. It could well be argued, indeed, that if a problem requires for its solution a great deal of fresh investigation and research, which inevitably takes time to complete, then a committee of inquiry is unlikely to be the best way of resolving it.

There is thus an inescapable difference between an academic inquiry which is essentially an outside influence on opinion and a committee of inquiry which, although formally independent of government, can never be completely detached from government. The value of a committee of inquiry's report as a source of information and ideas about the subject it has investigated is thus largely incidental to its central purpose. It is in the light of this that one should examine the kinds of criticisms made of individual committees which were referred to earlier.

COMMITTEES AS A MEANS OF PERSUASION

Such criticisms seem often to be based either on a view that the committee ought to have put forward a different solution or on a judgement that it did not investigate the subject thoroughly enough. The first suggests that although the committee analysed the problem adequately, it did not draw the right conclusions; the second implies that there were other and better ways of investigating the subject.

Those who look to committees to put forward bold new policies and suggestions for reform are naturally disappointed if committee reports fall short of what they consider to be necessary. They therefore tend to look for explanations either in terms of the failures of government to provide the committee with the right terms of reference and members or in terms of the failures of the committee members themselves to grasp what the problem was about or to get the relevant information or to draw the right conclusions.

These criticisms may or may not be justified for particular committees. But it is possible to suggest that they may rest on a mistaken view of the ways in which committees operate. For the most part, committees have in fact a relatively limited function, which is as much concerned with achieving a workable, practical accommodation between different interests and viewpoints as with raising more fundamental questions about the nature and effects of particular policies. Sensible well-argued proposals on limited topics may well be inadequate in the long term given the intractable nature of some of the problems faced by government. But governments rarely invite searching looks by committees of inquiry at vital areas of government, nor if they did is it likely that the committees would be able to agree on what was to be done, however educative the attempt might prove for public opinion.

To say that governments ought to make more use of committees of inquiry or to use them differently is to argue in fact for a major change of attitude to problems of government. For the moment, it is better to recognise that committees of inquiry play a limited but useful function in enabling the business of government to be carried on and, incidentally, in enabling certain topics to be given a particular kind of public airing.

The connection between these two also suggests that it is essential to view committees of inquiry in a context which is not static. The key word is persuasion. If governments operate largely by means of persuasion, this is a continuing process in which committees of inquiry have a definite part to play. In a characteristic situation, government may be under pressure from particular interests trying to persuade it to adopt a certain policy; government may be open to persuasion, but doubtful how far it should go in view of other arguments pointing in a different direction. A committee of inquiry is appointed and is then the target for those who wish to persuade it to recommend particular courses of action. The committee then has to reach a conclusion – which may mean much persuasion of some members by others – which will persuade the government and informed if not general public opinion.

The answer suggested here, therefore, to the problem posed at the beginning of this chapter is that the use and role of committees of inquiry have to be viewed primarily in terms of their instrumental value to government. The choice of such means of investigation and advice in comparison with, for example, the party political machinery does indeed carry certain implications for the way in which policies are evolved. However critical some people may be about the tasks given to particular committees or the way in which they have carried them out, however sceptical some committees indeed may feel about the usefulness of the procedure,[1] there is nevertheless a characteristic form of persuasiveness of committee reports. It is based on the fact that they are presumed to have sought out facts and views, to have argued the problem out among themselves and above all to have set out their arguments and conclusions in a public document. Differences of view cannot so lightly be ignored or passed over as they may be in a government White Paper; strong pressures from particular interests cannot so easily prevail as they may sometimes do behind the scenes of government.

Yet these characteristics are well known to government. It does not choose this means blindly but with an awareness of what it entails and the positive advantages which it can bring, as against alternative means of dealing with a problem. Hence it is not surprising that more emphasis should be placed here on the occasions when the educative consequences of a committee's report are likely to be welcome to government than on those possibly much rarer occasions when committee reports, though unwelcome to the Government at the time, are ultimately a factor at least in bringing about a change of policy.

The last point is a reminder that, although much can be said about the use made of committees of inquiry and their value, generalisation is possible only within fairly narrow limits. Certainly more needs to be done to examine the origins, operation and consequences of individual committees, despite the practical difficulties which have been amply commented upon in the course of this study, in order to throw more light on the nature of the problems discussed here and the tentative theories which have been put forward.

[1] Cf. the quotation at the beginning of this chapter from the Committee on General Medical Services in the Highlands and Islands.

THE NEED FOR POLICY STUDIES

Yet in the end it is perhaps true that the main interest in committees of inquiry must be in their contribution to policy-making, and more specifically to the ways in which changes of policy are brought about, and this contribution needs to be assessed in relation to particular areas of policy. Superficially, there is a great attraction in judging many committees to be unnecessary. Surely, it could be argued, it was not necessary to go through all the elaborate and formal procedures of appointing a committee simply to extend the qualifications for jury service or to find a new formula for remunerating milk distributors? Are not the resources of central government adequate to carry out the necessary investigations and consultations and to present ministers with reasoned arguments about the alternatives open to them so that they can decide what is to be done? And would not this be a quicker, more effective and less costly way of carrying on the business of government?

The questions emphasise both that there is more than one way of approaching a particular policy question and that each has different consequences and different advantages and disadvantages. Some matters are indeed settled by governments on the basis of information and advice available to them by less formal means than committees of inquiry. It does not follow that this is always or necessarily a quicker and more effective way of getting things done, or perhaps one should say it does not at all follow that speed and effectiveness go together.

From the limited evidence of this study it is certainly difficult to cite examples of committees of inquiry which have been the precursors of major new policies or changes of policy which had not already been canvassed or discussed. In other words, committees of inquiry are usually not so much innovators of policy as testers of ideas, examiners of the validity and practicality of proposals which others have, however sketchily, put forward. They are therefore very much part of the process by which public policies are moulded by the actions and interactions of government and the various interests and sources of pressure and persuasion, including both public opinion and political pressures. Governments may choose to announce policies with the minimum of previous consultation and investigation, but is it really possible to argue, as a general proposition, that one method is better than another? The policy which eventually emerges after a committee of inquiry has examined a problem may, and usually will, be a compromise between the ideal solution and one which can gain the maximum support.[1] This

[1] On the assumption that there will generally (but not inevitably) be a considerable difference between the two.

may be reasonable enough in some circumstances but not in others. Most governments find themselves compelled to carry out some policies which are unpopular with at least some of their supporters. It is hardly surprising therefore if on other occasions they seek solutions to problems which offer a reasonable chance of being acceptable and not too troublesome to put into operation. And committees of inquiry are a principal but not the only means which can help to achieve this. For advocates of a particular policy, governments may be judged to have acted too cautiously in settling for a compromise when to the critic it is quite clear what policy they should have followed and that they should have acted decisively to achieve it. The question is debatable, and is indeed at the heart of political debate, which is precisely about the policies which governments adopt and how and why they do so. But to move from debate about particular policies to generalisation about whether particular governments or, even more, governments in general not only produce the wrong policies but produce them in the wrong way requires far more specific evidence than is usually adduced.

The truth is that far too little study has been made of the way in which particular policies have evolved, and this is not surprising, given the practical difficulties of getting adequate information, at least until so long after the event that it becomes a matter of history rather than of contemporary politics and administration. There are certainly valuable accounts of such important policy-questions as the original organisation and structure of the national health service; [1] there are individual case-studies like that on the origin of commercial television chiefly designed to trace the influence of a particular interest group; [2] and there are some accounts which purport to show the influence of particular committees of inquiry on individual policy issues.[3] But perhaps even more we need a broader study of individual policy areas, like that published over ten years ago into the development of agricultural policy,[4] dealing with the various influences on policy and including the part played by committees of inquiry.

Without further detailed studies of individual committees, discussed earlier, and without sufficient of these broader policy-centred studies, we lack the effective basis for a full-scale analysis of the role of com-

[1] E.g. H. Eckstein, *The English Health Service* (Harvard University Press, 1959).

[2] Wilson, op. cit.

[3] E.g. Gerald Rhodes, *The Government of London: the Struggle for Reform* (LSE/Weidenfeld & Nicolson, 1970).

[4] Peter Self and Herbert J. Storing, *The State and the Farmer* (Allen & Unwin, 1962).

mittees of inquiry. Meanwhile, this study has indicated the scope and scale of such an analysis and suggested some of the hypotheses which it would be designed to prove or disprove. Such an analysis would not only contribute to greater understanding of the role of committees of inquiry but would also offer the best chance for drawing practical conclusions on their more effective use in future.

COMMITTEES OF INQUIRY 1959-1968

The main object has been to list as completely as possible committees of inquiry which were appointed in the ten years 1959–68 under broad subject-headings. For each committee four items of information are listed: 1 subject of the inquiry; 2 chairman of the committee; 3 year of appointment and report; 4 Command number(s) of report(s) (where applicable). Because, for reasons discussed in Chapter 2, the boundary between committees of inquiry and other committees is often hard to draw, an indication is given where a committee can be regarded as marginal either because it seems to be more advisory in nature or because it deals with a subject which is of relatively little importance in a policy sense. In addition examples are given where appropriate of committees which have been excluded on these or other grounds. Furthermore, because of the difficulty (also discussed in Chapter 2) of assigning some committees to one single category, an indication is given in certain cases of the links with other subject-headings. Royal commissions are indicated thus: (RC).

I INDUSTRY GROUP

The large number of committees falling into this group can be sub-divided into (a) those which affect industry generally, including industrial relations; (b) agriculture and fishing, primary industries with a special relationship to government; (c) transport, another important industry with a special relationship; (d) other specific industries.

(a) *Industry, general*

1	Truck Acts	D. Karmel	1959–61	—
2	Industrial Designs	K. Johnston	1959–62	1808
3	Noise	Sir Alan Wilson	1960–3	(1) 1780
				(2) 2056

not of course simply an industrial matter but has links with health (IIb) and general social policy (IIIb): there is also a strong specific link with transport (Ic).

4	Selection and Training of Supervisors	D. C. Barnes	1961–2	—

marginal advisory

5	(RC) Trade Unions and Employers' Associations	Lord Donovan	1965–8	3623
6	Patent System	M. A. L. Banks	1967–70	4407

(b) *Agriculture and fishing*

7	Experimental Importation of Charollais Cattle	Lord Terrington	1959–60	1140
8	Remuneration of Milk Distributors	Sir Guy Thorold	1959–61	1597

perhaps marginal in policy terms.

9	Fowl Pest Policy	Sir Arnold Plant	1960–2	1664
10	Fatstock and Carcase Meat Marketing and Distribution	W. R. Verdon-Smith	1962–4	2282
11	Scottish Salmon and Trout Fisheries	Lord Hunter	1962–5	(1) 2096 (2) 2691
12	Recruitment for the Veterinary Profession	Duke of Northumberland	1962–4	2430
13	Demand for Agricultural Graduates	C. I. C. Bosanquet	1962–4	2419

somewhat marginal advisory.

14	Statutory Small-holdings	Professor M. J. Wise	1963–7	(1) 2936 (2) 3303

links with local government (IV).

15	Welfare of Animals Kept under Intensive Livestock Husbandry Systems	Professor F. W. R. Brambell	1964–5	2836

one of the few committees in this subgroup with wider links, e.g. with general social policy.

16	Herbage Seed Supplies	Lord Donaldson	1966–8	3748
17	Reorganisation Commission for Eggs	R. Wright	1967–8	3669
18	Scottish Inshore Fisheries	Lord Cameron	1967–70	4453
19	Foot-and-Mouth Disease	Duke of Northumberland	1968–9	(1) 3999 (2) 4225
20	Use of Antibiotics in Animal Husbandry etc.	Professor M. M. Swann	1968–9	4190
21	Trawler Safety	Admiral Sir D. Holland-Martin	1968–9	(1) 3773 (2) 4117

Excluded : various standing advisory bodies making reports on limited subjects, e.g. *Antibiotics in Milk in Great Britain* by Milk Hygiene Subcommittee of Milk and Milk Products Technical Advisory Committee (1960–3), of importance for policy but advisory rather than inquiry.

(c) *Transport*

22	Rural Bus Services	Professor D. T. Jack	1959–61	—
23	Civil Aircraft Accident	D. Cairns	1959–60	—

investigation and licence control; links with central government procedure (IV).

24	Major Ports	Lord Rochdale	1961–2	1824
25	Traffic Signs	Sir W. Worboys	1961–3	—

a strong advisory element; more importantly it cannot be confined to an 'industrial' category; links with general social policy (IIIb).

26	Pilot Training	Duke of Hamilton	1962–3	—
27	Carriers' Licensing	Lord Geddes	1963–5	—
28	Civil Air Transport	Sir R. Edwards	1967–9	4018
29	London Taxicab Trade	A. Maxwell Stamp	1967–70	4483

Excluded : Traffic Signs for Motorways (1960) was basically advisory. *Traffic in Towns* (1963) perhaps deserves a special category as does the somewhat similar *Cars for Cities* (1967), but they are not committees of inquiry in the usual sense. *Road Pricing* (1964) was again basically advisory. *Better Use of Town Roads* (1967) was composed of officials. *Railway Policy Review* (in Annex to White Paper on *Railway Policy*, Cmnd 3439, 1967) is another unusual committee but is perhaps best regarded as advisory. *Highway Maintenance* (1970) was primarily concerned with local authority procedures. Altogether transport exhibits exceptional variety in types of committee.

(d) *Other specific industries*

30	Coal Derivatives	A. H. Wilson	1959–60	1120
31	Generation and Distribution of Electricity in Scotland	C. H. Mackenzie	1961–2	1859

perhaps belongs equally under central and local government (IV).

32	Contracts for Building and Civil Engineering Work	Sir H. Banwell	1962–4	—

marginal in policy terms.

33	Organisation and Practices for Building and Civil Engineering	W. M. Younger	1962–3	—

marginal in policy terms.

34	Aircraft Industry	Lord Plowden	1964–5	2853
35	Assessment of New Building Products (agrément)	Sir D. Gibson	1964–5	—
36	Shipbuilding Industry	A. R. M. Geddes	1965–6	2937
37	Cyclical Pattern of Machine Tool Orders	R. H. W. Bullock	1965–6	—
38	Pressure Vessels	R. W. Nichols	1966–8	—
39	Labour in Building and Civil Engineering	Professor E. H. Phelps Brown	1967–8	3714
	also links with I(a).			
40	Shipping	Lord Rochdale	1967–70	4337
	also links with I(c).			
41	Process Plant	R. W. Wright	1968–9	—
42	Delays in Commissioning Power Stations	Sir A. Wilson	1968–9	3960
43	Authenticating Engineering Products	Sir E. Mensforth	1968–70	—

II EDUCATION AND SOCIAL SERVICES GROUP

As with the industry group, this is a broad 'umbrella' heading to take in everything from education to social security.

(a) Education

44	Teaching of Russian	N. Annan	1960–2	—
45	Higher Education	Lord Robbins	1961–3	2154
46	Half Our Future (education of average 13–16 year olds).	Sir J. Newsom	1961–3	—
47	Teaching Profession in Scotland	Lord Wheatley	1961–3	2066
48	Day Release marginal advisory.	C. Henniker-Heaton	1962–4	—
49	Agricultural Education	Sir H. Pilkington	1963–6	—

in form a committee of a standing advisory body, but should probably be included; also links with agriculture (Ib).

50	Primary Education	Lady Plowden	1963–7	—
51	Primary Education in Wales	Professor C. E. Gittins	1964–7	—
52	Education of Deaf Children	Professor M. M. Lewis	1964–8	—

53 Psychologists in   Professor A.   1965–8   —
    Education Services   Summerfield
    marginal advisory.
54 National Film School   Lord Lloyd of   1965–7   —
                              Hampstead
    perhaps belongs equally under 1(*d*) i.e. as much a matter of
    relations between government and film industry as education.
55 Public Schools   (1) Sir J. Newsom   1965–70   —
    Commission   (2) Professor D. V.   (2 reports)
                              Donnison
    a difficult committee to classify because its task was mainly
    advisory, but it should probably be included in view of the
    nature of the subject and the inquiries carried out.
56 Education of Visually   Professor M. D.   1968–72   —
    Handicapped   Vernon

Excluded: Education generates many committees of an advisory
nature whether *ad hoc* or standing. Examples of the former are *Assistance
with the Cost of Boarding Education* (1960) and *The Government of Colleges
of Education* (1966). Examples of the latter are reports of the National
Advisory Council on the Training and Supply of Teachers and of the
committee on research and development in modern languages. Reports of
the Central Advisory Council for Education (England) have been
included but most of those of the corresponding body for Wales are truly
advisory (e.g. *Science in Education in Wales Today* (1965). Scotland has
numerous working-parties which are advisory or consist of officials (or
both) (e.g. *Appointment of Teachers to Education Committee* (1962),
Ascertainment of Maladjusted Children (1964)); and the committee on
Moral and Religious Education in Scottish Schools (1972), although not
simply advisory, is excluded because it was concerned narrowly with
practice rather than policy.

(b) Health Services

57 Mental Health   Mrs T. M. Allen   1959–61   —
    Services of Local
    Health Authorities
    (Scotland)
58 Accident and Emer-   Sir Harry Platt   1961–2   —
    gency Services
59 Field of Work of the   Dr Annis Gillie   1961–3   —
    Family Doctor
60 Health Education   Lord Cohen of   1961–4   —
                             Birkenhead
61 Hospital Pharma-   J. B. Grosset   1961–5   —
    ceutical service in
    Scotland

62	Administrative and Clerical Staff in Hospital Service	Sir S. Lycett Green	1962–3	—
63	Organisation of Prison Medical Service	E. H. Gwynn	1962–4	—
64	Senior Nursing Staff Structure	B. Salmon	1963–6	—
65	Drug Addiction	Lord Brain	1964–5	—

not just a health services subject; links with general social policy (IIIb).

66	General Medical Services in the Highlands and Islands	Lord Birsay	1964–7	3257
67	Relationship of Pharmaceutical Industry with the National Health Service	Lord Sainsbury	1965–7	3410

also links with specific industries (Id).

68	Care of Health of Hospital Staff	Professor Sir R. Tunbridge	1965–8	—
69	(RC) Medical Education	Lord Todd	1965–8	3569

links with education (IIa).

70	Psychiatric Nursing	Dr D. H. Clark	1966–8	—
71	Functions of the District General Hospital	Sir D. Bonham-Carter	1966–9	—
72	Suggestions and Complaints in Hospital (Scotland)	E. U. Elliott-Binns	1966–9	—
73	Hospital Scientific and Technical Services	Sir S. Zuckerman	1967–8	—
74	Hospital Pharmaceutical Service	Sir N. Hall	1968–70	—
75	Hospital Building Maintenance	D. W. Parish	1968–70	—

marginal in policy terms.

Excluded: For reasons discussed earlier in the study there are peculiar difficulties about drawing the line between committees of inquiry and advisory committees. Reports of the Central and Scottish Health Services Councils are mainly advisory (e.g. *Human Relations in Obstetrics* (1961), *Rheumatic Fever in Scotland* (1967)); those included above are mainly marginal (57, 58, 59, 60, 61, 68, 70, 71). At the same time, there are other, mainly *ad hoc*, advisory committees, some of unusual constitution.

Examples are: Working-party on the Organisation of Medical Work in Hospitals (first report 1967) appointed jointly by the Ministry of Health and the Joint Consultants Committee; Working-party on *The Responsibilities of the Consultant Grade* (1969).

(c) *Social Security*

76	Assessment of Disablement	Lord McCorquodale of Newton	1964–5	2847

mainly technical and advisory but included because of the political importance of the subject.

77–83 The following seven reports, all by the National Insurance Advisory Committee, are marginal in policy terms.

Doctors' and Midwives' Certificates	1959–60	1021
Long-term Hospital Patients	1959–60	964
Pension Increments for Wives and Widows	1960–1	1384
Time Limits for Claiming Sickness Benefit	1964	2400
Earnings Limit for Retirement Pensions	1966–7	3197
Conditions for Unemployment Benefit and Contribution Credits for Occupational Pensions	1967–8	3545
Time Limits for Payment of Benefits	1967–8	3591

Excluded: Other reports of NIAC on draft regulations are even more limited in character. Reports of the Industrial Injuries Advisory Committee are advisory and expert (e.g. *Byssinosis*, Cmnd 1095, 1960).

(d) *Other*

84	Local Authority and Allied Personal Social Services	F. Seebohm	1965–8	3703

ᘛ o links with central and local government (IV).

III   LAW REFORM, SOCIAL POLICY AND TREATMENT OF OFFENDERS

This is not really a cohesive group but the subject of law reform is closely connected with, and to some extent overlaps, that of general social policy; and it is also relevant to that area of policy which is concerned with the penal system and the treatment of offenders through the specialised field of reform of the criminal law.

a) *Law Reform*

85	Registration of Title to Land in Scotland	Lord Reid	1959–63	2032
86	Powers of Subpoena of Disciplinary Tribunals	Viscount Simmonds	1960	1033

87	Limitation of Actions in Cases of Personal Injury	Justice E. Davies	1961–2	1829
88	Jury Service	Lord Morris of Borth-y-gest	1963–5	2627
89	Positive Covenants Affecting Land	Lord Wilberforce	1963–5	2719
90	Legal Aid in Criminal Proceedings	Lord Widgery	1964–6	2934
91	Licensing Planning	J. R. Willis	1964–5	2709
92	Conveyancing Legislation and Practice (Scotland)	Professor J. M. Halliday	1964–6	3118
93	Law of Succession in Relation to Illegitimate Persons	Lord Russell	1964–6	3051
94	Mechanical Recording of Court Proceedings	Justice Baker	1964–6	(a) 2733 (b) 3096

marginal in both advisory and policy terms.

95	Scheme for Registration of Title to Land (Scotland)	Professor G. L. F. Henry	1965–9	4137

marginal in advisory terms.

96	Personal Injuries Litigation	Lord Winn	1966–8	3691

marginal in advisory terms.

97	Statutory Maintenance Limits	Miss J. G. Hall	1966–8	3587
98	Law of Contempt Affecting Tribunals of Inquiry *see also* 128.	Lord Salmon	1968–9	4078
99	Evidence (general)	Lord E. Davies	(1968)–72	4991

report of Criminal Law Revision Committee but included because of its importance and the inquiries carried out.

Excluded: Except for 99, reports of standing advisory bodies have been excluded since they are advisory rather than inquiry. They include the Law Reform Committee (e.g. *Evidence of Opinion and Expert Opinion,* Cmnd 4489, 1970), Law Reform Committee for Scotland (e.g. *Civil Liability for Loss Etc. by Animals,* Cmnd 2185, 1963); Criminal Law Revision Committee (e.g. *Order of Closing Speeches,* Cmnd 2148, 1963), and Private International Law Committee (e.g. *Draft Convention on Monetary Law,* Cmnd 1648, 1962). The reports of the Law Commissions are harder to classify, since they are not simply advisory and some at least of them have broader scope than those of the Law Reform Committees. However, it seemed best to exclude them here.

(b) *Social Policy*

100	Consumer Protection	J. T. Molony	1959–62	(1) 1011
				(2) 1781

typical of committees difficult to classify except under the broadest headings.

101	Scottish Licensing Laws	Lord Guest	1959–63	(1) 1217 (2) 2021
102	Sunday Observance Law	Lord Crathorne	1961–4	2528
103	Experiments on Animals	Sir S. Littlewood	1963–5	2641
104	Legal Status of Welsh Language	Sir D. H. Parry	1963–5	2785
105	Age of Majority	Justice Latey	1965–7	3342
106	Allotments	Professor H. Thorpe	1965–9	4166
107	Enforcement of Judgement Debts	Justice Payne	1965–8	3909
108	Immigration Appeals	Sir R. Wilson	1966–7	3387
109	Marriage Law of Scotland	Lord Kilbrandon	1967–9	4011
110	Cannabis	Lady Wootton of Abinger	1967–9	—

report of Advisory Committee on Drug Dependence.

Excluded : The main difficulty here is overlap between this subgroup and others (a great many committees can be said to have a bearing on general social policy). There is the added difficulty in some cases of drawing a boundary between inquiry/advisory. Cannabis (110) illustrates both these problems and is included both because of its wider investigations and the implications for the important social problem provided by the use of drugs. But other reports of the advisory committee (e.g. *The Rehabilitation of Drug Addicts* (1968), *Powers of Arrest and Search in Relation to Drug Offences* (1970)) are not included both because of their more limited scope and because they are more advisory in nature.

(c) *Crime and Treatment of Offenders*

111	Children and Young Persons (Scotland)	Lord Kilbrandon	1961–4	2306
112	Criminal Statistics	W. Perks	1963–7	3448
113	Scottish Criminal Statistics	Lord Thomson	1963–8	3705

these two committees are marginal in terms of policy.

114	Habitual Drunken Offenders	T. G. Weiler	1967–70	—

marginal advisory.

Excluded : Most of the committee reports in this group are advisory.

The advisory bodies include the Advisory Council on the Employment of Prisoners (e.g. *Organisation of Work for Prisoners*, 1964); the Advisory Council on the Treatment of Offenders (e.g. *Preventive Detention*, 1963); the Scottish Advisory Council on the Treatment of Offenders (e.g. *Organisation of After-care in Scotland*, 1963); and the Advisory Council on the Penal System (e.g. *Detention of Girls in a Detention Centre*, 1968). In a similar category are the reports of the Working-Party on the Place of Voluntary Service in After-Care.

IV   CENTRAL AND LOCAL GOVERNMENT

This group is intended to cover committees whose emphasis is on the administrative structure or procedures of central government, the legal system and local government, or on the organisation, recruitment, training, etc. of particular classes of public servants.

115	Probation Service	Sir Ronald Morison	1959–62	(1)	1650
				(2)	1800
	also has links with II(d) and III(c).				
116	Control of Public Expenditure	Lord Plowden	1959–61		1432
	marginal advisory,				
117	(RC) Police	Sir H. Willink	1960–2	(1)	1222
				(2)	1728
	also links with III(c).				
118	Magistrates' Courts in London	Judge Aarvold	1960–1		1606
	marginal advisory.				
119	Security Procedures	Lord Radcliffe	1961		1681
120	Representational Service Overseas	Lord Plowden	1962–3		2276
121	Organisation of Civil Science	Sir B. Trend	1962–3		2171
122	Police Cadets	F. L. T. Graham-Harrison	1963–5		—
123	Sheriff Court (Scotland)	Lord Grant	1963–7		3248
124	Organisation of Scientific Civil Service	Sir M. Tennant	1964–5		—
125	Court of Criminal Appeal	Lord Donovan	1964–5		2755
126	Management of Local Government	Sir J. Maud	1964–7		—
127	Staffing of Local Government	Sir G. Mallaby	1964–6		—

128	(RC) Tribunals of Inquiry	Lord Salmon	1966	3121
129	(RC) Local Government in England	Lord Redcliffe-Maud	1966–9	4040
130	(RC) Local Government in Scotland	Lord Wheatley	1966–9	4150
131	Civil Service	Lord Fulton	1966–8	3638
132	(RC) Assizes and Quarter Sessions	Lord Beeching	1966–9	4153
133	Fire Service	Sir R. Holroyd	1967–70	4371
134	'D' Notice System	Lord Radcliffe	1967	3309
135	Public Participation in Planning	A. M. Skeffington	1967–9	—
136	Overseas Representation	Sir V. Duncan	1968–9	4107
137	Method II Selection System	J. G. W. Davies	1968–9	4156
	marginal in policy terms.			
138	Government Industrial Establishments	Sir J. Mallabar	1968–70	4713

V MISCELLANEOUS

This group consists essentially of two distinct kinds of committees: those which can be assigned to a definite subject but one which has no strong links with any of the subjects listed above (e.g. water supply); and those which seem to belong equally to two or more categories.

139	Homes for Today and Tomorrow	Sir Parker Morris	1959–61	—
	subcommittee of Central Housing Advisory Committee.			
140	Levy on Betting on Horse Racing	L. E. Peppiatt	1959–60	1003
141	Solid Smokeless Fuels	N. M. Peech	1959–60	999
	marginal in advisory and policy terms.			
142	Financial Structure of Colonial Development Corporation	Lord Sinclair of Cleeve	1959	786
143	Company Law	Lord Jenkins	1959–62	1749
	links with I(a) but is much broader in scope.			
144	Broadcasting	Sir H. Pilkington	1960–2	1753
145	Workshops for the Blind	J. G. Stewart	1960–1	—
146	(RC) Press	Lord Shawcross	1961–2	1811
147	Training in Public Administration for Overseas Countries	Lord Bridges	1961–3	—

148	Decimal Currency	Earl of Halsbury	1961–3	2145
149	Sale of Works of Art by Public Bodies marginal advisory.	Lord Cottesloe	1962–4	—
150	Water Service in Scotland	Craig Mitchell	1962–6	3116
151	Impact of Rates on Households	Professor R. G. D. Allen	1963–4	2582
152	Housing in Greater London	Sir E. Milner Holland	1963–5	2605
153	Social Studies	Lord Heyworth	1963–5	2660
154	Remuneration of Ministers and Members of Parliament	Sir G. Lawrence	1963–4	2516
155	Turnover Taxation	G. Richardson	1963–4	2300
156	Preservation of Pension Rights	A. M. Morgan	1964–6	—
157	Our Older Homes	Mrs E. Denington	1965–6	—

subcommittee of Central Housing Advisory Committee.

158	Death Certification and Coroners	N. Brodrick	1965–71	4810
159	Housing Management in Scotland	E. Clark	1965–7	—
160	Scotland's Older Houses	J. B. Cullingworth	1965–7	—

159 and 160 are both committees of the Scottish Housing Advisory Committee.

161	The Needs of New Communities	J. B. Cullingworth	1965–7	—

subcommittee of Central Housing Advisory Committee.

162	Immigrants and the Youth Service	Lord Hunt	1965–7	—

committee of Youth Service Development Council.

163	Protection of Field Monuments	Sir D. Walsh	1966–8	3904
164	The Brain Drain	F. E. Jones	1966–7	3417

Working-Group on Migration of the (Advisory) Committee on Manpower Resources for Science and Technology.

165	Preservation Policy Group	Lord Kennett	1966–70	—

partly functioned as committee of inquiry.

166	Football	D. N. Chester	1966–8	—
167	Footpaths	Sir A. Gosling	1967–8	—
168	The Intermediate Areas	Sir Joseph Hunt	1967–9	3998

169	Council House Communities	Sir James M. Miller	1967–70	—

committee of Scottish Housing Advisory Committee.

170	National Libraries	F. S. Dainton	1967–9	4028
171	Legal Education	J. Ormrod	1967–71	4595
172	Third London Airport	Justice Roskill	1968–71	—

partly functioned as committee of inquiry.

173	Consumer Credit	Lord Crowther	1968–70	4596
174	Council Housing	J. B. Cullingworth	1968–9	—

sub-committee of Central Housing Advisory Committee.

Excluded: Housing, water and scientific policy all have important standing advisory bodies. In the case of housing their reports have been mainly included above since these have a strong inquiry element. On the other hand most of the science policy committees have been excluded since they are very largely advisory or concerned with providing technical information. Examples are the working-group of the Council for Scientific Policy on *The Flow of Candidates in Science and Technology into Higher Education* (Cmnd 2893, 1966); the manpower surveys of the Committee on Manpower Resources for Science and Technology (e.g. Cmnd 3103, 1966); and the Joint Working-Group of the CSP and the UGC on *Computers for Research* (Cmnd 2883, 1966).

SELECT INDEX OF NAMES

Note

All committees other than permanent standing bodies are listed by title under the heading 'committees'. Royal commissions are indicated thus: (RC).

All Acts of Parliament are listed under the heading 'Acts of Parliament'.

All government departments are listed under the heading 'government departments'; changes of name are not indicated.